IMPRESSIVE FIRST IMPRESSIONS

A Guide to the Most Important 30 Seconds (And 30 Years) of Your Career

Vu H. Pham, PhD, and Lisa Miyake

 PRAEGER

AN IMPRINT OF ABC-CLIO, LLC
Santa Barbara, California • Denver, Colorado • Oxford, England

Library of Congress Cataloging-in-Publication Data

Pham, Vu H.
  Impressive first impressions : a guide to the most important 30 seconds (and 30 years)
  of your career / Vu H. Pham and Lisa Miyake.
      p. cm.
  Includes bibliographical references and index.
    ISBN 978-0-313-37594-1 (hbk. : alk. paper) — ISBN 978-0-313-37595-8 (ebook)
  1. Career development—Psychological aspects. 2. First impression (Psychology) I. Miyake,
Lisa. II. Title.
HF5381.P492 2010
650.1´3—dc22   2009052369

ISBN: 978-0-313-37594-1
EISBN: 978-0-313-37595-8

14 13 12   3 4 5

This book is also available on the World Wide Web as an eBook.
Visit www.abc-clio.com for details.

Praeger
An Imprint of ABC-CLIO, LLC

ABC-CLIO, LLC
130 Cremona Drive, P.O. Box 1911
Santa Barbara, California 93116-1911

This book is printed on acid-free paper ∞

Manufactured in the United States of America

"Vu trains and speaks to thousands of people—from Fortune 500 executives, managers, and staff to university students—on *Impressive First Impressions*. Through these highly rated and interactive sessions, I've seen firsthand how the techniques presented in this book can impact and change lives. This must-read book will empower any professional to chart a better course for their career."

—Sean Gil,
Board of Directors,
Center for Research on Employment and the Workforce (CREW)

"This easy-to-read book is an invaluable guide and resource for individuals preparing to enter the workforce, sales and marketing personnel, and seasoned employees contemplating upward corporate mobility."

—Dr. Asad M. Madni,
Executive Managing Director & Chief Technical Officer,
Crocker Capital

"A must-read for all professionals and leaders. This book features truly insightful and practical strategies for crafting your First Impression—and advancing your long-term career."

—Kevin Shiu,
Director, Marketing Communication Operations,
IBM

"In an employment market where so many aspects feel out of our hands, our image and the impressions we make—both in person and virtually—remain one critical area we can control. Now is the time to see opportunity in change, to experience a professional rebirth, and this book is a great starting point. Congratulations to Vu Pham and Lisa Miyake for nailing this advice!"

—Donna Farrugia,
Senior Staffing Industry Executive and Career and
Workplace Expert

Contents

Foreword

Wisdom dictates, "you never get a second chance to make a first impression." Although true, this only barely scratches the surface of the depth and richness that encompass the study of first impressions. This book thoroughly engages this topic and proffers readers very practical strategies that are immediately usable. Grounded in years of research and training conducted by the authors, they call the book "pracademic." While it combines academic research, it translates the concept of first impressions for busy professionals who want an entertaining read that they can apply to their lives. As a reader, you will benefit from this book, whether you're a successful executive or a budding professional at the dawn of your career.

I can attest to the pracademic value of this book firsthand. Well before I read it, I had the pleasure of participating in the *Impressive First Impressions* course at the University of California–Los Angeles's Technical Management Program. As an Advisory Board member to the program, I audited this week-long course. The class comprised staff members and managers from major corporations, including Fortune 500, as well as others from government sectors. Based on participant reviews, the course ranked at the very top of over two dozen other leadership and management courses offered by the program. What you hold in your hand contains all of that knowledge—and more. I'm sure you will find great value and, I hope, professional transformation from reading this book.

One vital lesson that participants learned from the course, as I am sure you will from this book, is that *Impressive First Impressions* is more than a tool for professional advancement. It's a way of life.

The authors encourage readers to look at first impressions as a way of giving. They urge us to understand the motives and desires of others. They ask us to listen and observe what others want. This in itself is an act of giving and social generosity. More so, the authors want us to present our image and behaviors in a way that others would appreciate. Behaving in this manner ensures that we do more than respect others—that we give to them. Indeed, if every one of us led our lives in this manner, we would all advance with greater ease. I have always embraced the need to understand others and to present myself in a way that respects them. This belief and way of life have facilitated my success and this book reflects many of my values and the lessons that I've learned throughout my life. The authors passionately believe in this manner of life as I hope you will too.

Two groundbreaking chapters (10 and 11) that caught my attention are particularly noteworthy. The reader will learn how to leverage one's external environment in order to enhance first impressions. Equally important, the book translates first impressions into the digital information age as it addresses virtual first impressions. Yes, people form impressions of us even prior to meeting us. These represent just two of the areas of fresh insights and visionary thinking that this book presents. There are more that will positively change your professional and personal lives.

Enjoy your reading!

Dr. Asad Madni
President and Chief Operating Officer (Retired),
BEI Technologies, Inc.
Executive Managing Director and Chief Technical Officer,
Crocker Capital

Introduction
From First Impressions to Lasting Career Change

HOW TO GET OVER 300 PERCENT RETURN ON INVESTMENT WITH FIRST IMPRESSIONS

Our story begins with our sweet and popular protagonist sitting in a nondescript dining establishment (think classic crime noir novel). The protagonist quietly sits motionless in anticipation, knowing the dire destiny that awaits. Dozens will come with eager desire to devour our main character. They will experiment with the protagonist via cutting and consuming. Who is our pitiable protagonist? None other than chocolate cake.

This piece of chocolate cake represents the "soul" of Impressive First Impressions. What commonality do chocolate cake and first impressions share? Before answering this question, we need to examine some important research findings.

Results of a recent experiment reveal that food, such as chocolate cake, received significantly higher ratings and financial investment returns when presented in certain ways. The impression that the food made on people greatly biased their rating of the food. In an experiment conducted by Cornell University food psychologist Dr. Brian Wansink, diners clearly favored meals that made a stronger impression on them by using ambiance, language, personal biases, and presentation. The researchers showed that these factors strongly influence how people react to the food. Wansink worked with the crew of The Food Network's *Food Detectives* to prove that they could transform the food and its surroundings to elicit very different reactions.[1] The crew purchased food from a local club warehouse store. They asked diners to serve as a focus group for a restaurant menu and separated these diners into two groups.

The first group received a plain menu, literally labeled "Food," that listed their dishes in a very direct fashion. The menu listed these dishes as:

- Green Salad
- Fish Filet
- Green Beans
- Potato Casserole
- Chocolate Cake

To accompany the food, the crew served this group what they called "New Jersey Red Wine." Diners ate with paper napkins and drank wine from plastic cups. The crew plated the food on simple round dishes.

After the meal, diners rated this food an average of 3.4 out of a possible 10. One diner panned the food and declared that it felt as if someone cooked it in a microwave. Another exclaimed that they had tasted better frozen fish. A third stated that he would rather get a fast-food value meal. When asked how much they would price the meal, this first group averaged a little over $10.

The second group received a decidedly more gourmet ambiance. They began their meal with a more-palatable menu, which read "Today's Featured Menu." The list of culinary creations included:

- Crisp Mesclun Seasonal Greens with Italian Balsamic Vinaigrette
- Succulent Panko Encrusted St. Peter's Fish
- Haricots Verts
- Potatoes Au Gratin
- Belgium Black Forest Double Chocolate Cake

The wine accompaniment consisted of "Vintage Napa California Merlot." Of course, all food items came from the same warehouse store. The plating took slightly more attention to detail. The fish was served on top of lemon wedges. The beans looked more hand-arranged rather than scooped. Chocolate drizzle complemented the cake. The crew used square plates and actual wine glasses to hold the food and wine. More so, they added table cloths, flowers, and candlelight. Ultimately, this second group rated the meal an 8 out of 10. Moreover, they suggested an average price of $38 for the meal.

In total, the price boomed over 300 percent between Group One and Group Two. We conducted a similar experiment using chocolate cake with 35 seasoned employees at a Fortune 100 aerospace and defense company. The majority had over 20 years of experience and possessed a high level of attention to detail and critical analysis due to the nature of their work. The first group had undecorated cakes on paper plates and with plastic forks. Their menus labeled the dish, "Chocolate Cake." For the second group, we drizzled simple grocery store chocolate syrup and added two strawberries. We served the cake with silverware and china, labeled it "Double Chocolate Ecstasy Cake," and wrote a sumptuous description for it. We even added a little twist to the second group. We negatively biased the Group Two diners by stating that the cake was an experimental recipe from the chef.

The first group priced the cake at a little over $3, while the second cake was almost $8. Even with this negative bias, the second group rated their cake an average of over 250 percent higher in price!

This rule of great presentation applies to people as well as cake. Much research has addressed the significance of attractiveness. For example, students who appear more attractive get higher GPAs and grades from teachers.[2] These higher GPAs correlated less with genetic attractiveness than they did with grooming and personality. For boys, grooming made a larger difference than for girls. For girls, personality mattered more in earning better grades. In other words, attractiveness in getting good grades means how you groom and carry yourself. Your personality matters a great deal, and people judge your personality based on what they can observe: they can witness your behaviors.

Other studies about attractiveness corroborate these findings. Students receive higher grades on essays when accompanied by a more physically attractive photo. Attractive students also receive better treatment from teachers. Interviewers treat attractive job seekers better than less-attractive ones. Attractive prisoners earn lighter sentences as well.[3] Of course, as stated clearly, attractiveness in these cases consists of more than genetics, as they include our daily polish and practices. Impressions are thus made, not given. You can improve how others perceive your "attractiveness."

Let's return to the earlier question: What commonality do chocolate cake and first impressions share? Think of yourself as the cake. Like the cake, you can significantly enhance your impression with a little effort and some key strategies. The cake suddenly didn't taste better, but it earned a massive increase in perceived worth as a result of a few strategic actions. You can earn a higher perceived worth, whether socially or financially, by constantly striving to master your impression. The second set of studies on attractiveness shows that Impressive First Impressions extend well beyond genetics and physical appearance. We can generate a great impression through not only our looks but also our actions. As both studies demonstrate, the actions highly impacted how people perceived a meal and a person. This indicates that you can craft your impression through attention to nuances and behaviors. You could say the decorated cake and the well-groomed student both benefitted greatly from how they were presented.

These seemingly minor details extend to more than dressing up a dish or an individual, because like the elegant meal served to the second group in Wansink's experiment, people can leverage their ambiance—the environment around them. The second dinner employed subtle touches, such as candlelight and tantalizing language, that clearly influenced their audience, but in a nearly imperceptible way. Impressive First Impressions are more than vanity and clothing. They involve understanding how others view you and how you can appear better in their view through these seemingly minute details.

This book takes a much broader view of impressions, because we furnish you with techniques that go beyond dressing better. (Of course, it includes great tactics in these areas as well.) The book reveals ways to utilize your surroundings and improve your impression. It goes well beyond a list of professional dress "do's and don'ts," because it helps you to change your behaviors, leverage your immediate surroundings, and transform your way of life when it comes to presenting yourself. The extensive research, simple frameworks, proven cases, and practical strategies provide you with a readily usable tool kit. You will receive a sizable Return on Investment (ROI) in the way others treat you and how you treat others when you truly embrace and practice these frameworks and tools. We redefine ROI as *Return on Impression*. You will dramatically boost your social capital if you follow most of the advice within these pages. Imagine the professional possibilities when you arm yourself with these interpersonal tactics and wield them regularly to benefit yourself and others. Before we delve deeper into these practical strategies and possibilities, let's look at what we mean by Impressive First Impressions.

FROM "FIRST" IMPRESSIONS TO LASTING IMPRESSIONS

Right from the start, let's get to the primary point of this book:

> Impressive First Impressions mean that you must master an ongoing series of first impressions because these precious seconds will advance you throughout your life and career —and realize that it's an ongoing journey of continuous improvement.

What do we mean by that? How do Impressive First Impressions last throughout a lifetime career? It means continuously and actively taking account of our behaviors and surroundings throughout our careers, even on a second-to-second basis. Sounds challenging? We hope so. We challenge you to think of first impressions occurring more than during the first few seconds when we initially meet someone. First impressions happen even when we meet someone that we interact with on a daily basis. Our impressions "reset" each time we encounter the same person again. Mastering Impressive First Impressions means that you never truly master your impression, but instead, should always strive to improve it and tailor it to different audiences.

For example, if your colleagues see you at the office one day, they may witness you acting in a foul mood and observe very abrupt behaviors. Maybe someone dinged your car or nasty stop-and-go traffic delayed you an extra 30 minutes on your way to work that morning. You may scowl more often that day and barely acknowledge your colleagues. The next day, you may greet these same colleagues with a bright smile and bring donuts to share. Perhaps you found out that second morning that one of your stocks popped 30 percent or you received some good family news before leaving for work.

As you can see from this example, people create first impressions every time they meet with someone, even if they've worked with them for years and think they know them well. Our first impression "resets" after every interaction with others. Over time, you can change the way that colleagues and friends view you by resetting and reestablishing your first impression. You can transform how others perceive you over time, as you gradually change each and every encounter with that person.

Of course, we know many of you read this book to learn how to impress total strangers. That still remains at the core of first impressions, but we really want to shift the paradigm by reorienting the common view of first impressions. They're about more than 3 or 30 seconds, because they also constitute thinking more broadly about first impressions toward 30 (or more) years of career development.

Imagine the possibilities that arise when you can generate a fruitful and favorable impression during that first interface with a stranger—and follow-through with repeat impressions that continue to amaze them. That's what we mean by Impressive First Impressions that last a lifetime.

FIRST IMPRESSIONS FORM MUCH FASTER THAN WE COULD HAVE IMAGINED

One study discovered that we make judgments about others in milliseconds. In this experiment, researchers employed 90 different pictures of Caucasian males with neutral faces. These faces came from a previous test where participants had rated the faces a "3" on a scale from 1 (very negative) to 5 (very positive). The researchers then cropped the photos to only include faces, while excluding elements such as hair and ears. Participants did not receive any information about the purpose of the experiment. The researchers then asked the participants to rate the faces on their threat level from 1 (least threatening) to 5 (most threatening) based on their initial gut reactions. The results indicated that it took participants less than 39 milliseconds to form an impression about a face, even a neutral one.[4]

A different study demonstrates that we take milliseconds to make initial impressions about a person's trustworthiness. Our views of trust form even faster than attraction. This likely relates to our ingrained survival instincts when we first encounter a person. This study also shows that the more time exposure that participants had with the photos, the more confident they grew with their judgments.[5]

We pass judgment on objects similar to how we pass them with people. One recent study proved that people take approximately 50 milliseconds to form views about web pages.[6] We create these views from past experiences and information. This new information that we process in milliseconds already goes through complex filters and matrices that can even lead to judgments and actions. Our minds function more like a living collection of data that contain filters we all have but may not even be aware that we use.

Now let's relate these high-speed impressions to our professional lives. Have you ever wondered:

- How some master networkers and social butterflies dazzle a room within seconds?
- What techniques charismatic presenters and speakers employ to captivate their audiences immediately?
- Why particular people exhibit leadership qualities that make them shine and stand out?
- How it is that certain people project a magnetic presence and stand out from the crowd as soon as they step into a room?

With the quickening pace of our career development and work environment, we continue to adjust our judgments and decision-making equally fast. That certainly adds interesting insights, but should we succumb to such speed for success? Can we apply strategies to leverage these rapid reactions to our advantage? Can we truly wield this breakneck pace of perceptions to do more than improve our careers for only personal gain? Can we employ—and embrace—Impressive First Impressions as a *framework*, *philosophy*, and *lifestyle* to improve the lives of others as well?

Yes.

This book breaks down those intangible and invisible elements into processes that can be explained. It features practical techniques that you can immediately apply. The insight and strategies from this book stem from years of extensive research, experience from training and coaching thousands of participants, as well as the results we've achieved from applying a systematic framework for creating Impressive First Impressions.

With this book, we want to both help readers leverage this knowledge, and take a very different path by thinking of first impressions as more than a professional tool for personal gain. This book will help you to embrace first impressions as a framework, not just a snap judgment. A *framework* provides us with a more systematic way of perceiving and processing what we sense so that we can repeat our success with first impressions. A *philosophy* guides our beliefs and gives us deeper meaning than the seconds, or milliseconds, that we begin to process and act upon our surroundings. A philosophy gives depth and purpose to what we do. A *lifestyle* means that we practice what we believe and exercise these philosophies to make positive change for those around us. First impressions can create positive, meaningful change in the workplace and the lives of others.

We truly want readers to grasp the full value of first impressions as a *framework*, *philosophy*, and *lifestyle* that will benefit all parties involved. This underlying foundation distinguishes our book from existing views and the black-and-white "do's-and-don'ts" of image management, etiquette, or professional dress. Understanding how these milliseconds affect our lives can allow us to create profound professional change.

SECONDS TO IMPRESS, A LIFETIME OF IMPACT

That said, this book both discusses and goes beyond those first impressions, because it shows that these impressions have longer-term impacts (even as we ironically make even quicker judgments than originally thought!). Accordingly, we employ the term "Impressive First Impressions," not just "first" impressions, because we want to account for their lasting effects. On one hand, we can dismiss these as superficial, knee-jerk reactions that we left behind as we mature into adults. On the other hand, we can acknowledge that we still judge impressions and leverage this knowledge to benefit ourselves, as well as those around us. These initial impressions have deep and possibly permanent effects, so they're more than spur-of-the-moment reactions.

Beyond understanding these reactions, we want to promote Impressive First Impressions, because we want you, our readers, not just to understand how they work but to put them to work. To underscore this point, we capitalize "Impressive First Impressions" throughout the book because we want the term to stand out among the crowd of words. We want readers to leverage Impressive First Impressions as a system that can change professional careers.

If you repeat a consistent impression, it will eventually form a brand, which contributes to our notion that first impressions will lead to lasting ones. Repeat impressions form a brand. For instance, you may see commercials that run only 30 seconds yet run many times throughout the year. Similarly, when you drive down the freeway or cruise through a major intersection, you may see billboards that typically have only a few seconds to capture your attention. Still, the message stays simple and consistent, because the billboard stays in the same place, often on your same route to work or running a particular errand. In fact, these series of impressions have built brands that you can easily identify. See if you can link the following messages with the company or product. How many of the following can you get?

1. "A diamond is forever."
2. "____ makes hamburgers taste like steak burgers."
3. "The San Francisco Treat!"
4. "Breakfast of Champions"
5. "Double your pleasure, double your fun."
6. "Don't leave home without it."
7. "Bet you can't eat just one."
8. "I'm lovin' it."
9. "Just do it."
10. "It takes a lickin' and keeps on tickin' "
11. "Got ___?"
12. "How do you spell relief?"
13. "So easy a caveman can do it."
14. "Melts in your mouth, not in your hands."
15. "No more tears."
16. "Be all you can be."
17. "Snap, Crackle, Pop."
18. "The best part of waking up is _____ in your cup."
19. "They're g-r-r-r-eat!"
20. "You're in good hands with _____."
21. "U & us, ____"
22. "Like a good neighbor, _____ is there."
23. "M'm, M'm good!"
24. "Good to the last drop."

Here are the answers.

1. De Beers
2. A1

3. Rice-A-Roni
4. Wheaties
5. Wrigley's Doublemint Gum
6. American Express
7. Lays
8. McDonald's
9. Nike
10. Timex
11. Milk
12. Rolaids
13. Geico
14. M&M's
15. Johnson & Johnson Baby Shampoo
16. U.S. Army
17. Rice Krispies
18. Folgers
19. Frosted Flakes
20. Allstate
21. UBS
22. State Farm
23. Campbell's Soup
24. Maxwell House

How many did you get? Many people can get the majority of these, if not almost all of them. Consider how these companies convey frequent, consistent, and simple impressions that last only seconds at a time. These precious seconds have led to entire brands that exist as institutions. Coca-Cola and Pepsi. McDonald's and Subway. Target and Wal-Mart. Duracell and Energizer. We as daily consumers purchase from these companies and they influence our everyday lives. Some are so loyal to a product that they will go out of their way to make brands go back to their consistent messages. Remember when the Coca-Cola Company first introduced New Coke? People missed the original recipe for Coke so much that it spurred a wave of reaction to bring back the original Coke.

As the world grows increasingly fast-paced, and with our lives speeding forward faster with electronic technology, messages and images inundate us more. We rely on filtering these messages even faster and therefore make more snap judgments than ever before. Otherwise, we couldn't function with such a flood of information and data that could overwhelm us. First impressions, as a result, matter now more than ever. The old 30-second rule may even be too long to form an impression, as technology and the rapidly functioning human mind prompt us to act and react more quickly than ever before. Successful professionals need to stand out more than ever from the sea of information and their market-savvy competitors. As a result, we address an area that has barely received attention in the past: the virtual impression. We'll cover that in chapter 11.

In addition to advertising and marketing, entire institutions continually validate the notion that humans subscribe to these first and impactful impressions. These institutions heavily rely upon and/or study impressions, such as academia and private-sector corporations. Entire fields of research continually address impressions and their impacts, although not in such direct terms. For instance, many professionals nowadays know about the 30-second elevator pitch. In our fast-paced society, you'll need to impress your audience much more adeptly and quickly than in 30 seconds. Also, consider fields that study culture and social behavior, such as communications, psychology, and sociology, that contain numerous research studies on how our physical appearance and behaviors influence our reactions to one another.

Even fields that do not overtly claim relations to impressions actually find their very foundation on physical appearance and their social and cultural impacts, such as Gender Studies or Ethnic Studies. Organizations and practitioners that rely deeply on impressions include those from cosmetic dentistry and plastic surgery to architectural/interior design and entertainment, as well as sales and marketing. In addition to these institutions, private corporations focus on diversity efforts as well as comply with discrimination laws that actively address physical appearance, such as age, hygiene, and weight. First impressions permeate throughout almost every institution in our society.

We want you to apply these same principles to your own professional presence. This book guides you through the process, as it provides both insight and strategies that will transform your first impression into an Impressive First Impression.

WHAT MAKES THIS BOOK UNIQUE AND INSIGHTFUL?

How does this book stand out from others in the field? This book paves new paths about impressions, while also taking a very fact-based, rigorous approach to the topic. Plus, it's written in an accessible and practical way. The key points that make this book unique are its:

1. Systematic frameworks called the *Impressions Diamond Model* and the *Impression Zones*
2. Emphasis on Impressive First Impressions as a way of life
3. Discussion of the model and mantra: *Embrace Your ACE* (Audience, Culture, Environment)
4. Strategies for crafting your virtual impression
5. Approach that "you never get a second chance to make a first impression," but you can change and reset future impressions
6. Benefits geared toward BOTH individuals and organizations
7. Emphasis beyond "first" impressions
8. Practical, nuts-and-bolts strategies and advice
9. Extensive research

1. **Systemic Frameworks Called the *Impressions Diamond Model* and the *Impression Zones*:** Our book features a systematic framework for forming and leveraging impressions. You can easily follow the entire system or simply parts of it so that you can benefit from this carefully crafted yet practical framework. We call the two parts of this framework the *Impressions Diamond Model* and the *Impression Zones*.
2. **Emphasis on Impressive First Impressions as a Way of Life:** When people generally discuss professional image, presence, and impressions, this usually manifests itself in a list of do's and don'ts, as well as a means for individuals to get ahead in their professional lives. We believe that a true impressive impression depends on doing more than setting up smoke and mirrors. Embrace your impressions in order to change your behaviors, not just outer appearance but in ways that benefit others and impact your surroundings in positive ways.
3. **Discussion of the Model and Mantra: *Embrace Your ACE* (Audience, Culture, Environment):** The bulk of work on image management and first impressions focuses primarily on individuals wanting to improve their impression. They seldom account for ACE. This includes the

"A" of how to read an Audience, the "C" of understanding how Culture relates to this area, and the "E" of how to leverage your Environment, not just yourself. This advanced set of strategies will truly boost your impression. By the end, you will Embrace Your ACE.

4. **Strategies for Crafting Your Virtual Impression**: With the growth of telecommunications, we interact with people before we even meet them in person. They can judge us through phone calls, e-mails, instant messages, and video conferencing. True, virtual impressions existed before, with snail mail and photos, but we engage in much more frequent virtual communication today than ever before. Virtual impressions, therefore, matter more now than ever.

5. **Approach That "You Never Get a Second Chance to Make a First Impression," but You Can Change and Reset Future Impressions**: First impressions technically do only occur once. That doesn't mean that you can't change and improve them. We believe that first impressions reset, even when you interact with the same individual or audience. Your second and subsequent impressions allow you to modify your interactions. Although difficult to change, we really believe that, with time and effort, you can interact with the same individual and audience but change the way you subsequently approach them. You can gradually modify your first impression. First impressions can't be repeated, but they're not the final word.

6. **Benefits Geared toward BOTH Individuals and Organizations**: Books that deal with image and impressions generally focus on individuals getting ahead in their careers with knowledge about these issues. We focus on the fact that "a rising tide lifts all boats," because Impressive First Impressions will provide great value to organizations as well. Imagine if entire teams, departments, and companies implemented this concept. This would create more impression-savvy employees who each sport their individual flair.

7. **Emphasis Beyond "First" Impressions**: True, first impressions are very important, but we also employ the word "impressions," because the first few seconds can lead to much longer-term impact. These initial impressions can last a lifetime, so Impressive First Impressions can furnish a lifetime of positive results.

8. **Practical, Nuts-and-Bolts Strategies and Advice**: Busy professionals want convenient and useful strategies and advice. In our book, we feature many concise sections readers can access in short bursts of reading. Each section offers a *Practical & Tactical* area that stands out, so that readers can immediately apply these strategies.

9. **Extensive Research:** This book goes beyond our own experiences; it is the most extensively researched book on the topic that's geared toward professionals. We furnish a practical guide for crafting Impressive First Impressions, while backing our work with the most detailed research available.

Yes, part of Impressive First Impressions is to provide competitive advantages and differentiators. We practice what we preach, so that's why we just outlined these for our readers. This book will help you stand out in your own unique way, while assisting your organization in maximizing its employee self-awareness and awareness of others.

And remember that mastering first impressions can last a lifetime and you can continually change and "reset" your first impression throughout your life.

HOW WE'VE ORGANIZED THIS BOOK

For ease of reading as you build your Impressive First Impression, we organized this book by first focusing on strategic frameworks and philosophies. That way, you get a worldview of how to leverage your optimal impression. That summarizes Part I. In this part, you'll learn why first impressions matter and how they affect us every day. We articulate why they're the most important 30 seconds of your career and how they last throughout your professional life. We elaborate on the *Golden Virtues* and the *Impressions Diamond Model*. Who can resist valuable information in the form of precious stones and metals?

Moving to more specifics, we emphasize what we call the *Impression Zones* in Part II. These zones break up different parts of the body, as well as focus on overall behaviors and elements that contribute to your impression. We provide useful information for each element that we entitle "Insight & Information." Immediately after "Insight & Information," each element contains a "Tactical & Practical" section that offers specific advice. The *Impression Zones* also serves as a checklist for you to follow when you have an important event to attend. Just go down the checklist before you leave your home to attend that event and you'll minimize any faux pas.

Part III features frameworks and advice for a more advanced reader. It encourages you to "Embrace Your ACE." ACE stands for "Audience," "Culture," and "Environment." You'll learn that this book differs from other image, etiquette, or professional dress books in that we spend this time focusing on people, places, and objects around you. Gain awareness of these external factors and you will elevate your impression to the next level.

Also in Part III, we'll take impressions to an even further level, as we move toward virtual impressions. People make judgments of you before they even meet you. This happened with regular postal mail, but gains more importance with the proliferation of phone and electronic communication. Many people don't consider how much an e-mail or their phone presence affects how others perceive them. We will turn you into a virtual virtuoso when it comes to forming your impression.

NOTES

1. *Food Detectives*: Liquid Nitrogen Cocktails. Episode 209, first broadcast 24 March 2009 by Food Network.

2. Michael T. French and others, "Effects of Physical Attractiveness, Personality, and Grooming on Academic Performance in High School." *Labour Economics* (20 January, 2009), 373–382.

3. Richard A. Posthuma, Frederick P. Morgeson, and Michael A. Campion. "Beyond Employment Interview Validity: A Comprehensive Narrative View of Recent Research and Trends over Time." *Personnel Psychology* 55.1 (2002): 1–81; Michael J. Murphy, Don A. Nelson, and Thomas L. Cheap. "Rated and Actual Performance of High School Students as a Function of Sex and Attractiveness." *Psychological Reports* 48.1 (1981): 103–106. Ronald Mazzella and Alan Feingold. "The Effects of Physical Attractiveness, Race, Socioeconomic Status, and Gender of Defendants and Victims on Judgments of Mock Jurors: A Meta Analysis." *Journal of Applied Social Psychology* 24.15 (1994): 1315–1344.

4. Moshe Bar and others, "Very First Impressions." *Emotion* 6, no. 2 (2006), 269–278.

5. Alexander Todorov and others, "Inferences of Competence from Faces Predict Election Outcomes." *Science* 308, no. 5728 (10 June 2005), 1623–1626.

6. Gitte Lindgaard and others, "Attention Web Designers: You Have 50 Milliseconds to Make a Good First Impression!" *Behavior and Information Technology* 25, no. 2 (2006), 115–126.

Impressive First Impressions
Strategic Frameworks

Part I provides frameworks that underpin the entire concept of Impressive First Impressions, from how it impacts our everyday professional lives to how you can organize and leverage it. Impressions influence many facets of our lives, from common professional interactions and leadership scenarios to financial transactions and life-and-death situations. We firmly believe that Impressive First Impressions are more than a concept; they're a way of life. We explain that as well.

We infuse *Impressive First Impressions* with a framework that you'll find concise and easy-to-understand. Once you think of it at this strategic level, applying the nuts and bolts of it will come easy to you. (That's Part II of this book.) Briefly stated, impressions consist of combinations of images and interactions. It's more than how you look; it's how you behave. That's why we move beyond image, because impressions mean altering your interactions with others as well. When done right, a concept that seems as static as image transforms into a dynamic part of your daily life. Interactions, on the other hand, are inherently dynamic, because the word consists of "actions" that we share with others; thus the "inter" part takes great effect.

In Part I, you'll discover that Impressive First Impressions contain rich and complex nuances and strategies. Once you grasp these intricacies and simplified frameworks, you'll benefit greatly from this section.

Chapter 1

How Impressions Affect All of Us
Work, Money, and Death

WHOM WOULD YOU CHOOSE?

To truly understand the impacts of first impressions, gauge your own using the following photos. You're about to see several pairs of choices. For each pair, select the choice based on your initial reaction. We will provide no other information about these people and you will rely solely on their photos. You should spend no more than five seconds per choice. Be honest and go with your first reaction. Avoid over-analyzing your choice. (We'll discuss the choices immediately after you've selected one choice from each of the pairs.)

1. Whom would you select as your personal bodyguard?

(Shutterstock)

(Shutterstock)

2. If you had a toddler, whom would you choose for your child's babysitter?

(Shutterstock)

(Shutterstock)

3. Which person would you want as your financial planner?

(Shutterstock)

(Shutterstock)

In pair No. 1, the majority of people in our training sessions selected the muscular man. Think about the little details that would prompt such a choice. Here are some areas of note: They use words such as "tough," "rugged," "intimidating," and "scary" to describe him. They typically mention that his muscles mean that he stays physically fit and strong, so he can defend you against an attack. His sneer makes him look tough. He sports tattoos, which make him look tougher. Tattoos require enduring pain and we usually associate them with tough people. His intimidating looks would likely prevent any conflict or assault from happening. The lady, they assert, looks too weak and welcoming. A few people do sometimes opt for the lady, because they argue that she looks like she could negotiate through an attack. Others state that she looks welcoming and this may disarm potential attackers. They also fear that the muscled man may cause conflicts instead of prevent them. In general, however, most would choose the tattooed man over the formally dressed woman.

In pair No. 2, the large majority tend to choose the slightly older babysitter with collar-necked shirt. People we ask generally state that he looks "professional" and "responsible." They cite his collar-necked shirt as sending those messages, as well as the fact that he can afford a mobile phone. They refer to his open smile, which makes him seem trustworthy. They believe that the second babysitter, sporting a hood, looks shady. He resides within a dark environment and under a hood, so it makes him look less trustworthy. They associate hoods with bank robbers. His lack of smile counts against him because people believe his unsmiling face shows that he's hiding something and his hood and tough stare make him a difficult person to deal with. A few choose the babysitter with the hood. They state that the hooded man is younger in age and this will help him relate to their children. They don't like the fact that the other man talks on his mobile phone and may prove too distracted to watch their kids. Most, however, would choose the first babysitter.

In pair No. 3, the lady in the suit almost unanimously wins on this one. She looks the role of a financial planner and the other one … well, simply doesn't.

What commonalities do all of these images share? They all represent different career choices. Now think of yourself as an interviewer. You just made some snap judgments about each and every one of these people to select them for a specific job position, from bodyguard to babysitter. You engaged in making a choice of one person over the other within each of these pairs. Your inherent biases and experiences influenced your decision-making. Your quick judgments just determined someone's professional fate. We "bake in" certain assumptions when interacting with others. These assumptions come from our personal past experiences. If we rely on these experiences too much, then we remain closed-minded and incapable of change. If we ignore these past experiences, then we doom ourselves to make the same mistakes again and fail to see patterns. Of course, you would hopefully use as much data as possible about each person, but when you're pressed for time and have little access to more data, you'll have to sometimes make that quick choice. Our tendencies are to make snap judgments based on our experiences. Change roles just a little bit and place yourself in the position of any one of these photos. Now think about how others make extremely rapid judgments about you.

You may say, "I don't make decisions that fast and based on such unfounded judgments." Indeed, you may not, but you will base your final decision on a series of smaller judgments, just as people form quick impressions of each of these photos. If everyone were so unbiased and took a long time to make decisions, then why do many of us spend so much time on such subtle dress details before an interview? Why do we spend so many hours preparing for an interview that may last only 30 minutes? Many people seriously ponder what shirt and suit to wear. We allocate hours to anticipate and refine answers to questions that our interviewers may or may not even ask. These hours of preparation may culminate in an interview decision that takes less than 30 minutes to make. In fact, the interviewers may make up their minds in 30 seconds. We know that these nuances will affect judgments that combine to support the final decision.

These interviewers may not yet make a final decision within seconds, but they certainly are making a multitude of smaller decisions that contribute to the final decision. In fact, in one study of almost 80 job interviewers, job candidates' first impressions not only affected the decisions made by these interviewers, but the interviewers also actually changed their behaviors based on these impressions. When interviewers, for example, favored an interviewee based on a positive first impression, they treated these interviewees better. The interviewers exhibited more positive tones and words, asked fewer questions of the candidates and even attempted to sell their organization to these favored candidates more than the other job seekers.[1]

Your forthright eye contact and pleasant smile may endear you to the interviewer. Conversely, your frantic body language and worn shoes may scream to them that you lack attention to other subtle details. Ultimately, these smaller judgments about you lead to your success or failure in landing the job.

And why leave this wonderful impression behind after that initial interview? Why not project that Impressive First Impression every possible moment that you can while on the job? This will prompt others to treat you in a different, better light.

IMPRESSIONS AND MUSCLES

Making great first impressions will prompt us to change our short-term perceptions and behaviors, but if we make consistent efforts to change many of these short-term behaviors over time, that leads to long-term change. This can apply to our habits, quirks, and general lifestyle. You may ask, "How will some minor modifications in the way I act transform my life?" How does a series of regular short-term behaviors result in long-term change?

Take the example of the muscular man whom many have chosen as their bodyguard. He cultivated his physique through many hours of training and bodybuilding. You can see tangible and visible proof— his muscles. You can imagine how long it took him to develop these, since the human body contains over 600 muscles. When he first started working out, he likely had significantly less muscle mass. Sure, he could lift weights the first day, and as science shows, the initial boost in muscle size would instantly grow visible. Sure, his muscles may not transform him into who he is in the photo, but the quick rush of adrenaline and blood pumping through his veins in the few minutes following his workout would enhance this impact. Still, this muscular enlargement is both temporary and small compared to his build in the photo.

He probably experienced a lot of pain as well, because lifting weights means tearing your muscles before they can rebuild. The phrase, "no pain, no gain" fully applies here because he can only achieve this goal by pushing out of his comfort zone. Most people initially go to the gym, but ultimately many prefer comfort to effort. Fit-minded behavior tapers off as people spend less time doing it. The muscles shrink back and get softer over time.

The muscular bodyguard could let himself go and his muscles would shrink, but you can tell that he probably actively and consistently maintains his physique. His muscles solidify and grow over time. They remain strong and noticeable, even though he's not always lifting weights, because he's invested so much time into them. They can serve as more than his first impression, but constitute his brand. You could say that he engages in a series of short-term workouts that lead to a long-term lifestyle.

Relate this to what people normally consider an Impressive First Impression. Focusing solely on first impressions is like pumping iron one time to spark a temporary desired effect. Impressive First Impressions are more like engaging in a regular regimen of physical training so that the physique remains, even when the adrenaline and blood rush subside. Generating Impressive First Impressions means consistently sending your message and image to others so that they will "impress" these into their thoughts and feelings when they think about you. This regular behavior transforms a first impression into a lasting brand. Getting to this level takes pushing out of your comfort zone, exercising consistently, and investing time and energy. The results, however, will remain impressed in people's minds.

This book starts with first impressions, but takes them to the much-higher level of Impressive First Impressions. We want you to impress your first impression on others, which leads to your personal brand. We will take you from the impressions in the first few seconds to the decades of the tailored, unique brand called "you."

There's no secret or trick here. We provide you with scientific research, tested experience, and training results that form the foundation of this book. The rest, we leave up to you. You can read this book through and learn much, but to really benefit, you'll need to "impress" upon yourself that you need to seriously engage in and practice the contents within this book. Those many participants that we've advised and guided who really followed this process state that they achieved significant, positive results that have been life-changing. Results include weight loss, more self-confidence, more business, and promotions. If you take the time and energy to apply these concepts, you will create an Impressive First Impression.

Treat this process just like building muscle: You will see gradual growth rather than instant transformation. More so, view it as a domino effect of gradual change rather than one major transformation. One executive at a university spoke of his weight loss, change of clothing to more-fitted pieces, as well as increased self-awareness and self-confidence. His peers treat him better, he raises funds more easily, and he notices improved initial reactions from strangers he meets. He specifically attributes this "life-changing" momentum to learning about first impressions. Where does this function as a domino effect? For example, when you wear fitted clothes, you feel better and this may prompt you to get more physically fit. As you get more fit, you may trim down and wear new clothes that fit your new style and self-confidence. These all mutually reinforce one another in a web of change. You can also view this as an upward spiral of success. Just change one or two elements at a time—and keep it up—then tackle more. You'll see a domino effect of change.

DEBUNKING THE MISCONCEPTIONS OF FIRST IMPRESSIONS (AND FACING THE UGLY REALITY OF FIRST IMPRESSIONS AT WORK)

Some believe that first impressions consist of the first few seconds of interacting with someone. We challenge that characterization. To form a truly Impressive First Impression, we believe that you have to follow through with the impression that you gave. Impressive First Impressions entail the act of truly embodying and enacting the impression you first projected to others. We hope what you first projected reflected a great side of you that you already have. If you put your best foot forward during that initial encounter, do you make efforts to at least remain consistent with that in subsequent encounters? Beyond that, maybe you've improved since that first interaction with others. Impressive First Impressions mean truly living the impression you've shown others, and also learning and improving from it.

Let's start with an ugly reality that we should all face. In a study of over 3,000 participants, researchers tracked the success of New Year's resolutions. Fifty-two percent of participants stated their confidence in achieving the resolutions. By the end of the year, only 12 percent had actually accomplished their beginning-of-year goals.[2] That's barely more than 1 out of 10 people! Many start with a bang and ring in the New Year by jogging in the morning or hitting the gym. This new behavior pushes us beyond our comfort zone (straining and paining our bodies), stems from a timeline and specific event (the ending of one year and beginning of another), and has yet to fit into our practiced routines (probably overwork or engaging in sedentary behaviors). Usually within weeks to months, we revert back to our regular habits of bodily complacency. If you regularly go to the gym, you've probably noticed that it's significantly more crowded at the beginning of the year than the fall or end of the year.

What does this have to do with our professional lives? Like a physical workout, our professional work starts with a similar big bang, yet often continues in small pops. Let's consider a common professional reality—interviews. Many professionals who land great jobs exhibit the following attitudes and behaviors: they show up not even punctually, but early. In predictable fashion, they dress in crisp business wear and pay attention to subtle nuances in their attire. These polished folks speak with care, consideration, and respect. They choose their words carefully and listen very well to their prospective bosses.

Enthusiasm and ambition exude from their voices, faces and overall body language. They truly want to come into your office and work with you. Sounds a lot like the New Year's resolution to exercise more, doesn't it?

So what's so ugly about this reality? Like the New Year's exercise resolution, they are first attempts that usually peter out over time. People won't step outside of their comfort zones and instead choose complacency. They project their best first impression for a specific event called the job interview. Over time, they return to their less-attractive habits.

These professionals mostly showcase these attitudes and behaviors *before* they land their jobs. They exhibit these positive attributes during the one day that results in a successful interview and perhaps a job offer. They create a stellar first impression on that day, but as the months and years pass, they let some of these sparkling attitudes and behaviors deteriorate. They may start to come to work tardy more often. They may use the Internet and phone more than necessary for personal communication. Enthusiasm diminishes. Conflicts and lack of respect proliferate. For many people, one of their best-performing days in their position at work occurrs before they even started.

Why do many of us limit our workplace behaviors to only the early stages of our job? Just because we know more about our jobs as we gain more experience and efficiency, why does that lead many people to grow complacent? Did we overexaggerate and oversell ourselves?

Envision a workplace where our usual attitudes and behaviors align with those that we represented during that interview when we made that excellent first impression. Why just view that great interview day as a fleeting moment when you can live that moment every day? Yes, it will take effort, but recall that those efforts consisted of carrying yourself better in dress and behaviors. These actions landed you the job, so they likely will yield you better assignments, promotions, and professional relationships. As you assume these more desirable roles, you'll also improve from where you were during that first impression.

We want to transform that ugly reality into the ideal one. That starts with creating an Impressive First Impression. So let's debunk a myth. Some people truly believe that making Impressive First Impressions merely consist of wowing others in the first 30 seconds and then it's done. As a result, people believe that managing first impressions merely means sending superficial and manipulative messages about yourself. And look what happens when people put their best foot forward during job interviews, only to slack off when they're on the job.

Yes, these people used a great first impression, but they forgot that the word "impression" contains the word "press" in it. They sure did press their image and message into the minds of their prospective employers, but did they press hard enough to make these stick? This takes effort and the consistent "pressing" and "impressing" of others is more than superficial. If you only impress a message on someone once, they may quickly forget. On the other hand, if you continue to impress a message frequently and consistently, it leads to lasting impacts . . . and that's an Impressive First Impression. Engage in repeated and consistent impressions and you start to form a personal brand. People will begin to identify you with that personal brand. More so, if you improve upon that Impressive First Impression, people will take note of that, too.

Impressive First Impressions should last for more than those first 30 seconds or 30 minutes. Aim for something more like your next 30 years. By gradually transforming your first impression more positively, we want you to live that impression consistently and regularly. In the chapters that follow, we'll provide you with effective and practical strategies that will improve your professional impression. We'll give you tools and concepts to influence those around you in ways that benefit everyone. Only you, however, can truly make these changes to create that impression you want to make. From the thousands of participants we've trained to improve their first impression, we hear and know that they truly grow when they take the first step by implementing and consistently practicing what they've learned and committing to change.

Take, for example, partners at top accounting or law firms. To stay abreast of their industry and continue to increase their clients and rates, they're always reading new material, learning from their clients, and engaging new ideas. In gaining new clients, they constantly have to engage in business development. Another way of looking at it: They have to constantly interview to win a client's trust and business. To maintain their clients, they're always performing at their best to please them. And in doing their best, they're improving and delivering results for clients. In turn, they receive client references and support. All this sounds simple and it is. As one executive stated to us, it takes consistent effort, motivation, and practice. It takes consistently making an impressive impression, and once you develop that, it grows into your personal brand of reliability. Continuous improvement serves as the cornerstone for Impressive First Impressions.

The same applies to the best employees in a company. These best employees frequently seek to augment their skills and learn new ones. This represents what organizations call continuous learning and improvement. They treat every day at work as an opportunity to learn and grow. They step past the borders of their comfort zones. They always behave and interact as if they're interviewing. They stay at the top of their game, because they've learned that success and improvement means that they need to advance. If they made New Year's resolutions, these top performers would likely keep them. These successful professionals do more than create their first impression; they live that impression with their best behaviors, be it before or after the interview. And if they adopt new techniques and strategies to improve themselves, they integrate them into their daily lives.

The Impressive First Impression that lasts leads to an impressive brand. We want you to experience this profound change and continue to improve. You picked up this book because you wanted to improve your impression, so we challenge you to actively engage this book. We challenge you to be a top performer in forming an Impressive First Impression and a lasting brand. We challenge you to join that 12 percent of people who keep to their resolutions (whether New Year's or otherwise) and transform their lives. This book goes far beyond guiding you to craft that Impressive First Impression—it helps you to live it.

FIRST IMPRESSIONS IMPACT OUR EVERYDAY LIVES

First impressions are worth much more than most of us realize. Why do some professionals of equal qualifications (or even sometimes lesser ones) get further ahead than others? Why do some divisions and departments in our organizations succeed over others, despite the fact that they may perform no better (or even not as well) as others? Does this fit a logical, rational way to run an organization? Of course not. The impressions that people make greatly impact their perceived value. Our impressions can make or break careers, cost or make millions of dollars, and even save or destroy many human lives. Research repeatedly demonstrates that humans make snap judgments of one another based on mere seconds (or less) of interaction. In today's intergenerational workforce, the facts and research indicate that these impressions are vital across all generations. What are these impressions worth to us? Let's examine some examples here in the United States:

- **Over $4,734 Per Year for Just 6 Inches of Height:** Ever notice that world leaders and business leaders tend to stand taller than the average person? Men in these major leadership roles tend to be of above-average height for men and women leaders tend to stand taller than average women. From a different, but related perspective, ever notice that fewer major leaders stand below average in height? One study found that Fortune 500 male CEOs tend to stand at slightly over 2 inches above the average American male height of 5′9″. In the United States, 14.5 percent of men measure above-average height, whereas 58 percent of these Fortune 500 CEOs measured above-average height.[3]

  We even embed height and leadership into our language, such as the term "Napoleon Complex," which signifies a shorter man who over-compensates for his height by acting more aggressively. We lack a similar term or complex for a tall man who behaves aggressively. We advocate "standing tall" when presenting our views, instead of "shrinking away" from challenges. Our society tends to create barriers for shorter people, even in our language.

  One 2004 study found that each inch of additional height yielded approximately $789 per year in earnings.[4] Just think about this: someone 6 feet tall makes $4,734 more per year than someone 5 feet, 6 inches tall, controlled for age, race, and weight. And remember to adjust for salary increases and inflation, as this number would be higher by today's standards. Over 40 years of a person's career, this means hundreds of thousands in compounded earnings! In a similar study of white males, researchers found that the difference was $850 per inch, per year—based on 1996 dollar values.[5] Indeed, our reactions to, and perceptions of, height shape our impressions of others. Thank goodness for legal and organizational diversity initiatives to challenge these height differences. We've never encountered any organization that advocates treating people differently by height, but we do want to highlight this as a general and individual perception that leads us to act differently. As humans, we're thinking animals and may unconsciously treat others differently based on height. We hope this book raises awareness and changes perceptions about height, as well as provides practical tips to address these differences.

- **Job Interviews and Work Performance:** Even before we start a job that launches our professional careers, impressions already determine if we even land that job. Just look at almost any career or job website. Virtually all of them make some mention of first impressions and how interviewers often make up their minds within the first few minutes of the interview. As with the research we previously cited, how "attractive" a person seems does affect how well others will treat and evaluate them. For instance, male judges were asked to rate essays written by purportedly attractive or unattractive female authors. The attractive author was rated by male judges as significantly better than the unattractive one. Studies demonstrate that even since childhood, teachers tend to assess attractive children at a higher level.[6] Other studies have proven that more attractive people tend to function as more persuasive communicators.[7]

- **The Same Rings True with Recruiters:** As with how organizations judge interviewees, the impressions that companies make on these prospective job recruits matters. In fact, the cultural impression that organizations leave on job seekers matters more with the younger generations than they ever did with the older ones. According to a recent article in *Talent Management*, college recruits and younger employees care a lot about work-life balance, development opportunities, and job flexibility.[8] For instance, think about how people portray certain companies. Google conjures images of a youthful environment that drives innovation and collaboration, a casual dress environment, flexible schedules, and open work spaces. On the other hand, when you think of Merrill Lynch, you may think in terms of trust, time-honored foundations, long-term relationships, exclusivity, formal dress, and structured work spaces that connote wealth preservation and confidentiality. Clearly, these two work cultures reflect their founders, historical contexts, and individual industries, but both also convey clear impressions that attract different types of employees.

- **Intelligence and Credibility:** Although students deemed more attractive earn higher grades, those considered more intelligent also likely fare well. Studies demonstrate that people view those who wear glasses as more intelligent and honest than those who don't. One experiment by ABC News clearly demonstrated this. They asked a pair of young, identical twins to wear identical outfits. One, however, wore glasses and the other did not. The newscasters then asked two classes of students which twin they would select to help them with their homework. Thirty-six out of 38 chose the twin with glasses.[9]

- **How We Elect Our Presidential Leaders, Past and Present:** From historical to present presidential elections, we partly choose our leaders based on what impressions they make on us, not just the content of their messages or actions. We see this in different cases, from decades ago to recent elections. Let's start with the first televised presidential debate and compare this with more-recent debates. In the 1960 U.S. presidential election debate, Richard Nixon lost to John F. Kennedy by a narrow margin—and his appearance influenced his political demise that year. Those who listened to the debate via radio favored Nixon. Those who viewed the debate on television awarded the debate's victory

to Kennedy. Impression reigned. During the debate, Nixon sweated pro-
fusely and inadvertently sported a five-o'clock shadow. Television viewers felt that Nixon seemed nervous and untrustworthy as a result of his
appearance. Those who had less data to form an impression of Nixon
(such as visual cues from their televisions) relied more on his content
and rewarded him with their support, while those with more data
formed judgments more heavily based on his impression than his content. The latter group tipped the scales in favor of Kennedy.

Even in current years, we encounter many people who may not be
able to articulate the position of a particular president or presidential
candidate on serious issues from domestic economics to foreign policy,
but these same people can certainly characterize their impressions that
they form about these same leaders. For instance, people think of
Hillary Clinton as a cold candidate or as a strong woman (depending on
whether or not they support her). Many describe George W. Bush as
either a straight talker or simpleminded. People call Bill Clinton "Slick
Willie" or a charming figure and label Ronald Reagan as a nice person
or a deceptive actor. Do many of us really know where they stood on
more than a couple of issues? When we speak of these leaders, do we
really only speak about their content or do we also look at their perceived character? We certainly do both.

One study correlated the outcome of U.S. congressional elections to
the level of perceived competence of each candidate's face. The researchers provided participants with random samples of actual congressional
candidates from 1996 to 2006 elections. They used over 167,000 binary
choices for participants and found correlations between the candidates'
faces and their attractiveness, honesty, and likability. Most surprising,
the researchers discovered the strongest correlation between candidates'
faces and their perceived level of competence. The perceived competence
also correlated with the outcomes of the elections, as the candidates
with the more competent-looking face won their elections.[10]

Relate how we select U.S. presidents with how we select people for
jobs, promotions, or just simply how we treat people. We gravitate
toward people every day the same way we elect people to jobs. Given a
choice between yourself and one other job candidate or colleague up for
promotion, would it prove more advantageous to have others to treat
you like Kennedy rather than Nixon? If that's the case, it leads naturally
to your appearing and behaving the way the job requires. It takes a
conscious effort to appeal to those around you at work to look and act
the part.

- **Billions of Dollars:** Impressions are becoming increasingly important
  to our daily lives. We see this from the growth of industries such as
  cosmetic surgery, health, and beauty. Americans spent approximately

$12.4 billion on cosmetic procedures in 2005. According to the American Society for Aesthetic Plastic Surgery, between 1997 and 2005, total cosmetic procedures increased by 444 percent! These procedures were primarily to enhance a person's looks rather than for health reasons. For instance, the top five surgical procedures in 2005 were:

1. Lipoplasty (Liposuction) with 455,489 procedures performed.
2. Breast Augmentation with 364,610 procedures.
3. Blepharoplasty (cosmetic eyelid surgery) with 231,467 procedures.
4. Rhinoplasty (nose reshaping) with 200,924 procedures performed.
5. Abdominoplasty (tummy tuck) reported 169,314 procedures.

   Similarly, the health, beauty and wellness industry generated over $45 billion in 2005.[11] Yes, Americans are not only increasingly aware of their impressions, they are actively spending dollars to alter their physical being to improve these impressions. Those who undergo cosmetic surgery may have numerous reasons for engaging in these procedures. We're not advocates or detractors of plastic surgery, but we think it's an important indicator that Americans grow increasingly conscious of their images and the impressions that these images form.

• **Numerous Human Lives:** What trait often comes to mind when one sees a person who wears glasses? Practically everyone responds "intelligent" or "smart" (of course, some point out the reality of bad ocular genetics . . .). In the 1970s, Cambodian leader Pol Pot believed that glasses and knowing a foreign language reflected intelligence and education. He believed that people armed with these capabilities would prove threatening to his governmental rule. For that reason, he killed anyone who wore glasses. Although a brutal dictator, Pol Pot was a shrewd man who risked exterminating innocents to minimize the risk of rebellion to his regime. Similar perceptions hold true today, as research shows that people who wear spectacles are viewed as more intelligent than those without them. Pol Pot's perceptions about eyeglasses were reflected 30 years later, in ABC News' experiment involving glasses, twins, and homework help.[12]
   As in the case of the Nixon-Kennedy election, a leader's impression directly impacted millions of people who judged these very leaders. Whether matters rest on the perceptions about or by these leaders, impressions can truly influence the fate of entire nations and populations.

   As we demonstrated, first impressions are not just about money and power but a multitude of human lives. Hair stubble and sweat have hindered a person's road to leading an entire country. Wearing eye glasses has resulted in genocide. At minimum, first impressions affect our daily professional lives. The book addresses questions such as: How do impressions affect our lives and what are the benefits and consequences? What practical strategies can help us with these impressions? They affect all of us virtually every day, with immense benefits and consequences.

HOW TO BENEFIT FROM AND LEVERAGE AN IMPRESSIVE FIRST IMPRESSION

Within the extremely short time it takes to form an impression, people will make assumptions about one another in multiple ways, from a person's intelligence and communication skills to their education and income level. As human beings, we make these judgments and either reap the benefits or suffer the consequences from these very judgments that stem from the first impressions we make on others.

When people form these first impressions about others, be they fact or fiction, their impressions can prove very positive or negative. Leveraging those precious seconds can lead the way to success. As they say, you don't get a second chance to make a first impression. This first impression tends to stay in the mind of others. The primary purpose of this book is to assist professionals with navigating through the process of establishing an Impressive First Impression. As mentioned, impressions produce lasting impacts, so as you repeat a consistent and powerful impression, you form a brand. Yes, repeat impressions culminate into a brand that endures in the minds of others and that's why we go well beyond "first" impressions. Instead we advocate for our brand, which is Impressive First Impressions, because they stem from initial interactions with others and also create lasting impacts on others.

On an individual level, if you harness only a fraction of knowledge and strategy about generating Impressive First Impressions, you will help your professional development, improve your career prospects, and grow your network. For an organization, this book will help employees appear and act more polished, grow their confidence, and collaborate toward forming a common brand identity. We've poured countless hours in researching, training participants in impressions workshops, and developing our systematic framework so that you can quickly learn and leverage all of these elements within one easy-to-grasp guide.

IMPRESSIVE FIRST IMPRESSIONS AND PROFESSIONAL DEVELOPMENT

We gear this book toward both current working professionals and aspiring professionals, such as students and job seekers. Day to day, people encounter numerous impressions but only pause to think about them. As busy professionals, we even more rarely stop to plan and carefully create the impression that we want. We took the time to research, analyze, and frame the science and art of impressions. If you can take the time to read this book, then take the time to do the same about your individual impression.

This book provides both a powerful framework and practical techniques that will lead to professional advancement. That said, Impressive First Impressions benefit individuals and institutions alike. Making Impressive First Impressions is more than about individuals, because it will greatly enhance the workplace team, department, and organization as a whole. What are the primary professional benefits of this book?

- **Individual Professional Development**: Anyone who works in a setting in which presenting oneself as a polished professional will benefit. Almost everyone interviews for a job and this requires polish. Polish does not mean simply wearing a suit and tie or dressing formally. We define polish as the optimal image that a particular organization wishes their employees to project. Polish varies by organization. For instance, polish in a video game company may mean hip, cutting-edge casual fashion and hairstyles to reflect the creativity and innovation of its designers. Polish in a law firm may mean donning a conservative suit and tie with fine details. It's a major step toward career advancement to make a strong impression and build credibility with our supervisors and colleagues. Whether you're in a casual or formal work environment, Impressive First Impressions will benefit almost anyone. Whether you already have a job or are seeking a job, Impressive First Impressions will benefit almost anyone.

- **Team Management and Leadership**: A strong leader needs to make a strong impression. Any good leader and supporter should embrace this notion. A leader or manager who projects behaviors or images that do not align with the team can lose credibility. For instance, most leaders may dress slightly more formally than their team or may project an air of confidence and enthusiasm that functions as models for those around them.

- **Sales, Marketing, and Client Relations**: This book helps anyone engaged in business development of any kind understand that buyers of services will judge their vendor within seconds. It will help refine business developers' approaches.

- **Organizational Cohesiveness:** Projecting the same repeat impression leads to a brand identity. Inculcating impressions into the minds of others will ensure that you and your organization send a strong, consistent brand message.
- **Confidence-building:** Sometimes, the basics hold true. Anyone wanting to build confidence should understand how others perceive them, as well as what they can do to generate these impressions within others.
- **Health:** Health relates to building confidence and looking good to others. The age-old sentiment that if a person looks good, they feel good, still holds true for most of us. Creating an impressive impression means staying fit and isn't just about our looks and behaviors when trying to impress others.

The impressions most individuals make on others can cost them tens or hundreds of thousands of dollars, if not literal millions. Losing out in a job interview because you didn't "fit" what the interviewers wanted can cost tens to hundreds of thousands for most people, and even more to some. Failing to close a prospective client deal because you presented yourself poorly can cost similar amounts. Many of us have been or know one of these people. Take these real-life examples that most working professionals can relate to:

Case No. 1: No Suit, No Tie, No Promotion

One person in his early 30s asked us why his colleagues did not take him as seriously as others and why he kept getting passed up for management-level promotions. After much discussion, we identified several primary areas that he could change to create a better impression. For instance, he looked young compared to others of his age, so he needed to alter that perception.

More interestingly, when asked if people wore suits and ties to work, he told us that about 4 out of 5 men did at least wear ties, if not suits. He refused to do so because he thought it was uncomfortable and unnecessary. If 80 percent of his office wore ties and he was part of the 20 percent who didn't, how could others promote, let alone follow, someone who dressed more casually than they did? This point proved more significant when the office culture espoused dressing more formally.

Third, he similarly refused to wear a watch, because he deemed it uncomfortable. We asked the other participants in the training session what wearing a watch signifies to them. They unanimously agreed that it demonstrated punctuality and an awareness of time management. The gentleman said that he simply pulled his mobile phone from his pocket to get the time. Have you ever seen someone look at their phone under the table during a meeting? People generally view this as someone sending an e-mail or text message while others were talking. They often perceive this act as one of inattentiveness and may not even realize that this gentleman was simply keeping track of time. The perception did not align with the reality, but the consequences of the perception affected him in the workplace. He distracted and annoyed others at the meeting.

Simple features such as ties and watches can have an immense impact on how others perceive us, whether negatively or positively.

Case No. 2: "How Blunderful to Meet You"

One woman arrived at a job interview twenty minutes late with her shirt on inside-out (and yes, the tag stuck out too). Needless to say, she didn't get the job at this Fortune 500 company, but that's only one outcome of the story. Immediately after she left, the five people on the interview panel kept talking about her tardiness and lack of attention to basic details. They barely even commented on any of her responses or thoughts, but instead continued to express shock at how poorly she presented herself. Needless to say, the job seeker maintained her position—as a job seeker.

Not landing a job can come from similar factors, such as mismatched clothing, poor grooming, bad body language, or even bad body odor. Think about the earning potential lost each time someone does not land a job. Worse, if they're not currently employed, consider how long it takes to land another job interview and their time suffering stress and anguish as bills pile up and self-esteem drops from being unemployed. According to the American Psychological Association, 81 percent of Americans are stressed from a bad economy.[13]

Case No. 3: Overdressed for Success

One of our training participants recounted how when he first went from a job at a consulting company to a biotech company, he wore a suit and tie to work the first day. His boss and co-workers laughed at him and told him to dress casually. Unlike the first example, this person came to the office overdressed. Employees in some office cultures, such as young, hip Internet or video-game companies or creative departments in advertising firms, may balk if you sport a fancy suit and tie to work. Dress appropriately so that you can form strong team bonds with your colleagues. You can dress slightly more polished and formally than they do, but not too much more. One rule of thumb says to dress 10 percent better than your peers and clients. If the typical employee wears T-shirts and jeans, then you can wear polos or casual button-up shirts with slacks. A tie may prove too formal. Similarly, a culture where people wear suits without ties means that you can add a tie for more effect. Sure, when in Rome, you should do as the Romans do, but we believe that you should do a little bit more to create an impressive impression.

Case No. 4: Real Estate Mistake

Virtually everyone has dealt with the slimy salesperson. One gentleman we interviewed recounted how he spent an afternoon house hunting with his two children. He found an ideal home after some online researching, so he entered the place during the open house. Surprisingly, nobody greeted him, so he and his children explored the downstairs on their own. They admired the wonderful home's layout and proceeded upstairs into the first bedroom and bathroom. As they casually walked further along the upstairs hallway, a woman walked out of the master bedroom.

She was still putting on her shoe and her hair seemed disheveled. An equally tousled man followed her out of the bedroom a few moments later. Clearly, the couple did more than simply try to sell the house. They got plenty of personal use from it as well. What a horrible impression to make on this gentleman (and his two children)! This serious buyer took his business elsewhere and the couple lost tens of thousands in potential commission.

As seen in this story, most of the factors with interviews apply to business development and sales. When we hear the words "slimy salesman," what makes a person say these words? It can come from some of the same factors as a job interview, whether from clothing or body language. Have you dealt with a vendor or salesperson who made that first impression in a negative way?

These cases represent common work scenarios and costs that result from bad impressions. Let's go back to the process we discussed earlier—the job interview. Almost every working professional needs to go through this process, but just interviewing won't land people jobs. Successful interviews depend on understanding the interviewers' expectations, maximizing your polished image, interacting well with others, and influencing them to hire you over the hordes of qualified and hungry candidates that could be knocking down their doors.

NOTES

1. Thomas Dougherty and others, "Confirming First Impressions in the Employment Interview: A Field Study of Interviewer Behavior" *Journal of Applied Psychology* 79, no. 5 (1994), 659–665.

2. Richard Wiseman, "New Year's Resolution Experiment" *Quirkology* (2007), http://www.quirkology.com/UK/Experiment_resolution.shtml (Accessed June 12, 2009).

3. Malcolm Gladwell, *Blink: The Power of Thinking Without Thinking*. New York: Little Brown and Company, 2005.

4. Timothy A. Judge and Daniel M. Cable, "The Effects of Physical Height on Workplace Success and Income: Preliminary Test of a Theoretical Model" *Journal of Applied Psychology* 89, no. 3 (2004), 428–441.

5. Nicola Persico and others, "The Effect of Adolescent Experience on Labor Market Outcomes: The Case of Height" *Journal of Political Economy* 112, No. 5 (2004), 1019–53.

6. Robert M. Kaplan "Is Beauty Talent? Sex Interaction in the Attractiveness Halo Effect" *Sex Roles* 4, no. 2 (1978), 195–204.

7. Joann Horai and others, "The Effects of Expertise and Physical Attractiveness Upon Opinion Agreement and Liking" *Sociometry* 37, no. 4 (1974), 601–606.

8. Lindsay Edmonds Wickman, "On the Hunt for Talent" *Talent Management* 4, no. 3 (2008).

9. "What Glasses Say About You: Putting Perceptions About People Who Wear Glasses to the Test" ABC News (2009). http://cosmos.bcst.yahoo.com/up/player/popup/?cl=12304452.

10. Alexander Todorov and others, "Inferences of Competence from Faces Predict Election Outcomes" *Science* 308, no. 1623 (2005).

11. American Society for Aesthetic Plastic Surgery. 2005 http://www.surgery.org/download/2005stats.pdf (Accessed June 4, 2009).

12. Stuart J. McKelvie. "Perception of Faces with and without Spectacles" *Perceptual and Motor Skills* 84, no. 2 (1997), 497–498.

13. Kimberly Garza, "Secrets of Chillaxation" *Spirit Magazine* (2009).

Chapter 2

The Impressions "Diamond" and Systematic Impressions

THE IMPRESSIONS DIAMOND MODEL

This chapter provides the four key elements of understanding impressions. We call these the four "I"s; this foursome of elements work together to form the *Impressions Diamond Model*.

Many professionals express frustration that some people naturally possess social skills and easily showcase these skills with minimal effort. The reality is that people who engage in seemingly seamless social interactions often have years of experience and practice. They have ingrained these skills until the skills become habits. Remember that social skills are still skills—and we can learn any skill with understanding, training, and practice. Part III provides you with tools with which you can practice (called the *Impression Zones*), but first, we'll help you understand the concept of impressions through the Impressions Diamond Model.

THE FOUR "I"s OF IMPRESSIONS

Just remember four "I"s in the shape of a diamond—that's the basis of how impressions work. The diagram in this chapter offers a simple and memorable visual that will help you understand the process of how impressions function. Then, we define and explain each of the four "I"s.

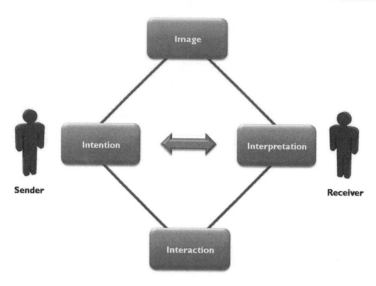

1. **Intention**: A message almost always has an intention behind it. This book defines an intention as the reason behind how you choose to act or behave. True, sometimes we send unintentional messages, but it's important to be fully aware of what intentions we have before we can effectively design the messages that we send. This concept applies to impressions as well. All impressions have intentions, so we start with the fact that there is usually some intention involved with impressions, whether or not the communicator can fully grasp the nuances of the intention.

   The message sent does not always openly reflect the intention. For instance, when a person wants comfort and to save money, he may decide to wear his favorite old, red shirt rather than buy a new one. The intention is to seek comfort and save money, but wearing this red shirt can be interpreted in many different ways, because we don't always know what's going on in the audience's minds.

2. **Image**: Many people conflate the term "image" with impression. Image is only one part of an impression. An image consists of the physical and behavioral elements that an individual engages in without anyone present. The image exists regardless of how others interpret them. For example, if we take the previous case of the person who wants comfort and financial savings, he dons the red shirt to satisfy his own wants, not necessarily because someone else directly influenced this action. The wearing of the red shirt is the image, which accompanies the person's intentions. The physical element is the red shirt and the act of wearing it is the

behavioral element. The image does not involve others, but only the person wearing the shirt.

Of course, an image does not always reflect the intention. For instance, if you are stopped in a traffic jam and reach for an item in your glove box, you may accidentally honk your horn. The intention of honking the horn was because you wanted an item, not because you wanted to honk the horn. Thus, the image and the intention do not always align. In this case, the image here is simply the act of honking the horn and the sound of the horn.

3. **Interaction**: The interaction consists of the image with others present. The image is an action that you may take, but it can occur without anyone around to witness it. For example, when the person wears his old red shirt at home, but then walks downstairs and his spouse observes him, this creates an interaction. In other words, the act of the person encountering his spouse in his red shirt is when both people form an interaction. With the case of the horn, the interaction is not simply you honking it, but when others hear you honk your horn.

4. **Interpretation**: The interpretation is what others think about the interaction. This happens when another person interacts with us and witnesses the image we send. That other person can now conjure an interpretation. With regards to the red shirt, the wearer's spouse may interpret the shirt as that person being slouchy (instead of comfortable) or too cheap to buy a new shirt (instead of frugal). With the horn-honking, it may have occurred by accident, but a person in a neighboring car may think you're honking at him. He could become nervous, thinking he did something wrong, or he could grow angry and reply with a furious counter-honk or obscene gesture.

Once you understand this very simple yet useful framework, you can see that first impressions mean more than simply primping yourself in a vain way. Carefully ascertain and analyze how others view you and craft your image and interaction. An impression consists of more than image but instead encompasses all four factors of the Impressions Diamond Model.

Chapter 3

Impressive First Impressions
"Gold" and Way of Life

IMPRESSIVE FIRST IMPRESSIONS AS A WAY OF LIFE

Impressive First Impressions mean much more than a list of rules or advice to follow. They represent philosophies that run deep, and a mastery of these beliefs means that we can change our worldview and behaviors to create more impactful shift to our surroundings. Yes, this may sound philosophical and zen, but in actuality, if a person does not *embrace* a framework and philosophy, then how can she change her behaviors? If a person holds an attitude of cynical skepticism toward ideas, how can she truly expect to improve and benefit from these new ideas? Bottom line: If you don't believe that you can improve your first impression, then you probably wouldn't have made it this far. That's already a major milestone of progress because you remain at least open, if not intent, on further pursuing this change.

We discussed earlier that job interviews can be among one of the best-performing days for professionals, yet attitudes and behaviors often deteriorate as some employees get too accustomed to and complacent in their jobs. If they took the first impression projected during the interview and used it as a model to behave at work, the workplace and their individual experiences would improve. It makes sense that employers hire their employees partly based on that interview and the way that it aligns with the organization's culture and environment. The question remains: can we live up to the impression that we projected during our interview? Employers hire employees based on the persona showcased during the interview. Can you make a truly conscious effort to be that person every day?

Take another example: the idea of diets. Every year, several new diet trends come out in the form of various books and models. They each have their signature benefits, but somehow Americans increasingly grow more obese each year. It's often not the model that's flawed, but whether or not a reader actually follows the model. Although adhering to a dieting system would likely yield results, many people fail to do so. If so few follow these models, imagine how few actually *embrace* and make changes that lead to healthy lifestyles, not just temporary diets. Nutritionists, fitness trainers, and health experts have not changed their fundamental position that the basis of good health and diet come from proper eating and exercise. Most people know that they can improve their weight and health if they take this advice, but how many of us truly make profound changes to our eating and workout habits? How many of us truly *embrace* this healthy lifestyle? The ones who do are fit and healthy.

We make a similar assertion with Impressive First Impressions. We can provide frameworks, philosophies, and practical advice, but if readers go through the book and reject the advice throughout, how can they expect to make profound changes and advancements to their professional lives? Some may say that their content, abilities, and skills are what truly matter in the workplace, while changing their image and interactions are superficial smoke and mirrors.

Of course we agree that what professionals produce matters a great deal, but why discount and dismiss another tool? A hard drive makes a nice product, but doesn't a hard drive encased in a beautiful frame look better and attract more buyers? If we were always so logical, wouldn't more-compact, higher-quality Beta tapes have beaten out larger, less-crisp VHS tapes? If you had to select a job candidate from two clones, but one clone was late to the interview, would you honestly hire the tardy candidate over the punctual one? Impressive First Impressions should not supplant strong content, abilities, and skills, but they do provide another enhancement and tool for professional advancement that make these attributes even stronger.

THE FOUR GOLDEN VIRTUES OF IMPRESSIVE FIRST IMPRESSIONS

This book compiles the core tenets of Impressive First Impressions into four key concepts. To complement our four "I"s from the

Impressions Diamond Model, this book presents the four Golden Virtues that will help you understand how to construct Impressive First Impressions. The Diamond and Gold in this book will make you shine. The four Golden Virtues of Impressive First Impressions are:

Golden Virtue No. 1: Humans Are Thinking Animals
Golden Virtue No. 2: Content May Be King, but Impressions Are Aces
Golden Virtue No. 3: Impressions Are About More Than the Individual
Golden Virtue No. 4: Repeat Impressions Form a Brand

Golden Virtue No. 1: Humans Are Thinking Animals

Pop Quiz: Mountain Lions and You

Thousands of years ago, Aristotle believed that we're just "thinking animals." Even today, he's still quite right.

Quiz: A parent leisurely walks down a hiking trail with his beloved toddler when the pair spots a mountain lion a few dozen feet away. The creature beholds both parent and child as well. With mere seconds to act, what should they do?

The gut reaction often leads us to the "Fight or Flight?" response. In training sessions about first impressions, some participants choose to flee, hoping that they can outrun the lion. As is often the case, four legs prevail over two and probability dictates that the feline will fetch its prey. How can the average professional desk jockey prevail over a professional hunter that kills to survive? Most of us feel lucky to survive the week into Friday. Mountain lions love to leap on the backs of their victims and clamp down on the victim's neck with suffocating pressure. Their flexible spine runs on par with the cheetah so that they can swiftly maneuver around obstacles and quickly change direction in mid-sprint. And yes, they climb trees too. This choice will likely result in the pair becoming lion lunch.

Some participants choose to fight and defend their child from this perilous panther. (They're also called cougars and pumas, but who can think of taxonomy at a time like this?) Weigh the odds: in one corner, we've got an average human of working professional fitness with relatively little to no hunting and fighting skills. In the other corner, awaits *Felis concolor*, a vicious carnivore with exceptional speed and strength. Oh yes, it sports claws and fangs that do go straight for the jugular. Not many would bet on the human in this case.

Some participants do go for option three, the road less traveled. Throw the toddler at the hungry lion and hope that's enough to keep it sated as they escape. We'll let you form your own opinions about this answer.

The Right Answer: The parent can prevent an attack with an impressive impression. The best method for repelling a lion attack, and even preventing the attack altogether, remains in projecting oneself as a formidable figure. Rather than a vulnerable being to protect, the parent in this case can think of the toddler as a valuable asset. The parent should place the toddler on his shoulders and have her wave her arms so that both appear larger, while the parent makes calm noises and shouts. In many cases, the lion will leave humans alone. Size does matter and it produces not just an impressive impression, but a practical one as well. You can also throw objects at the mountain lion. It can't throw objects, but you can, which suddenly establishes your dominance and advantage during this situation. Talk to lion trainers and they will give you similar advice.

From Crime to Careers, Humans All Discriminate

Impressive First Impressions influence more than animals, because they influence humans as well. As our Greek philosopher so correctly believed, we often rely on our instincts the way animals do, but we like to think of ourselves as rational beings. In reality, we sometimes act more like instinctive animals than rational beings.

Let's move from lions to humans. Humans have to engage in some form of discrimination to describe others. Many confuse discrimination with prejudice. To discriminate literally means to tell the difference. We have to discriminate between day and night or near and far to function on a daily basis. Prejudice occurs when we first discriminate and then treat others unequally. Discrimination has received a very negative connotation, but here, we distinguish it from the term "prejudice." We have to tell the difference, or discriminate. For example, how would the victim of a mugging describe the suspect to the police? When law enforcement asks victims of a crime to describe the suspect for a sketch, what elements often enter into this suspect sketch? Height, weight, race, hair and eyes all play into the description. Suspect sketches on the news often state these dimensions to assist the public in finding the suspect. There are few other ways to describe the person, but these can often be changed, such as clothing and accessories. Are we that much better than the mountain lion who discriminates its prey based on size?

From crime to careers, these physical judgments affect our everyday lives. So what does this have to do with Impressive First Impressions in the workplace? Recall the example of how tall people make more money than shorter ones (filtered for race, gender, and age). Do you honestly believe that many managers consciously reward taller people more than shorter ones? These unconscious behaviors demonstrate that we may think we behave rationally, but our subconscious and instincts still influence our actions to some extent. Like the mountain lion, we equate height with power and tend to respect these taller people. On the other hand, like how we deal with mountain lions, we can consciously plan, strategize, and practice how to change our impression to influence others subconsciously and get what we want.

Does it make us better than animals if we discriminate based on these physical characteristics such as height and weight? Does this mean we should unabashedly discriminate against others? Not at all. As champions of diversity, we believe that people need to resist stereotyping while leveraging and promoting diversity. Still, our psychology as humans remains similar to an animal's because we still judge others based on physical characteristics. We do want you to acknowledge that our animal instincts get us to form impressions and stereotypes that we can think through and understand.

The lesson here is that animals rely on their instincts when judging impressions. We can use this to our advantage by systematically analyzing how others may instinctively react; thus we can leverage these instincts to help with our impressions. On the other hand, we can also see through and dissect impressions so that we can better understand what others may present to us on the surface.

The statement "humans are thinking animals" means that we do make snap judgments based on our instincts. On one hand, we can leverage this to our advantage to create an impressive impression. On the other hand, we can employ our rationality to think through and analyze impressions to benefit ourselves and those around us.

Golden Virtue No. 2: Content May Be King,
but Impressions Are Aces

Sometimes, we get so distracted by a person's image that we actually can't fully focus on what they're saying. When someone has a piece of food on their lips or caught between their teeth, it grows increasingly difficult to listen to their words as they flash damp, dark spinach bits sandwiched between their teeth. How about when we fixate on that stain on their shirt or the smell of their breath? During the 2008 Super Bowl, a *Tide* commercial featured an interviewer and an interviewee with a stain on his shirt. The stain became so distracting that it started to develop a voice of its own. The stain's voice gradually grew louder than the interviewee's voice, making it almost impossible for the interviewer to hear the words coming out of the interviewee's mouth. Given that the Super Bowl and its commercials appeal to a mass audience, this comical commercial reflects that most Americans do understand impressions at some level because they would need a basic understanding to appreciate the commercial's humor.

In the daily workplace, people often present ideas during regular meetings—some fail miserably and some succeed, sometimes despite the quality of their content. On a similar note, many people have heard and cited the crucial "elevator pitch" because it generally works. The elevator pitch consists of what to say to grab the listener's attention within 30 seconds or less. Advertisers state that freeway billboards should ideally incorporate no more than eight words to send their message to cars that zoom by these signs. Both of these cases seem to involve impressions. And involve rapid ones at that.

Why does a concise and powerful "elevator pitch" by a salesperson usually capture someone's attention much more effectively than the engineer who prepared a 43-slide PowerPoint presentation or the accountant who formulated financial statements with hundreds of line items? That one eye-catching visual cue or value statement will almost always trump detailed content.

Think about it this way. If you receive frequent pitches and presentations, you would likely tire of reading long-winded and detailed documents. Instead, what if someone told you that you could triple your investment return with no risk? How about if they stated that your bottled drinking water costs more per gallon than your car's gasoline? How about if they stated that they could save your company $1.8 million a year? Would you now at least take a few seconds to listen?

These three statements are all true. One magazine used that investment tagline and when readers opened to the article, the article recommended that they transfer their low-interest-bearing savings accounts to higher-interest Certificates of Deposit. This was not at all a profound insight, but it drew readers' attention. Similarly the water and gasoline example got many people who complained about gas prices to question their bottled-water consumption. We're sure some started drinking tap water again. Finally, the $1.8 million savings resulted from a company that simply needed to hire a retired employee as a consultant, since no current employee had the knowledge of how to develop a product properly. The failed product tests prior to the consultant's hiring cost the company over $1.8 million.

Almost every one of us has had some distracting gaffe like the stain or the copious PowerPoint at some moment in our lives. More importantly, what are the costs of these faux pas? What if it cost a person their potential job because of a bad interview, a potential client sale or even just chipped away at the respect of their colleagues? Without dispute, content plays a critical role, but impressions precede content. Content may be king, but impressions are aces. We need both content and impressions to succeed.

Remember that "content may be king, but impressions are aces." Before you go into exhaustive details, check to see if you have effectively captured your audience's attention first.

Golden Virtue No. 3: Impressions Are About More Than the Individual

Sometimes, people get self-conscious thinking about themselves, which can make working with impressions difficult for people with this state of mind. Often, it's easier to think about others than to focus on ourselves; this segues directly to Golden Virtue No. 3. In order to effectively leverage impressions, think beyond yourself by understanding the perspectives of others. Experts and researchers have constantly emphasized that people should know their audience. We apply a similar notion by conveying that understanding others can better help us to shape our own impressions.

We take this further by asserting that we should *help others to help us with our own impressions.*

For example, many Americans believe that white has a celebratory connotation such as for weddings, but in certain cultures, white symbolizes death and has a place at funerals. Therefore, if an American goes to an Asian celebratory event wearing white, it may send a tragic message rather than a festive one. Think about the person you want to impress and what that person wants. This will facilitate what steps to take in making a good impression.

We also believe that people can leverage their friends and colleagues to help themselves, as well as those friends and colleagues, form a strategic impressive impression. Think of yourself as a halo that sits atop your friends, or vice versa. They never physically touch you or are a physical part of you, but they shine their light on you. We call this the Halo Effect. Most people define the Halo Effect as a person's set of traits, either positive or negative, that influence how others perceive this person's subsequent traits. In other words, once they see a person as good, they continue to view further actions by that person as good, even if those actions may not be good. Similarly, once others view that person as bad, they will view subsequent actions, even good ones, as bad.

We define our Halo Strategy as a Halo Effect, but as it relates to people rather than traits. When others see you with a positive person, they'll likely perceive you as positive. When they encounter you with a negative person, they'll likely perceive you as negative. Whom you engage with and associate with will color others' opinions of you. The Halo Effect does indeed apply to impressions, which further reinforces our belief that impressions are more than about the individual.

Take for example, the case of Heidi and Phillip. If Phillip just met others and discussed how smart and humble he was, as well as stated all of his accomplishments, we're sure the words "arrogant" and "self-absorbed" may not even describe him enough. Instead, if his friend Heidi introduced Phillip to others and spoke about his same intelligence, modesty, and accomplishments, he would shine. Heidi would also shine, because she spoke highly of others rather than only about herself. Wouldn't Heidi now be a person that you would likely want in your corner as a colleague or friend? The case of Heidi and Phillip also works in reverse. If Heidi spoke poorly to others about Phillip when he was absent, then she would be a negative gossiper. If you were one of those listening to Heidi talk about Phillip, would you trust Heidi? She could gossip about you to others when you're not around. The bottom line is to be the positive Heidi. You will look good and earn trust because you helped others look good. We'll discuss this tactic in a subsequent section of the book, but for now just remember that impressions are more than about the individual.

First impressions with impact require that you really think about others and how to leverage one another's trust and generosity to create a Halo Effect of impressions. When you think about how to make others look better, you'll do more than look like that positive and encouraging person—you'll act and become more like that person. Seek trusted people and those that you truly want to help, and you'll actively go out of your way to enhance their impressions to others. In the process, you'll benefit, but give first and you'll get later. It's not all tit for tat, though. As you truly embrace Impressive First Impressions, your heart will guide you toward helping a friend.

This concept of tapping into a positive halo exists all around us and in our daily lives. We just need to gain awareness and consciously practice it. Look at testimonials on book covers from well-known folks. People delivering the testimonials support their friends' books and lend their credibility to these authors. In doing so, the person quoted on the testimonial also gets his or her name in print and enjoys a positive and encouraging impression. Both the person delivering the testimonial and the author benefit as they mutually increase book sales and recommendations.

Even more commonly, we use job references on résumés, as well as endorsements on professional sites such as LinkedIn. With tens of millions of users and a function on this website that encourages endorsements, good social networkers know that generating a warm and glowing halo for one another pays off and propagates goodwill. You'll also see these comments (good and bad) on user reviews of products and services, such as those on consumer sites. The collection of positive comments will steer you toward purchasing a particular product or service. And who better to recommend these than a user who has experience with these same products and services?

The age-old, but time-tested, advice of knowing your audience also comes into play. When we say that "Impressions are about more than the individual," we also assert that you should understand your audience. Good speakers know that tailoring their message and delivery method to their audience goes a long way. For instance, if you're a corporate executive speaking to nonprofits about fund-raising, you should consider that talking about profits and the bottom line may not appeal. Nonprofit staff generally didn't join their organizations for money but rather to support a cause that impassions them. Instead, this same corporate executive should focus on her passion for what she does and how nonprofits can parlay their passions into winning over donors. Similarly, virtually all professionals, from good authors and teachers to savvy advertisers and marketers, know that embracing the audience's wants and needs will lead to success. These successful professionals construct their impression or the impression of their messages with others in mind.

Success at appealing to and impressing others means understanding others. This means the act of being conscious and considerate of others' attitudes and motivations. This takes time and energy, but also creates empathy and giving because you will share the underlying values of your audience. Going beyond yourself also means giving, because you're giving your time and energy to others, simply by even thinking about them when they're not present. If you can dedicate that time to your audience, then picture what will happen when you're actually interacting with them. Think about more than yourself and you'll improve your impression.

We go into detail in Part III where we encourage you to "Embrace Your ACE," which means to embrace your "Audience," "Culture," and "Environment."

"Impressions are more than about the individual," because if you make others look wonderful, you'll likely look just as wonderful. You'll generate generosity and understanding, which leads to benefit all around you. It's a simple rule, so simply adhere to it.

Golden Virtue No. 4: Repeat Impressions Form a Brand

When you present an impression with a consistent message and consistent frequency, it can form a personal brand. For example, one corporate executive at a Fortune 500 company transformed a perceived weak habit into a powerful personal brand. Others always commented on how this executive talked very emphatically with his hands. In fact, this habit extends well back into his childhood. At a friend's birthday party when he was 6 years old, he played charades with the other boys. One of the boys swung his arms around wildly, and instantly all of the other boys laughed boisterously.

They all screamed that executive's name. For years, he struggled with the internal conflict of either moving his hands and feeling self-conscious or restraining his hand movements and feeling accordingly constrained. His staff, who saw his hand movements, began to tell him that they associated him in positive ways with hand movements. He grew increasingly confident in gesturing with passion and energy. He labored to optimize his hand movements and colleagues, both within and outside of his company, began to recognize that his hand gestures accompany his excellent presentation skills. He has increasingly been an in-demand speaker at many venues.

Would you like your colleagues to think of you every time they see or hear elephants? One executive we work with at a different Fortune 500 company does. He views elephants as his biggest asset and not just because of their size. When traveling abroad, he discovered some beautiful elephant figurines that could fit into the palm of his hand. He brought home a few to give to friends and colleagues. People around the office began to associate him with elephants. More so, they began to talk about how he remembered his employees, friends, and colleagues, even when he traveled. When he returned to that foreign country, he brought home dozens more elephants and began keeping them on a stand in his office. When people visiting him saw these multitudes of mammoth mammals, he told them the story and would offer them an elephant as a gift. By repeating the same action, he branded himself with the elephants and at the same time cared for and gave to those around him. Elephants may supposedly have great memories, but in this executive's case, his colleagues remember him for his elephants.

Others sport a personal brand that ties intimately with their impression. Think about famous figures and our associations with them. These people repeatedly act a certain way, state specific messages, or wear and carry a certain item that signifies their signature message. Here are just a few:

- Musician Elton John: Sunglasses
- Wonder Woman: Golden Lasso
- Superman: Red cape and "S" insignia and his phrase, "Up, Up and Away!"
- *American Idol* Judge, Simon Cowell: Harsh comments
- King Arthur: Camelot and Excalibur
- The Philippines government official Imelda Marcos: Shoes

- Former President Bill Clinton: Pointing with his thumb
- Former President Ronald Reagan: Jelly beans
- Donald Trump: Hair and real estate
- Arnold Schwarzenegger: "I'll be back"

To truly create Impressive First Impressions, you can elevate repeat impressions to form a consistent and bold personal brand that conveys a "uniquely you" message.

In this chapter, we emphasized the importance of embracing the four Golden Virtues of Impressive First Impressions. Through internalizing and believing in these, you will optimize your mastery of first impressions and truly benefit those around you. To summarize, the four Golden Virtues of Impressive First Impressions are:

Golden Virtue No. 1: Humans Are Thinking Animals
Golden Virtue No. 2: Content May Be King, but Impressions Are Aces
Golden Virtue No. 3: Impressions Are About More Than the Individual
Golden Virtue No. 4: Repeat Impressions Form a Brand

PART II

The Impression Zones
From Insight & Information to Tactical & Practical

In chapters 4 through 7, we present a series of short, quick bursts of practical advice. These chapters feature two key learnings:

1. **Insight & Information**: These sections contain research, common issues, and scenarios that affect professionals in the workplace.
2. **Tactical & Practical**: Equally important, we focus on strategies and techniques that anyone can use in their daily lives, which we call *Tactical & Practical*. This complements *Insight & Information*, because you can take your understanding of the issues and facts to the next level, as you apply strategies and techniques provided in this section.

We divide Part II into bite-sized pieces that you can quickly read, digest—and practice. This creates immediate value and positive change that you will notice rapidly. Again, we emphasize practice, because reading and digesting comprise only a couple of vital components. Implement these strategies and techniques in your daily life and you will begin to notice a difference.

Treat this section like both a step-by-step guide and a reference manual. It's step-by-step because you can focus on small changes rather than thinking of it as an overwhelming transformation. Pick one section and commit to making that change rather than trying to do it all at once. Imagine if you implement just one part of this section per month, that's a dozen changes in one year!

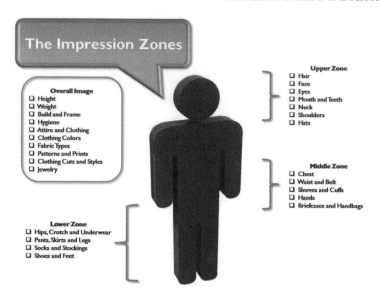

Moreover, we provide a systematic approach to tackling these changes. We call these *Impression Zones*, where you can focus on one zone at a time, or specific elements in one particular zone. We also feature practical details through *Insight & Information*, as well as *Tactical & Practical*, in areas that do not necessarily fit into the Impression Zones. We call this section the Overall Image, which focuses beyond one specific area. This section of our book provides real-life applications to critical areas of Impressive First Impressions.

Why did we divide our specific advice into the key zones? We believe that if you go head-to-toe in a systematic way, you'll get more consistent results. Think of it as a checklist that you can follow. You have checklists for quality control in manufacturing and design, so why not have one for people as well? We can systematically improve ourselves. Plus, if you simply focus on one element within a zone per month, that's twelve elements that will improve your impression over the course of a year. No need to tackle everything at once. The Impression Zones create a step-by-step process where you can gradually grow. Recall the web-like model, where if you enhance one area of your image or interactions, this will positively impact other areas. In addition, you can skip around to areas where you need the most work rather than reading this section linearly.

Chapter 4

Overall Image

INSIGHT & INFORMATION
HEIGHT

This book's introduction covered some research on height, so a more concrete set of cases and examples should further reinforce the notion of how height plays into a workplace impression. We hope that raising awareness about our perceptions and reactions to height will make us more equitable, but many people will still follow their instinctive reactions to height.

Recall Aristotle's statement that humans are thinking animals, which we've adopted as one of the Golden Virtues in making an Impressive First Impression. We instinctively react to height the way animals do. Animals of all kinds assert their presence by increasing the appearance of their height. Tarantulas stand on their hind legs when threatened. Peacocks flare their feathers to look larger. We may think that these behaviors promote aggression and conflict, but in actuality these kinds of behaviors prevent conflicts. Asserting one's height can prove beneficial in that way as well.

We can see the importance of height anywhere from primitive mating rituals in the animal kingdom to something as sophisticated as voting in one of world's most powerful democratic nations. This rang particularly true in the 2004 presidential election, as the 5-feet, 11-inch George W. Bush debated the 6-feet, 4-inch John Kerry. Though Kerry stood significantly taller than Bush in real life, they looked surprisingly similar in height during the televised debates. How so? Bush's representatives demanded that the lecterns stand 50 inches tall and

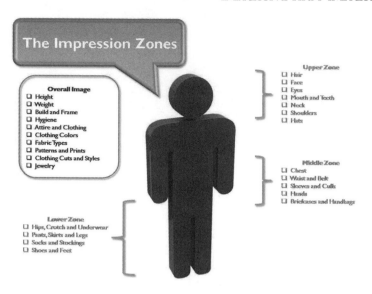

The Impression Zones

Overall Image
- Height
- Weight
- Build and Frame
- Hygiene
- Attire and Clothing
- Clothing Colors
- Fabric Types
- Patterns and Prints
- Clothing Cuts and Styles
- Jewelry

Upper Zone
- Hair
- Face
- Eyes
- Mouth and Teeth
- Neck
- Shoulders
- Hats

Middle Zone
- Chest
- Waist and Belt
- Sleeves and Cuffs
- Hands
- Briefcases and Handbags

Lower Zone
- Hips, Crotch and Underwear
- Pants, Skirts and Legs
- Socks and Stockings
- Shoes and Feet

be placed 10 feet apart, so that the television audience would less likely notice (or be influenced by) the height difference.[1] Why was this strategy so critical to the Bush campaign? It turns out that historically size does matter in presidential elections, as the taller candidate has won the popular vote every time since 1888 with two exceptions.[2] In the end, Bush won the 2004 election; his campaign's strategy of addressing height in televised debates may have had a little something to do with his success.

Even our rationality takes a holiday based on the way we treat taller people in the workplace. We've discussed the research that indicates the annual pay differential for height, as well as the research on business and political leaders who benefit from height. When we intersect gender with height, women in the United States are approximately 4 inches shorter than men. Now consider that women in the workplace can wear higher heels to level the playing field. One CFO that we interviewed at a major company recalls how when she began to wear heels to work, people treated her better. She conveyed that it had a positive impact on her career advancement. However, consider one important caveat: occasionally, we pose the question, "What is the socially acceptable maximum heel height that a woman can wear to work?" Almost everyone cited 3 inches and some cited only 2 inches. (We've only encountered a few women who have stated 4 inches—and they work in the entertainment industry, where people take more fashion risks.) Many describe women who wear taller heels as less credible, as they use words such as "loose," "promiscuous," or "unprofessional." We hope society gains more tolerance here in the future. The social limitation of heel height does maintain gender differences: Given the 4-inch difference in height between men and women, coupled with the "norm" of wearing no more than 3-inch heels, women still have a slight height disadvantage.

Spread the word on these height and gender-based discrepancies, so that people will more thoughtfully consider their own height biases and perceptions. As stated, we're not at all advocating heightism (prejudice against one's height), but rather we aim to raise awareness so that all of us can check our assumptions and knee-jerk reactions to height. Still, the reality of height and pay differences exist, so the dilemma of balancing social change and professional practicality remains an issue that we hope readers will address in the workplace.

Bottom Line: We often pay heed to racial and gender differences in diversity efforts and workplace discrimination. We hope that organizations surface the often less-discussed issue of heightism. We also know that there are practical and acceptable strategies to modify the perception of height. These modifications are already built into the workplace, from higher heels to pinstripe suits, so we provide tactical and practical recommendations for leveraging those norms.

TACTICAL & PRACTICAL
HEIGHT

It's unfair that a man makes an additional 1.8 percent or around $800 in annual wages for each extra inch of height. Drinking gallons of milk may not help us increase our height at all, but don't despair. If you do want to look taller in the workplace, here are some suggestions on how you can make yourself appear taller. Of course, regardless of your height, even if you may not stand as tall you should certainly stand proud. We offer practical advice to increase the perception of your height but also caution that perhaps it's better that we all become more aware of heightism.

Men and Women:

- **Get rid of that extra weight.** Those extra pounds are noticeable and make you look shorter than you really are. We wish that there were a different perception, but consider an aesthetic principle about height:

if you took two lines of the same height but made one of the lines wider, that line would also look shorter.

- **Sit and stand up straight.** Mom was right. Good posture is important, especially because it helps us look taller. The military emphasizes good posture to make more-confident soldiers and you do remember what scares off the mountain lion? It's standing up taller and more erect.
- **Wear clothes that fit you well.** Avoid wearing baggy clothes, because they may make you look slouchier, less crisp, and shorter. Oversized clothes will overwhelm your body.
- **Wear vertical lines!** Better yet, keep your blazer or suit jacket unbuttoned to maximize your vertical lines. Vertical lines generally add the effect of making people look taller.
- **Dress in one color.** The continuity of monochromatic outfits makes you look lengthier and therefore taller. The colors coordinate rather than only complement each other. Too many colors break up your body into shorter segments.
- **Wear a thin belt.** Thick belts can slice you in half visually, thereby making you look smaller.

Women:
- **Wear heels.** But don't overdo it. If you fall flat on your face because you tripped on your extra-long heel, you won't be looking very tall. Also, some people in the workplace view heels that are too high as inappropriate. Many cite three inches as the maximum heel height a woman should wear to work. We leave the choice of heel height to what you and your co-workers deem appropriate.
- **Wear pantyhose hues that match your skirt, pants and/or shoe color.** This has a similar effect as monochromatic outfits, which make you look lengthier and taller. They create one unified line that gives your lower area a longer feel.
- **Wear skirts that are longer than they are wide.** This will make you look longer than you are wide. Plus, a lengthy skirt looks more professional than a short one.
- **Elongate your neck.** This can be done via v-necks, long necklaces and/or pendants. Be careful with your v-necks, though. If they're too low, they could be deemed inappropriate for the workplace.

Of course, do all this in moderation. If you wear a low v-neck with a long necklace and pendant, complemented by a long skirt and three-inch heels with matching pantyhose, you may look a little mismatched.

INSIGHT & INFORMATION
WEIGHT

Weight discrimination may run much more rampant than any other form (perhaps alongside height) as a major issue that receives much less attention than racial and gender discrimination. The National Institutes for Health (NIH) Obesity Research Taskforce estimates that approximately 65 percent of Americans are obese and this number continues to grow.[3] This indeed calls to attention the likelihood of weight discrimination. Studies indicate that obese employees make anywhere from an average of 10–24 percent less than their slimmer colleagues. (It's gendered, since morbidly obese women make 24 percent less than slimmer counterparts, but the massive 24 percent wage disparity applies only to women, as morbidly obese men suffer less of a gap.) Put into a concrete dollar amount, this means that an individual who makes $80,000 could be making up to $20,000 less than her counterpart because of her weight. According to a recent *Wall Street Journal* article, research by the National Association to Advance Fat Acceptance (NAAFA) found that only 9 percent of upper-level male executives are overweight.[4]

Interestingly enough, society used to view bigger as more beautiful because a voluptuous body was associated with affluence, beauty, and health. Not until the mid-1900s did this change, as Western countries began to prefer a slender body. This cosmetic preference, along with data showing the negative implications of a high body-mass index (BMI), changed society's perceptions of weight.[5]

There is a cost to obesity in the United States, which the NIH estimates at $117 billion in 2003, based on both direct and indirect costs.[6] These costs include, for example, the treatment of medical conditions such as diabetes and heart disease. As obesity swells in the United States, this number will expand accordingly. This compounds the stigma and emotional stress and depression caused by this stigma. We hope that society and professional workplaces discuss this as part of their diversity initiatives, but like heightism, we also recognize that people will treat one another differently based on weight. We're not medical doctors, but strongly believe that creating a good first impression when it comes to weight also promotes physical, mental, and emotional health. This can come from discussions inside and outside of work, but we hope to help by providing practical tactics for improving your professional impression. Despite prejudice by others that sometimes remains beyond our control, this book can help you with practical advice on what you can do.

As a country, we've become obsessed with weight loss and looking trimmer. We spend billions of dollars on weight-loss procedures, pills, gym memberships, exercise equipment, health books and magazines, and diet food. Why? Because research has found that there's a strong correlation between money, health, and weight. Though we don't recommend that people obsess over their weight, we do recommend that they take heed of important weight-related statistics and their health.

Bottom Line: Besides the $117 billion (and increasing) cost of obesity, we believe that professionals should seriously address prejudices about weight in the workplace. Promote acceptance. Taking individual action on what you can control as an individual, in the meantime, can benefit both you and those around you. Besides, there are links between obesity and loss of productivity at work (mostly through health issues and sick days), so good health and productivity can come with watching your weight. Plus, exercise makes people happier!

TACTICAL & PRACTICAL
WEIGHT

We know that obese individuals, particularly women, make less than their thinner counterparts. This isn't fair. Like height differences, the dilemma of raising weight discrimination and applying weight perceptions and judgments is ultimately an individual choice. Remain aware of these issues but also know that many treat people differently based on weight. That's not a company policy; it's a human snap judgment. So, what can you do about it? You can actually lose weight, which helps with your health anyway; in the meantime, you can use these tips to look your best.

How Exactly Can One Look Thinner?

Any of the aforementioned advice on how to look taller (without actually growing taller) also applies to weight. Anything that emphasizes your length, rather than your width, really helps. This entails items from clothes and color to posture and stance.

Fit

Don't buy a size because you used to wear it. Just because you were a size 2 in 1989 doesn't mean you're the same size now.

Clothing that's too tight on you emphasizes oversized areas. However, clothing that's too big makes you look bigger. Try to buy the right fit, even if it means getting your clothes tailored. It's well worth the investment. Think about the salary difference over the years. Although there's no guarantee you'll make more money, it will at least afford you the opportunity.

Colors

Wearing monochrome has a slimming effect but if you think that's too bland, blend shades of the same color. Which color, you may ask (unless you've already read ahead to the "Colors" section)? Black or dark colors are the most slimming. White and bright colors can make you look bigger.

Jackets

Long-line, single-breasted jackets with hidden pockets are usually the way to go. If you absolutely need pockets, the bosom pocket is usually the best pick, since it keeps the figure looking trim. You want your jacket falling below the waist, because that mitigates the attention given to your waist and midsection.

Pants

Avoid wearing wide-bottom pants because they'll make your bottom look … well, wide. Go for the straight or boot-cut leg pants for a more slimming effect. Try to avoid pockets or zippers in your crotch area, since they draw more attention to your waistline.

Skirts

As we mentioned in the "Height" section, skirts should be longer than they are wide. This means that fuller skirts should be longer, while straight skirts can be shorter. Don't wear pleats if you're bottom-heavy. Go for A-line skirts instead.

What If You Still Want to Lose Some Weight?

If you do want to lose a few pounds, keep in mind that weight loss is not all about dieting. That's most of the battle. Other factors include: cardio exercise, weight training, vitamins and supplements, psychological factors, such as stress, as well as support, such as working with a trainer.

INSIGHT & INFORMATION
BUILD AND FRAME

The human body is a living organism that's constantly moving and changing. As such, it is quite possible to modify and alter the shape of your body over time via techniques like diet, exercise, and bodybuilding. Society tends to put pressure on us to sport certain body builds and frames. We as people tend to favor larger, muscular men and petite women. Of course, exceptions do exist, but these tend to be the preferences in American culture. As a result, people spend much time, energy, and money on dieting, fitness, and even plastic surgery to improve their bodily builds.

Bodybuilding serves as one important example of how our culture strongly focuses on our builds. Inherent in its name, bodybuilding uses progressive resistance exercises to help develop and build one's muscles. Many bodybuilders train for personal pleasure and health, while others train for competitive purposes. Non-bodybuilders who lift weights, both men and women, generally prefer tone bodies and engage in body sculpting rather than building larger muscles.

Bodybuilding originated in Europe in the late 1800s along with the development of photography. This new medium helped distribute images of muscular men, which increased bodybuilding's popularity. Born in 1867, Eugen Sandow became the first famous bodybuilder after transforming his gymnast's build to that of a bodybuilder. He was dubbed the "World's Most Perfectly Developed Man" and pioneered bodybuilding into a profitable enterprise.[7]

One of the most famous bodybuilders of our time is Arnold Schwarzenegger. Awarded the title of Mr. Universe at age 22, he went on to win the Mr. Olympia contest seven times.[8] Since then, he starred in numerous action films including *Conan the Barbarian* and *The Terminator*. The former world-famous bodybuilder and Hollywood star now governs the state of California. His build no doubt attracts a lot of attention, both as a celebrity and as a politician. This example, although extreme, reflects how much we pay attention to our builds in this society.

In general, people with larger builds tend to demonstrate more presence. They literally take up more space and so the human eye naturally notices them more readily. We tend to associate large, muscular builds with strength and confidence on one hand. On the other, they can elicit perceptions of that person appearing as a threat or as less intelligent. As we've already discussed in a previous section, we view obese builds somewhat differently. Smaller builds often allow people to blend in the crowd and tend to be viewed as more scholarly, which makes sense, given that they would less likely participate in many sports competitions that demand larger builds. People view these small builds, however, as weaker and less prominent. We tend to attach large versus small builds based on our evolutionary tendencies toward "survival of the fittest," where size often reigns supreme. In modern society, size still matters, but we take into account more than build. Of course, build still matters and people hold these general perceptions about it.

We are generally bound by our natural body frames and build, so there's only so much we can do to change that. Bone structure varies in size and density, and your frame can affect your ideal weight. Use the information in Tactical & Practical to help you better understand your frame and how it affects you.

Bottom Line: People judge one another's build as one of the first factors when making that initial impression because it's easy to spot from afar. You can, however, alter your build to create a more-positive impact and reaction.

TACTICAL & PRACTICAL
BUILD AND FRAME

We've all heard people jokingly exclaim, "I'm not fat. I'm just big-boned." Well, there's definitely some truth to that statement. Though a lot of the tips in the Weight section can apply to those with larger frames, larger-framed individuals should take other factors into consideration.

First of all, how do you know if you're overweight or just have a large frame? How can you figure out your frame size? Search for a "Frame Size Calculator" on the Internet and input your gender, height, and wrist circumference or elbow breadth. From there, it'll calculate your frame size for you.

Once you figure out your frame size, consider some of the following tips to complement your frame size with clothing and accessories.

Large Frame:
- Take note of the fabrics and overall proportion of your clothing to make sure they look right on you. Clothing could fit well in one area, but could fit poorly in another. For example, the shoulders of a shirt could fit perfectly, but the shirt may appear boxy at the waist.

- Wear larger accessories to complement your frame so that your frame will not overwhelm the accessory. One larger-framed woman carried a very small backpack and it looked tiny compared to her build. If you have a larger frame, then wear larger accessories to best complement your frame.
- Men, the Ivy League cut or Brooks Brothers "sack" suit is ideal for you. Also look into the European suit with squared, padded shoulders and a more tapered waistline.

Small Frame:

- Wear petite accessories, so they don't overpower your frame. A large medallion around your neck and chest, for example, will take up much of your torso.
- Men, elongate your appearance by wearing a single-breasted pinstripe suit with double buttons. Too many buttons overwhelm your body. Double-breasted suits make you look smaller, because that extra fabric and fold make you boxier.
- Avoid large patterns, such as large panes, because you'll only sport a few pattern squares, when compared with larger-framed folks who can showcase many more squares on their bodies.

INSIGHT & INFORMATION
HYGIENE: SCENTS AND SMELLS

The nose may know, but "Ignorance is Bliss." Making an impressive impression means more than looking good. Impressions come in all shapes, sizes—and smells.

Imagine yourself in this actual situation. Body odor abruptly victimizes you on a bicoastal business flight from Florida to Los Angeles. The passenger seated in front of you just finishes stowing his bag in the overhead bin as you claim your seat. However, he leaves a rank preflight surprise as he sits. You literally run into the lingering wall of smell radiating from his body. Your stomach churns as your nose burns.

Optimistic, you hope the seats can block the odorous stench. No such luck. The laws of diffusion favor his raunchy body gas as it creeps around and stalks your nose. You brace for impact with dread and despair as the plane ascends for its foul five-hour flight.

You try to read a magazine, but the gripping odor clenches more than your nose, it paralyzes your mind with only the thought of this odor. But wait! A gift from the heavens emerges as you find that this magazine happens to contain a perfume sample. Desperation breeds innovation; you grin and think, *Fight smell with smell.* You wave the sample and counter the wall of smell with your own olfactory barrier.

The floral-scented remedy quickly transforms into a malady. Your stomach rebels in nausea from the cheap perfume that might as well be toxic fume. Only time comes to your aid as you eventually escape from this airborne prison after five grueling hours. Your plane flight from hell ends only when your escape flight from smell begins (in other words, you deplane).

Luckily, this situation only lasts for five hours, but what if this person is your coworker, or what we call a "Stinky Stan" or "Stinky Sally?" If you work with this person five days a week in your office, how can anyone engage in effective communication, let alone teamwork? How can you even share ideas or handle meetings with such an unbearable stench from your colleague? The cost of smell to your organization compounds the individual's impression and decreases productivity. How can anyone concentrate with nasty odors piercing their noses?

Interestingly enough, according to researchers, there's actually sometimes a strong relationship between the offensive odor and the scent of perfume. Skunks emit concentrated sprays unbearable to our noses, yet in trace doses, odors such as those are what we call musk in perfumes. Musk used to come from ingredients such as the glands in the abdomen of the male musk and near the anus of the African civet cat.[9] Before you pass severe judgment on that odorous colleague, take a deep breath (proverbially) and be sympathetic that what stinks to you may smell wonderful to someone else.

As negative odors can distract and decrease productivity, positive odors can increase productivity. Psychology professors demonstrated that fragrances can boost performance at a rate similar to a cup of coffee. One study concluded that, when given a 30-second burst of peppermint, subjects improved performance by 15–25 percent and showed a smaller decline in work performance as the tasks progressed. The Shimizu Technology Center yielded boosts in keypunch operators by 21 percent with lavender bursts, 33 percent with jasmine and 54 percent with lemon.[10]

Bottom Line: Don't be that stinky colleague; adhere to good hygiene in the tips that follow. Interpreters form impressions with all of their senses, including smell. Whether from natural body odors or manufactured colognes and perfumes, the nose knows. If you have a colleague who stinks, you may want to inform a third party who has been tasked to deal with this, such as a manager, a specialist in human resources, or a friend of that person (careful that it is for positive purposes to help that person and not idle gossip). If you have strong integrity and a lot of courage, you can tell that person yourself. Again, be sympathetic that a person's musk perfume can come from an animal's anal gland, so there's a fine line between aromatic scent and appalling stench.

TACTICAL & PRACTICAL
HYGIENE: SCENTS AND SMELLS

As research demonstrates, certain scents can increase productivity and improve collegial psychology. Many professionals bring and offer mints at work. You should too, because the mints:

- Reduce halitosis (the fancy term for bad breath), which can prevent distracting smells from your mouth.
- Promote social generosity, because when you offer mints to others, it can help them with any of their halitosis—and it shows your generosity and consideration. Even if their breath smells fine, the offer of a treat can make someone a bit happier.
- Invigorate and refresh people, which increases productivity.

Real estate agents sometimes bake cookies when showing a home, because it prompts prospective buyers to associate the house with a warm, homey feel. It recalls times of comfort.

Smell matters more than some of us may think. In a survey of over 1,500 people conducted by *Psychology Today*, about how others perceive appearances, the most surprising result came from the high number of words about hygiene—this came from the written comments, since the study didn't even ask any questions about this topic![11] All of these odor-related opinions came from women. Some mentioned that poor hygiene trumped bad appearances as the primary turnoff. People tend to overlook their own personal hygiene because it's a baseline that a majority of people don't consciously address—but as this study shows, it *is* an important baseline to think about.

Maybe you don't have a perfectly symmetrical face or the body of a supermodel. Even so, you can still improve how others perceive your appearance by engaging in basic hygienic practices that can make your scent more appealing to those around you. Complete the checklists below to ensure that you don't end up smelling like Stinky Stan or Sally.

You will reduce your chances of smelling bad if you:
- **Shower.** Remember that many societies didn't always bathe regularly, so it's not a given.
- **Wear deodorant or antiperspirant:** Sweat by itself emits little smell, but when the bacteria eat away at the sweat, we begin to stink. Staying dry can help prevent this.
- **Brush your teeth, floss, and use mouthwash.** Make sure you brush your tongue and underside of your upper mouth because halitosis is partly caused by germs on these oral softscapes. Flossing also removes bacteria between your teeth that lead to odorous breath.
- **Wash your clothes.**
- **Don't smoke,** especially before going into a meeting with a prospective client or employer. Be aware of the fact that smoking often makes your clothes smell as well.

You will smell significantly better than Stinky Stan if you:
- **Use cologne/perfume sparingly.** Colognes and perfumes react differently to our individual body chemistries, so what may smell great on Person A might smell like a dead skunk on Person B. And, even if you think it smells great, your supervisor might hate it . . . or be allergic to it.
- **Bring along breath mints or gum, and tissues** in case you spill something that could leave an unpleasant odor on your attire.
- **Stay away from pungent foods** such as garlic, salsa, onions, and spicy foods.
- **Avoid stress and caffeine** (if possible)—these both increase body odor. Stomach acids can make your breath smell.

If you encounter Stinky Stan in your workplace, make sure you:
- **Let human resources know.** They have experience with smelly co-workers. An online poll of 633 human resources managers revealed that 74 percent of them have had to confront an employee about body odor.[12]
- **Let him know . . . in private,** of course. In a poll of over 400 people, 75 percent of respondents said they would want to be notified by a friend if they smelled.[13]

INSIGHT & INFORMATION
HYGIENE: SIGHTS AND SOUNDS

Reenter Stinky Stan, that unhygienic person from our last section. He learns that deodorant remains a staple of the savvy professional. With his newfound knowledge, he always applies antiperspirant. His current confidence shatters into a thousand pieces when his coworker politely points out the armpit stains on the shirt that he's wearing.

No problem, I'll just wear a different shirt from now on, he thinks (at least he now thinks instead of stinks). Uh-oh. Almost all of his shirts have pit stains. Mortified, he worries and ponders, *Am I so filthy that my sweat stains my shirt?*

This common concern comes from chemistry, not just natural body-fluid excretions. The interaction between your armpit sweat and the deodorant/antiperspirant that you wear can generate an armpit stain on your shirt. He may be clean, but he certainly doesn't look clean. His image leads to a dirty impression. Similarly, food stains, lint, and holes in clothing are also sights that create a less-hygienic impression, even though you may be very hygienic. These negative perceptions can also come from your unknowing actions. Some people scratch their heads constantly, which can emit dandruff or leave gel residue on their fingers. Others pick their ears without realizing they do it. Still, others pick their crotch and noses as a regular habit. (People see this more often than you'd think.) It's the impression that these visual cues give that lead to people treating you poorly because they think you're unkempt.

What about sounds? You know those, from burps to flatulence. We know to keep those to ourselves. Sometimes, however, people engage in very subtle behaviors that they may not realize. One colleague we know would burp, and although he held it in, he would then blow the gas out the corner of his mouth like a smoker blows away smoke. Even though he steered the gas away from his colleagues, he called attention to his burping. He would be best served to excuse himself and go to a restroom. Even a subtle sound and sight that sometimes seems acceptable, although not completely inappropriate, does seem odd and draw unnecessary attention.

Bottom Line: Even though a person may be clean and hygienic, others may not perceive them as hygienic. From wrinkled shirts and pants to disheveled hair and nails, your image can contribute to an impression that lacks cleanliness. Do you think co-workers want to spend any more time than necessary with an unhygienic colleague?

TACTICAL & PRACTICAL
HYGIENE: SIGHTS AND SOUNDS

As Stan quickly learned, you don't necessarily have to smell stinky in order to look or sound stinky. Armpit stains are tricky because the item that causes you to smell better (deodorant) may be the very culprit that causes you to look smelly with those armpit stains. How can you minimize armpit stains? Allow enough time for your deodorant to dry before putting on a shirt. And, wear a short-sleeve shirt underneath your dress shirt to prevent your dress shirt from staining.

Your Attire Can Have a Significant Effect on Just How Hygienic You Look

Wash your clothes, not just to remove smells but to remove stains as well. After washing your clothes, consider ironing them, too. Wrinkled shirts are unsightly and an iron can do wonders. However, an iron is not a miracle-worker. If your attire has gone through too much wear and tear and is beyond repair, let it go. If the wear and tear is minor, like loose stitching or fibers, be sure to mend them as soon as possible.

Also, for decency's sake, don't reveal your underwear. With the rise of low-rider pants, jeans, and skirts, people are exposing more underwear. Men, no one really needs to know if you're wearing boxers or tighty whities. And women, we really don't need to see your lacy thong or flowery panty either. Actually, they now make low-rise thongs in case you wear low-rise jeans and pants, but you probably don't want a thong uprising to ruin your professional impression.

It's Not All Clothing. Your Accessories Matter, Too

Make sure you clean, fix, and replace your bags, briefcases, shoes, and accessories as needed. If your favorite bag or briefcase from the 1980s looks like it's falling apart at the seams, maybe it's time to let go and buy a new bag. The same rule applies to shoes and accessories, which you should keep polished.

Your Body Parts Are Important

Hair, teeth, and nails are all important parts of your body. If your hair is disheveled because you forgot to brush it or if you have something green stuck in your teeth after eating some of that delicious spinach artichoke dip or if you still have some gunk in your nails from who knows what, you probably look pretty unhygienic. If you want to fix these hygiene faux pas, make sure you don't groom yourself in public. If you have an opportunity to make a few quick touch-ups in the bathroom, we suggest that you keep a small upkeep kit that includes a nail clipper, toothbrush, toothpaste, floss, and stain remover. You can also add fabric sprays that kill bacteria and refresh clothing.

And Remember, Hygiene Is Not All About How You Smell or Look. It's About How You Sound, Too

Maybe you're one of those special few who have been blessed with burps and farts that don't smell . . . or at least don't smell very much. Regardless of whether your farts smell like classy perfume or dead skunks, they *sound* unhygienic. So when it comes to burping and farting in public, just don't do it.

INSIGHT & INFORMATION
ATTIRE AND CLOTHING

Let's face it: The workplace grows increasingly more casual as we shift from business to business casual (and even casual in some workplaces). Consistently, we train and hear professionals both criticize this shift, as well as commend it. Critics cite that it promotes issues such as reduced professional behavior and a lack of respect for customers. Advocates state that going more casual increases comfort and productivity. Another issue is social acceptance, as some employees fear their peers would perceive them as standoffish and treat them differently if they overdressed.

The common wisdom of dress to the role you aspire still holds true in many cases. On average, do executives dress more polished than others at a company? Most people we ask answer with a resounding "yes." So, you should ideally dress it up just a notch as well. As you advance in your career, are you more concerned about blending in with your lateral peers or progressing to a higher position? This is a personal decision that you'll have to make according to your personal goals and motivations. Here's something to keep in mind. Do you tend to disclose more information to your managers or lateral peers? Usually it's the latter, because it often feels easier to establish rapport with peers rather than one's manager. With that said, if you become a manager, your employees may tread lightly around you when deciding whether or not they should share detailed or personal information with you. As you advance, you'll have to struggle to make sure that it's not "lonely at the top." Again, this decision of career advancement is personal, but we're assuming that many of our readers want to consider advancement.

Research supports the correlation between notched-up attire and career advancement. According to a survey conducted by Wirthlin Worldwide, of 150 executives surveyed, 70 percent believe that attire affects an employee's state of mind and behavior. Similarly, 63 percent believe that those who dress more professionally advance more in their careers.[14] As casual as our workplace becomes, the top executives and managers do tend to dress better and more-polished than their employees. Even if it's a casual-jeans culture, executives who wear jeans are wearing designer jeans that are pressed and more fitted. There's even a better casual than casual—some call it CEO casual or executive casual. Dressing more professionally generally helps, and even if your work culture espouses casual dress, isn't it generally better to look at least somewhat more polished than your peers? Simply put, do you want to blend in or stand out in an acceptable way?

Companies have dress codes for a reason: professional clothes reflect professionalism. We've heard people complain that they don't want to be just another suit in a "sea of suits," but wearing professional attire is more than just a matter of conformity. It demonstrates that you can work well in a team—both in ethic as well as dress. Your shared dress can reflect shared ideas, as well as your ability to collaborate with others. Of course, we encourage diversity and individuality in dress . . . but all within professional reason. We break down dress tips by specific zones in the rest of the *Insight & Information* and *Tactical & Practical* sections.

Bottom Line: Dress to the role you aspire.

TACTICAL & PRACTICAL
ATTIRE AND CLOTHING

We all know that wearing a suit and looking sharp are critical elements to creating a positive first impression during job interviews. However, dressing the part isn't only critical when looking for a job; it's important once you land that job, too. Studies show that dress plays an integral role in getting promoted. 93 percent of executives interviewed in one study said that the way a person dresses significantly impacts on whether or not they will receive a promotion.[15] Another study determined that salaries increased from 8 to 20 percent when employees traded their inferior suits for more professional attire.

Five Quick Tips on How You Can Look Great in Your Workplace:

- **Dress appropriately for your audience so that you avoid overdressing or under-dressing.** For instance, dress at least slightly more professionally for your clients. If you want to impress your boss or an executive at your company barbecue, avoid overdressing in your suit.

- **Look the part you'd like to have:** Don't dress for your current position. If you want to be an executive, you have to *look* like an executive. Of course, overdressing can make you stand out too much, so make sure to not overdress too formally when compared to your peers. As a rule of thumb, dress 10 percent better than your peers. This number reflects a subtle extra touch, such as pressed clothes when your peers don't iron, or a collar-neck shirt when your colleagues wear t-shirts.

- **Dress more conservatively when meeting with foreign business partners** than you normally do. It's better to play it safe.

- **Clothing separates give you more bang for your buck.** With these pieces, you can make a variety of business-attire combinations. Just make sure they match. To make sure they match, buy within a similar family of clothing fabrics and colors.

- **Go shopping for business attire in the morning** rather than the afternoon. People are usually more perceptive and analytical earlier in the day, which makes you a more discerning shopper. We're a little taller in the morning as well, so it's a better time to shop for clothes, so you know they'll fit when you're at your largest. For shoes, however, your feet tend to be bigger at night, so that may prove the best time to shoe shop.

Four Things You Shouldn't Wear in the Workplace,
Even on Casual Fridays:

- **Exercise clothing.** You're there to work, not to work out.
- **Midriff-baring clothing.** Save it for the weekends.
- **Sandals, flip-flops, slippers** ... whatever you like to call them, they don't belong in the office. Keep your toes to yourself.
- **Denim or shorts.** These are not business casual. These are casual. Nowadays, some workplaces allow for jeans but they're generally seen as too casual for work.

Three Ways You Can Avoid Overdoing It in the Workplace:

- **Avoid wearing fur or diamonds during promotion period.** You don't want to look like you have millions when your boss is trying to decide if he should raise your salary by a couple thousand. Plus, you may offend some animal lovers.

- **Don't boast about the designer brand of your clothes.** No one needs to hear about it.
- **You don't have to have all of the latest fashions.** Just keep up to date. If you buy clothing that's too trendy, it'll probably go out of fashion soon enough. Classics count, so use them as a foundation and add contemporary accessories to accent them.

INSIGHT & INFORMATION
COLORS: ROY G. BIV, THE COLORS OF THE RAINBOW

According to the Institute for Color Research, "people make a subconscious judgment about a person, environment, or product within 90 seconds of initial viewing and that between 62 percent and 90 percent of that assessment is based on color alone."[16]

Colors can communicate and connote diverse messages that vary as much as the color spectrum. They can reflect and communicate your general personality or your current mood. Perhaps you wear bright colors when you're more cheerful and dark colors when you're blue. Colors speak volumes and we label them "loud" or "muted."

People you encounter react in certain (and sometimes very different) ways to colors. Research shows that orange most easily catches our attention, from hunters who sport vests that exclaim, "don't shoot me," to life jackets that scream, "save me!" Blue generally connotes cool and red often means hot, while green tends to represent fresh and natural.[17]

If nothing else, colors can make the human eye believe it's seeing something different than what's there. Dark colors make objects and people appear smaller and slimmer, while light colors do the opposite. Clashing colors can create a disruptive, but eye-catching effect or just emit an incongruous image. For instance, certain colors can clash with certain skin tones.

Just be aware that a single color can have different meanings depending on the individual and communities that interpret them. Someone from China may view red differently than someone in the United States (i.e., the Chinese usually associate red with luck, while Americans may view red as aggressive or passionate). Perhaps people who wear red aggressively pursue their goals. According to *Psychology Today*, research shows that sports teams who wear red jerseys tend to win more often than those who wear blue.[18]

The classic colors of the rainbow represent the color spectrum. The acronym ROY G. BIV serves as a mnemonic device that sounds like a name and indicates the main colors of the spectrum from end to end (R=Red, O=Orange, Y=Yellow, G=Green, B=Blue, I=Indigo, V=Violet).

As Constance Ramos states on her television show, *Color Correction*, rather than think about right or wrong colors, we should consider "wrong color choices." Learn to choose and use the right colors and you'll improve your image.

Bottom Line: Once you learn about the connotations and functions of colors, you can wield them to your advantage. They will act as an arsenal at your command, which can enhance the impression you leave on others.

TACTICAL & PRACTICAL
COLORS: ROY G. BIV, THE COLORS OF THE RAINBOW

Remember that color connotations vary across cultures, so we're going under the assumption of traditional "American" views about the subject matter. We list some common associations of the ROY G. BIV colors, so you can use these connotations (and combinations of them) to evoke different emotions on your clothing, presentations, and office spaces:

- **Red:** passionate, angry, aggressive, hot, bloody, violent, and exciting
- **Orange:** warm, energetic, warning, hopeful, hospitable, and cautious
- **Yellow:** bright, cheerful, sunny, warm, prosperous, and cowardly
- **Green:** natural, calm, relaxing, fresh, peaceful, pleasant, restful, lucky, monied, and envious
- **Blue:** cool, peaceful, calm, restful, serene, tranquil, truthful, formal, sad, depressed, and highly esteemed (navy)
- **Indigo/Violet:** royal, dignified, powerful, rich, dominant, dramatic, mysterious, wise, and passionate

Aside from these color connotations, one study found that the level of positive responses ranked in the following order, along with their general connotations: 1. Green (relaxation, peace), 2. Yellow (happiness, sun and summer), 3. Blue (ocean and sky), and a tie between Purple (children and laughing) and Red (Valentine's and love).[19] Keep these in mind. You'll probably want to wear clothing that reflects the emotion or mood you want to convey. Wear the appropriate color to elicit the appropriate response. For example, you may want to wear blue, since it will help calm both yourself and the interviewer. Red and purple may excite passion in your day-to-day work experience. Green may showcase your creativity to clients.

In a professional environment, many want to project a more serious tone, therefore they tend to decorate and dress with darker colors. Be careful when using excessively vibrant colors in the office, as they can either distinguish or extinguish your career. Some office environments, such as design and advertising firms, accept or even encourage bright colors. Either way, observe the work culture and decide how much you would like to blend in with or stick out from your peers.

One simple, yet effective tactic: Go to a home-improvement store and take different samples of color cards from the paint section. Place these colors on against your face and hands to see which ones match best. Make sure you do this in natural, outdoor light, as well as under indoor fluorescent lighting. This way, you can see how colors complement or clash with your skin tone both indoors and outdoors.

You can also go to the mall and ask the makeup counter specialists for advice.

INSIGHT & INFORMATION
COLORS: BLACK AND WHITE, DARK AND LIGHT

Black or white? Dark or light?

From the Heart of Darkness to the Garbs of the Grim Reaper, black often gets a bad rap. Yes, people in the Western world often associate black with evil, fear, and foreboding.[20] The phrase, "good guys wear white" stems from a reaction to good guys who normally sport this color. Similarly, the "Prince of Darkness" connotes the devil. Studies do corroborate these Western perceptions to some degree. For instance, one study found that people who watched a violent act perceived the act as more violent when the violent person wore black over other colors.[21]

Another research project closely examined the color black in competitive sports and observed that this color related to increased penalties and aggression.[22] The researchers looked at NFL football teams and NHL Hockey teams, with a particular eye toward those who wore primarily black uniforms. They measured the yards penalized in football and the minutes in hockey and found that sports teams who wear black tend to be penalized more than those who wear white. Accordingly, those who wear black tend to exhibit aggressive behavior. The players in black uniforms exhibited more aggression and meaner behavior. As this study shows, sometimes black brings out the "darker" behaviors in us, whether we're the players or the referees. The behaviors around, and reactions to, the color black could also mutually reinforce each other and lead to further aggression.

On the other hand, this effect doesn't apply to every situation, since we will unlikely view people wearing black at funerals or black-robed judges as more aggressive. On the positive side, black clothing also can indicate cutting-edge fashion and create a slimming effect on our bodies. Like any other color, these cultural connotations remain relative to the person, group, and context.

Many favor dark colors such as black, gray, and navy for interview suits. In fact, according to Goldman's "Million Dollar First Impression," statistics and studies show that those who wear navy to an interview are the most likely to get the job. Why are dark colors good for a professional first impression? It's because dark colors exude a degree of seriousness, so we're more likely to take others seriously when they wear such colors.

So how about black's opposite, the color white? Westerners generally attach cleanliness and goodness to white. Think hospitals and angels. Many etiquette and image specialists assert that white is the most formal of all colors. Think white wedding gowns and tuxedos. Of course, we sometimes depict drug lords as wearing white suits. Clothing in this color also makes a person look larger, so watch out for that weight-enhancing white!

Research shows that adults generally perceive light colors more positively and dark colors more negatively.[23] This rings true especially for women, who viewed light colors even more positively and dark colors even more negatively than men. Think about how pastels symbolize spring and rebirth. Party colors generally consist of brighter shades and neons. Even the shades and brightness of colors impact how others perceive us and vice versa.

Bottom Line: We all know the world isn't simply black and white, so why should you limit yourself to the binary black-and-white conceptions? Still, we do tend to tie dark colors with more negative associations than light colors, so use this knowledge to your advantage—darker colors make you look more serious and professional, while lighter colors make you look livelier.

TACTICAL & PRACTICAL
COLORS: BLACK AND WHITE, DARK AND LIGHT

Just as each color of the rainbow entails different connotations depending on the context, the same holds true for some of the less colorful hues of black, white, and the in-between gray. Some common associations with these colors include:

- **White**: pure, innocent, youthful, faithful, open, honest, and peaceful
- **Black**: dignified, sophisticated, mysterious, tragic, serious, sad, old, strong, gloomy, and evil
- **Gray**: modest, mysterious, neutral, sad, ambiguous, vague, and old

Though most image specialists will tell you that white is the most formal of colors, many perceive black as the default formal color because it's a classic. Some say that black suits are too formal for everyday business attire while others call it a safe bet for all business occasions. So, should you always bet on black? Keep these thoughts in mind before you do:

- Monochromic colors, or shades of gray, often give off a sophisticated vibe while dark colors showcase an authoritative look. Which one are you going for?
- Look around you. What colors are appropriate for the business settings in which you often find yourself? Do you stand out or do you blend in? More importantly, do you want to stand out or blend in?
- Studies show that those who wear dark colors to interviews most likely land the job. Dark suit colors are considered classics for a reason.
- To play it safe, keep with basic colors as a foundation, which include black, white and gray. You can layer additional colors on top of these foundations to add flair.

INSIGHT & INFORMATION
FABRIC TYPES

Studies show that kinesthetic learners make up 10 percent of the U.S. population, while an additional 65 percent identify as visual learners.[24] It's no surprise, then, that the look and feel of fabrics play an integral role in the quality of our clothing.

Each fabric type has its own unique history and usage. Though the origins of cotton are not very clear, scientists in Mexico found bits of cotton balls and pieces of cotton cloth dating back at least 7,000 years.[25]

Cotton's role in our everyday lives demonstrates its versatility. From towels and sheets to blue jeans and shoe strings, you'll find cotton almost anywhere. Similarly, people associate silk with its smooth elegance. Silk has a long history as well. Archeologists recently found a small ivory cup carved with a silkworm design dated between 4,000 and 5,000 BC.[26] Though it lacks cotton's versatility, silk is used to make some articles of clothing as well as curtains and cushion covers. Cotton and silk provide just two examples of fabrics with different purposes, backgrounds, and feels.

Many often equate the feeling of certain types of materials with specific emotions or memories. When you touch a soft, feathery pillow, what do you think of? How about fine leather? Rough carpet? We have a strong sense of touch, and the feeling of different materials can have different associations—both positive and negative. The same goes for the fabrics of suits and other clothing you wear in the workplace. For instance, we often link leather clothing to rebels and those on the cutting edge, like rock stars and biker gangs. Silk spawns images of softness and delicacy. The crisp and wrinkly feel of linen shows casual summer sophistication.

Though your colleagues won't necessarily caress their hands along your workplace attire (at least they shouldn't), they can still see the type of fabric you're wearing. Silk may convey a sense of luxury, while scratchy wool may make you seem a little stiff. In addition to the look, you want a fabric that feels right for you. We'll give you a feel for the different fabrics out there in Tactical & Practical.

Bottom Line: The look and feel of your fabrics reflect your personal look and feel.

TACTICAL & PRACTICAL
FABRIC TYPES

Consider fabric type as an integral part of your outfit, not only for your impression but for your comfort as well. We primarily focus on suits because business casual depends on the specific workplace and can run volumes in debates and discussions as to what people deem most suitable.

Suits

As a general rule, most people favor light wool and cotton as suit fabric types because they look and feel great. In addition to looking at the fabric type itself, make sure you look at the stitching, seams, and hems for the suits (and shirts) that best suit you.

Why Wool?

It wrinkles less than most fabrics. To be sure, use the scrunch test. The fabric shouldn't hold too many wrinkles after your scrunch and release it. In addition to its wrinkle-free quality, wool feels comfortable and lasts longer than polyester and blended-material suits.

Cashmere for Class?

Cashmere affords softness and fineness to your suit, which make it more elegant.

What's the Best Fabric Type for Shirts?

As a general rule, cotton, silk, and linen shirts are better than acrylic ones. Use cotton's versatility to your advantage—it works in both summer and winter weather. Plus, it breathes, so you can avoid sweating and sport a softer, more natural feel.

What Type of Shirt Fabric Works Best for Professional Settings?

Unembossed, plain materials look more professional than patterns and textures. They provide a crisp, clean appearance with their smoother surfaces and cleaner patterns. Patterns give texture, however, and can add variety to make you stand out from the crowd. Shinier fabrics add a little more fun into your work wardrobe.

What Types of Shirts Should You Avoid?

Try to avoid sheer shirts for professional settings. Actually, it's frowned upon in business casual settings, too, since people can see through it. Undergarments should remain under, so be careful that you don't flaunt them. The same rule goes for fur. In some parts of the United States, it could stir controversy. Your colleague may support animal-rights and could find it offensive. Minimally, animal lovers may cringe at that mink trim on your coat.

How Can You Add Physique to Shirts?

Men should wear undershirts beneath their dress shirts to prevent itchiness and stains from sweating, and to add shape to the shirt. Also, avoid low-quality fabrics that tend to cling to the body.

INSIGHT & INFORMATION
PATTERNS AND PRINTS

If you think back to the 1990s and some of its childhood pastimes, what do you think of? You probably think of Nerf guns and Tamagotchi pets. Do you also remember the popular Magic Eye series? These books, originally released in 1993, allowed people to see 3D images by focusing on 2D patterns. The books featured images called autostereograms, though most people simply knew them as Magic Eye patterns. Psychophysicist Christopher Tyler first created autostereograms in 1979, but they didn't become popular until the 1990s. Since then they have been featured on videos, postcards, lunch boxes, and neckties.[27] Magic Eye isn't necessarily all about fun and games, though. They're frequently used for vision therapy by orthoptists and vision therapists in the treatment of binocular vision and accommodative disorders.

Though not as popular or complicated as autostereograms, tessellations frequently appeared in elementary classrooms as well. A tessellation consists of pictures or tiles that cover a plane symmetrically without overlapping gaps.[28] Some of you may remember looking at repeating patterns of birds or lizards, while learning about tessellations at school.

These patterns stimulate the eye and spark intrigue, particularly on clothing. You may not frequently find autostereograms or tessellations on everyday clothing (aside from on unique ties), but you may still see animal prints while going through clothing racks at the mall. Animal prints survived the 1980s and 1990s, and are one of the longest-standing and more noticeable patterns you'll find today.[29] Zebra stripes. Leopard spots. Tiger prints. You can find all sorts of animal prints on everything from headwear to shoes.

Though animal prints aren't too popular in the workplace (or with animal activists), you'll still find some patterns and prints at work. These and other daring prints send a bold message and tend to show more playful and youthful tastes. Stripes, including the pinstripes commonly used on suits, are probably the most common pattern you'll find. You'll find some plaid patterns, too, though we often caution careerists to consider how this pattern looks on their body type before buying too many plaid shirts.

Bottom Line: Patterns and prints can prove fun, interesting, and unique. However, consider their look and the message they convey before donning them at work.

TACTICAL & PRACTICAL
PATTERNS AND PRINTS

In what may often seem like a monochromatic workplace, some-times we feel the urge to stand out. Showcasing personal brands and individual preferences can bolster your impression. On the other hand, standing out too much may also bear its own set of consequences. The balance between fitting in and standing out varies by workplace and that's why we suggest paying heed to our Golden Virtues of Impressive First Impressions. Think about how others will view you when selecting the most-appropriate patterns in the workplace. That doesn't mean that you shouldn't take a risk, but it does mean that you should to some degree fit in with your organization's culture. For patterns, we provide some tips to consider before you pair that bright orange shirt with intricate tessellations with green plaid pants.

1. The jury's still out on whether or not you should stick to one or two patterns when wearing an outfit. However, experts all agree that you shouldn't wear more than three patterns layered on top of one another unless you *want* to look like a clown.

2. If you wear more than one pattern, make sure your patterns have a common color in order to imply that you deliberately put together. You don't want to look like you pulled the only two clean articles of clothing from your closet.

3. Carefully consider wild or complex prints on pants, shirts or ties. If your shirt hurts your eyes when you look at it, it's probably not safe for work. You can wear playful clothes, as long as the articles with complex patterns do not overwhelm.

4. If you're a short or slim person, shirts with large patterns or prints may overwhelm your body. For instance, if you wear a plaid pattern with larger squares, you'll have fewer squares on your body, which will make you look smaller.

5. Start with smaller patterns that conform to your body size. In general, solids provide a practical foundation to any outfit and can accompany any pattern.

6. Dots and circles add a fun and playful feel to your outfits.

7. Paisleys also represent playful, yet more-abstract, patterns.

8. Herringbone and houndstooth furnish clothing with a more-textured and sophisticated feel.

9. Crocodile skin signifies adventurousness and daring.

10. Plaids are practical and down to earth.

INSIGHT & INFORMATION
CLOTHING CUTS AND STYLES

If you look at fashion over time, you can often observe trends of a particular decade . . . and see them return several decades later. The short-lived (and sometimes hideous) trends will blip on the fashion radar and disappear forever. Others will have a permanent impact on the fashion industry. You may remember some of these trends—whether you lived through the decade or heard about it—such as the Coco Chanel look of the 1920s, puffy sleeves of the 1930s, cocktail dresses of the 1940s, white t-shirt/Levi's/leather jacket combo of the 1950s, miniskirts of the 1960s, sportswear of the 1970s, power suit of the 1980s, and grunge wear of the 1990s.[30] Even if you didn't live through the decade, you could have easily worn one of these popular outfits a few decades later.

Suits follow fashion trends, too, though the differences over the years often appear more subtle than ones observed in trendy clothing for the masses. With the passage of the 14th Amendment in 1920, women gained suffrage and their sense of equality showed. Women entered the workforce and often donned an androgynous look. For men, the trousers in the 1920s tapered down tightly at the ankles and pinstripe suits became popular thanks to gangsters like Al Capone. Many didn't have discretionary funds to spend on clothes or shoes in the 1930s due to the Great Depression, and this showed in workplace attire. Conservative dress became even more widespread in the 1940s, since the U.S. government needed extra material to support World War II troops. For the most part, one could no longer find cuffs, collars, buttons, or other niceties on dresses. Men's suits went from four pieces (jacket, vest and two pairs of pants) to just two pieces—jacket and pants. This trend differed greatly from the "power suits" of the more-prosperous 1980s, during which both men and women donned boxier suits.[31] Since then, most of the shoulder pads have been removed from today's suits and closer fits (often with the help of a tailor) remain popular.[32]

We shared with you the history of styles over the decades, but we'd like to point out that for the most part, they should remain just that—*history*. If you wear the same clothes you had from 20 years ago, that's aged. If a younger person wears your clothing from 20 years ago, that's retro. Yes, it's a double standard, but avoid resurrecting your old clothes from decades ago. Leave them to the next generation. Revamp your wardrobe whenever necessary, because outdated attire can have negative connotations. What do you think when you see a man's jacket with elbow patches? What about a woman's suit with oversized shoulder pads? You may think: old, outdated, 1980s. You may also think that the wearer of such clothing lacks fashion consciousness or doesn't care about professionalism, because they don't pay attention to some of the more obvious features of their attire. Don't let this happen to you.

Bottom Line: The trends of both everyday wear and suits are interesting to observe over time. We'd like to emphasize, though, that trends of the past should be observed more than donned. Still, retro looks can offer a fun alternative to classic daily wear. These retro outfits blend elements of contemporary and classic. We recommend that you keep your suit updated in both fit and style.

TACTICAL & PRACTICAL
CLOTHING CUTS AND STYLES

You could buy a $1,000 suit but if it doesn't fit right, it won't look right. Find the perfect size, cut, and style to create the right look for you. We'll take you through the basics of finding the right size before walking through more specific cuts and styles.

Clothing: Too Small? Too Big?

Often times, tight clothing results from someone buying a size that is too small and thinking that they'll eventually "slim down" to fit into it comfortably. Before that happens, they'll try to squeeze into that size 6 when they know it's time to be realistic about their weight-loss plan (or lack thereof) and buy a size 10. It can be painful to buy a size or two up, but if you keep on insisting that you'll lose weight and be able to wear your clothes comfortably in the near future, they may perpetually look a little too tight and less flattering on you. It's probably even more *physically* painful to wear clothing that's too tight, and it can decrease comfort and therefore productivity in the workplace. You'll look better in a size-appropriate 10 than a way-too-tight 6. You could have the opposite problem as well. If you recently lost a lot of weight, then a too-big 10 won't look right on your size-6 body. Simply put, make sure you wear the right size for your body. One issue of GQ *Magazine* showed a photo of a man the photographer met in a subway station. He wore a suit two sizes too large for his frame, so the suit made him look boxy and chunky.

When the magazine refitted him in an ideal suit for his frame, they actually discovered that he had an athletic physique underneath.

Below, you'll find some tips for men and women regarding appropriate cuts and styles.

Men:

- For an all-around solid look, go with an updated British/American-style suit. The lower button positions and longer lapel fit most body sizes.

- Double-breasted suits also elongate the lapel line and look appealing. These, however, primarily work for taller, more trim men. On shorter men, the excess fabric overwhelms their bodies and makes them look boxy.

- For an executive style, stick to a classic and timeless look. Tailored suits, navy blazers, button-down oxfords and ivy-league ties are some ways you can obtain this look.

- Though every body type differs, as a general rule, square-shoulder cuts usually create a better fit than the soft-shoulder style. This gives structure and makes professionals look more substantive toward their upper bodies. This draws attention to the face and can give an inverted pyramid look rather than a triangle. People usually perceive the former as more powerful and confident.

- When buying a matching vest to go along with your suit, make sure the arm holes don't sag and the vest doesn't wrinkle when you move around. The cut should be comfortable and fitted, without too much room. They should still allow you to move, however.

Women:

- For a great traditional look, go with the single-breasted jacket.

- For an executive look, try shirtwaist dresses, oxford shirts, tailored shirts, A-line skirts, and cardigan sweaters.

- Careful when wearing clothing that's too short, too low, or too see-through. Skirts should fall mid-calf to slightly above the knee. Low-hanging necklines and see-through shirts simply aren't acceptable in a professional environment.

- Avoid tiered-hem skirts, excessive ruffles, and puffed sleeves. You want to look like a professional, not a princess.

INSIGHT & INFORMATION
JEWELRY

Metals have meaning. The jewelry you wear can reflect your personality and style. Learn a little more about your gem or metal of choice, and make sure you're conveying the right message with your personal flair.

- **Diamonds and Precious Stones:** The diamond's extravagance often steals the show as the centerpiece of most jewelry. Other precious stones, from rubies to emeralds, furnish people with a more playful and colorful impression.

- **Platinum** symbolizes prestige. It is considered rare and more precious than gold or silver. Popular culture references such as credit card rankings and musical album sales reflect the image of prestige and exclusivity that people associate with platinum.

- **Gold** provides a classic look that represents style, luxury, and tradition. Because of its color, it adds a warmth and richness to your ensemble. The fineness of gold is determined by the proportion of pure gold to other metals added to increase durability. You'll find 24 karats in pure gold, while lower numbers represent the number of parts per gold.

- **Silver** connotes a coolness and sleekness that people often associate with the moon, especially in western countries. It is often perceived as mysterious and sometimes "ethnic." Silver is popular due to its availability and relatively low cost compared to gold. Fine silver consists of 99.9 percent silver, while sterling silver is made of 92.5 percent silver and 7.5 percent copper or other metals.

- **Stainless Steel** has a modern, technological and futuristic vibe. This is fitting for a metal that was developed by technological and manufacturing advances. Because this steel contains more than 10 percent chromium, it usually doesn't rust and is easy to maintain. Stainless steel offers daily functional uses. You'll find it in the kitchen in sinks and knives. Although not a precious metal, it sends a functional message when adorned.

- **Titanium** also has a modern vibe, because it is very high-tech and one of the newest metals available. Strong as steel but 45 percent lighter, titanium resists corrosion and demonstrates versatility because it can be anodized into colors. Though titanium is not technically considered hypoallergenic, many still consider this a great metal for those with metal sensitivities. Eye glasses frequently contain titanium for their durability and lightweight properties.

Jewelry shapes also send signals to others about you. Rounded shapes tend to soften your appearance and show a more gentle attitude. Edges, such as in triangles and squares, generally make you appear more cutting edge and risk-taking.[33]

Bottom Line: Jewelry, although typically small and subtle, can enhance and accent your overall impression, as long as you understand the basics of materials and shapes.

TACTICAL & PRACTICAL
JEWELRY

Accessories, particularly jewelry, can add a little sparkle to your usual business attire. Though a little flair looks good, too much sparkle and jazz can be distracting. We believe strongly that you should also sport a watch, which exhibits that you're punctual and mind your time. If you think you can get away with using your mobile phone in lieu of your watch, read the chapter on virtual impressions and you'll understand why that's not a great idea. Here's some advice on how to spice up your look with some jewelry, without overdoing it.

Jewelry (including bracelets and necklaces)

Wear jewelry and watches that are . . .

- **Appropriate for the situation.** Jewelry should accent the rest of your ensemble but not outshine it.
- **Made of quality material and stones.** People will judge you based on the quality of your jewelry.
- **Gold-toned with black stones, if you're wearing a black suit.** They look great together.
- **Color-coordinated.** If you decide to go with more colorful stones, make sure they match the color of your outfit.
- **Made of gold or silver,** and then match your accessories accordingly.
- **Simple, yet elegant.** One elegant, unusual piece of jewelry looks more polished than a number of dangling pieces.

Earrings

Wear earrings that are . . .

- **No bigger than the size of a nickel.** You don't want long, dangling earrings because they're distracting. Wear smaller earrings if you wear glasses.
- **Made of real 14 karat gold or sterling silver.** Quality is key.
- **Made of precious stones,** which are considered luxurious.
- **Made of pearls.** You can easily match these to pearlized buttons on your suits as well.

- **A pair,** meaning don't wear more than one pair of earrings per ear. You don't want to draw too much attention to your ears. Less is more in this case.

For men, we recommend that you avoid wearing earrings as well as large or colorful pieces of jewelry to work. The main exception to this rule would be workplaces in creative fields, such as fashion and entertainment.

Rings

Wear rings that are . . .

- **Your wedding ring or your class ring.** These are appropriate for the workplace.
- **Reasonable in size.** Don't wear a large ring on the right hand that will prevent another person from shaking your hand firmly. Large rings could also get in the way of typing, writing, and other daily work functions.
- **Made of black leather or metal bands.** These typically complement business attire

NOTES

1. Karen Tumulty and John F. Dickerson, "Inside the Debate Strategies" *Time* (26 September 2004), http://www.time.com/time/election2004/article/0,18471,702075-1,00.html (Accessed June 14, 2009).

2. Katie Herman, "Presidential Candidates Have Large Height Difference" *The Fed* (22 October 2004), http://www.the-fed.org/articles/volume20/issue2/presheight.html (Accessed June 15, 2009).

3. National Institutes for Health Obesity Research Taskforce, "The National Strategic Plan for NIH Obesity Research" *National Health Institute* (August 2004), http://www.obesityresearch.nih.gov/About/Obesity_EntireDocument.pdf (Accessed June 13, 2009).

4. Nancy Voros, "Weight Discrimination Runs Rampant in Hiring" *Careerjournal.com: The Wall Street Journal* (2000), http://208.144.115.170/myc/climbing/20000905-voros.html (Accessed June 13, 2009).

5. Thomas Einhorn, "Brain, Bone, and Body Mass: Fat Is Beautiful Again" *The Journal of Bone and Joint Surgery* no. 83 (2001), 1782.

6. National Institutes for Health Obesity Research Taskforce, "The National Strategic Plan for NIH Obesity Research" *National Health Institute* (August 2004), http://www.obesityresearch.nih.gov/About/Obesity_EntireDocument.pdf (Accessed June 13, 2009).

7. Mike Emery, *Men's Bodybuilding: A Short History* (2003), http://bodybuildingreviews.net/Bodybuilding.html (Accessed June 10, 2009).

8. Oak Productions, Inc. "Athlete" *The Official Website of Schwarzenegger*, http://www.schwarzenegger.com/en/athlete/index.asp?sec=athlete (Accessed June 9, 2009).

9. Natalie Angier, "Powerhouses of Senses, Smell, at Last Gets Its Due" *The New York Times* (14 February 1995), http://www.nytimes.com/1995/02/14/science/powerhouse-of-senses-smell-at-last-gets-its-due.html (Accessed June 13, 2009).

10. Howard J. Pierce, *The Owner's Manual for the Brain: Everyday Applications from Mind-Brain Research* (Austin: Bard Press, 2000).

11. Michael Pertschuk and Alice Trisdorfer, "Men's Bodies—The Survey" *Psychology Today* (1 November 1994), http://www.psychologytoday.com/articles/pto-19941101-000022.html (Accessed June 2, 2009).

12. HR.BLR.com, "Sorry, But You Stink" *hr.blr.com* (14 April 2005), http://hr.blr.com/news.aspx?id=15057 (Accessed June 10, 2009).

13. Jared Sandberg, "Sure, Hold Your Nose, But Colleagues' Odors Pose Serious Problem" *The Wall Street Journal* (21 July 2004), http://online.wsj.com/article/SB109035944035168974.html (Accessed June 10, 2009).

14. Society for the Advancement of Education, "Bosses to Workers: Lose the Flip Flops" *USA Today* (November 2003), http://findarticles.com/p/articles/mi_m1272/is_2702_132/ai_110531012 (Accessed June 10, 2009).

15. Accountemps, "Dressing the Part: Office Attire" *Careermag.com*, http://www.careermag.com/articles/dressing-the-part-office-attire-1669-article.html (Accessed June 10, 2009).

16. Jill Morton, "Why Color Matters" *Color Matters* (2005), http://www.colormatters.com/market_whycolor.html (Accessed June 4, 2009).

17. Jill Morton, "Why Color Matters" *Color Matters* (2005), http://www.colormatters.com/market_whycolor.html (Accessed June 4, 2009).

18. Michelle Bryner, "Sports Psych" *Psychology Today* (1 September 2005), http://www.psychologytoday.com/articles/pto-20050831-000017.html (Accessed June 4, 2009).

19. Naz Kaya and Helen H. Epps. "Color-Emotion Associations: Past Experience and Personal Preferences." *AIC 2004 Color and Paints, Interim Meeting of the International Color Association*.http://www.fadu.uba.ar/sitios/sicyt/color/aic2004/031-034.pdf (Accessed on June 12, 2009)

20. Aldert Vrij, "Wearing Black Clothes: The Impact of Offenders' and Suspects' Clothing on Impression Formation" *Applied Cognitive Psychology*, no. 11 (1997), 47–53.

21. Aldert Vrij and Lucy Akehurst, "The Existence of a Black Clothing Stereotype: The Impact of a Victim's Black Clothing on Impression Formation" *Psychology, Crime, and Law*, no. 3 (1997), 227–237.

22. Mark G. Frank and Thomas Gilovich, "The Dark Side of Self and Social Perception: Black Uniforms and Aggression in Professional Sports" *Journal of Personality and Social Psychology* 54, no. 1 (1988), 74–85.

23. Michael Hemphill, "A Note on Adults' Color-Emotion Associations" *Journal of Genetic Psychology*, no. 157 (1996), 275–281.

24. Marilyn Snell, "Innovator: Judy Kranzler" *Democratic Leadership Council: Blueprint Magazine* (1 September 1999), http://www.dlc.org/ndol _ci.cfm?kaid=110&subid=181&contentid=1234 (Accessed June 5, 2009).

25. "The Story of Cotton" http://www.cotton.org/pubs/cottoncounts/ story/index.cfm (Accessed June 4, 2009).

26. The Silkroad Foundation, "History of Silk" *The Silkroad Foundation* (1997), http://www.silk-road.com/artl/silkhistory.shtml (Accessed June 4, 2009).

27. Magic Eye, "Frequently Asked Questions" *Magic Eye*, http://www .magiceye.com/faq.htm (Accessed June 4, 2009).

28. Seth Bareiss, "Tessellations" *Tessellations*, http://www.tessellations .org (Accessed June 9, 2009).

29. Tegan Louise, "Why Animal Print Fashion is Popular" *Ezine Articles*, http://ezinearticles.com/?Why-Animal-Print-Fashion-is- Popular&id=2279317 (Accessed June 4, 2009).

30. "Fashion through the Decades: 1900–1990" http://www.angelfire .com/ok5/coenfashionfiles/faafiles/faaunit1/fashionthroughthedecades.pdf (Accessed June 4, 2009).

31. Jenny Gallagher, "A Brief Look at the Fashions of the Twentieth Century from the 1920's–1990's" *Fashion Through the Decades*, http://drake .marin.k12.ca.us/students/gallaghj/fashion/fash_thru_decade.html (Accessed June 10, 2009).

32. "Fashion through the Decades: A Crash Course on the History of Fashion" *Belle de Four* (22 October 2007), http://fashionbella.blogspot .com/2007/10/fashion-through-decades-crash-course-on.html (Accessed June 4, 2009).

33. "The Meaning of Metals" *EncycloBEADia*, http://www.fire mountaingems.com/encyclobeadia/beading_resources.asp?docid=8A18 (Accessed June 5, 2009).

Chapter 5

Upper Zone

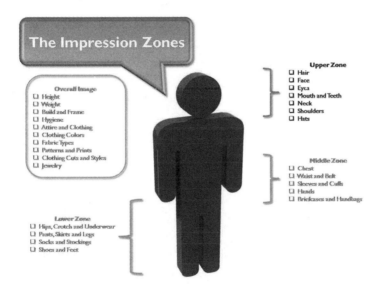

The Impression Zones

Overall Image
- ❑ Height
- ❑ Weight
- ❑ Build and Frame
- ❑ Hygiene
- ❑ Attire and Clothing
- ❑ Clothing Colors
- ❑ Fabric Types
- ❑ Patterns and Prints
- ❑ Clothing Cuts and Styles
- ❑ Jewelry

Upper Zone
- ❑ Hair
- ❑ Face
- ❑ Eyes
- ❑ Mouth and Teeth
- ❑ Neck
- ❑ Shoulders
- ❑ Hats

Middle Zone
- ❑ Chest
- ❑ Waist and Belt
- ❑ Sleeves and Cuffs
- ❑ Hands
- ❑ Briefcases and Handbags

Lower Zone
- ❑ Hips, Crotch and Underwear
- ❑ Pants, Skirts and Legs
- ❑ Socks and Stockings
- ❑ Shoes and Feet

INSIGHT & INFORMATION
HAIRSTYLE

Hairstyles, particularly those of women, have changed over the years. Here's a brief timeline of hairstyles throughout the decades to give you a sense of how far we've come.[1]

1990s: Big hair was replaced by an angled, layered, shag haircut made popular by Jennifer Aniston.

1980s: Big hairstyles, such as the mullet, were ... big.

1970s: The advent of the hair dryer allowed for a looser, feathery look.

1960s: Hairstyles shifted from flips, bouffants, and beehives to long, straight hair parted down the center.

1950s: Elegant and immaculate hairstyles reflected women's ideal homemaking techniques.

1940s: Elegance, sophistication, and Victory Rolls represented Hollywood glamour.

1930s: Finger waves and pin curls radiated voluptuous femininity.

1920s: The bob, inspired by renowned ballroom dancer Irene Castle, represented bold femininity.

1910s: Women cut their hair short, similar to American nurses in Europe.

1900s: Wealthy women adorned their hair with jewels and hats with veils and lace.

Bottom Line: Hairstyles change with time, so make sure you update yours periodically. Ever notice how some folks wear the same style for years? Make sure to talk with your stylist or flip through magazines from time to time.

TACTICAL & PRACTICAL
HAIRSTYLE

Believe it or not, your hairstyle says a lot about you. A good hairstyle can flatter your look and reveal the degree of your personal hygiene. An out-of-date hairstyle, on the other hand, makes it seem like you lack interest in new developments. We could write volumes about hair, but we'll provide brief tips here. Your hairstyle is arguably more important than your outfit, because it's something you wear on a daily basis.

Men:

Keep it simple; short hair is the way to go. For those who border on no hair or have receding hairlines, stick with your natural hairline. This demonstrates confidence and acceptance. Right now, total baldness is also a very popular look for men. If you think this works well with your head shape, you can give it a try. For those with more hair, gel keeps hair under control. Just use a little bit, so you avoid making your hair look like a greasy mop.

- *Parts*: You should avoid using a comb, because it creates harsh lines. Instead, use a brush, or even just run gel through your hair with your fingers, to showcase your hair's texture. When parting your hair, stay away from a hard-line part that shows scalp. Instead, allow your hair's natural line to dominate and cover up that hard part with some hair.
- *Short and Long*: Long hair softens a man's face and makes for a more-youthful look. Short hair generally looks more masculine—think military crew cut.

Women:

Go natural! Some of the best hairstyles look very natural, in both cut and color. If you do decide to change your hair color, make it gradually. If you change your hair drastically, not to select a look that will shock others too much. Of course, sometimes, a little shock value goes a long way. It depends on whether you're aiming for a gradual shift or the surprise of shock. While changing the color, make sure that it complements your skin tone and accentuates your eyes. Make sure you maintain the color as well, since your different-color roots will begin to reappear every couple of weeks.

As a general rule, people consider short or shoulder-length hair the most professional look for women. Women ask us if they should go long or short and we say it depends. Long hair looks more youthful and fun. On the other hand, very few successful female executives keep their hair long. However, because women's faces come in different shapes and sizes, we're providing you some tailored tips that match your face shape. If you have . . .

- A *round face*, stick with long hair to add length to your face. Bangs will help with this as well. Hair flipped inward makes the face look narrower.

- A *heart-shaped face*, go with long hair or a style that draws attention away from your pointy chin. Go with a look that accentuates your strong cheekbones.

- An *oval face*, you're in luck. Pretty much all hairstyles look great on you and even the more-difficult curly hair is an option for you. Keep hair away from your face, though; this includes bangs and long hair. You have a great face shape, so make sure your hair doesn't cover it up.

- A *square shape*, avoid bangs because they'll soften the edges of your face.

INSIGHT & INFORMATION
FACE SHAPE

Your face plays a critical role in your first impression, because it's the part of your body that another person usually notices first and looks at the most. In certain cultures, people will employ the shape of your face, among other facial features, to ascertain your personality and read your fortune. People in these cultures revere the accuracy of these face-reading skills that have existed for thousands of years. These readers believe that a shape plays a prominent role in how others perceive your personality and destiny. Rounder faces generally show more friendly and gentle people, for example. Sharper faces tend to display ambitious and sharper personalities.

Whether or not you believe in face reading, you can leverage knowledge about face shape to your advantage. Two important rules that we've frequently come across in regards to facial attractiveness are the "Rule of Symmetry" and the "Rule of Opposites."

Widespread studies by Randy Thornhill of the University of New Mexico and Karl Grammer of the University of Vienna have found that the symmetry of one's face has a strong correlation with what people deem "attractive."[2] The more symmetrical a face, the more people find it appealing. Why? Because people perceive physical symmetry as a reflection of youth, fertility, health, and strength—all of which serve important evolutionary functions.

How exactly does symmetry reflect our genetics? Our genes encode perfect symmetry, but environmental factors are usually inconstant. Because of this, our ability to look symmetrical despite these chemical, physical, and biological factors demonstrates our health and strong genes. Symmetry isn't just a matter of looks, though. According to Thornhill and Gangestand, symmetrical people also smell better. In their study, women preferred the scent of symmetrical men and vice versa.[3]

Needless to say, most people aren't perfectly symmetrical. There are, however, other ways to continue looking good without necessarily possessing a 1:1 ratio. Similar to the "Rule of Symmetry," the "Rule of Opposites" also plays off the concept of balance—but from less of a genetics perspective and more from an aesthetics perspective. People's features don't necessarily need to be symmetrical to look balanced. By utilizing "opposites" as explained in Practical & Tactical, people can showcase a different kind of aesthetically pleasing balance.

Bottom Line: People tend to show favor toward face shapes with symmetry and balance.

TACTICAL & PRACTICAL
FACE SHAPE

Altering the appearance of your face shape doesn't necessitate cosmetic surgery. You can make your face look a little more symmetrical by employing the following tips:

- **Shape and tweeze your eyebrows evenly so that they appear symmetrical.** Because your eyes are one of the most noticeable parts of your face and body, it's important for your brows to look symmetrical.

- **Conceal markings or blemishes that may cause you to look asymmetrical.** You're probably dabbing concealer on your blemishes anyway; this is just another reason why you might want to mask imperfections.

- **Place even amounts of makeup on both sides of your face.** Uneven amounts of makeup, especially lots of it, can make you look asymmetrical and funny.

The rule of opposites allows you to use external methods to create more balance in your appearance. Research shows that people favor statistical averages of face shapes. That said, if your face has one shape, then use external measures that accentuate shapes opposite to yours. Here are some ways to adapt the rule of opposites into your personal style:

- **Try square glasses if you have a round face, and round glasses if you have a square face.** Complementing shapes give your face a balanced look. Glasses can create the effect of a more balanced look if you choose the right pair to accompany your face.
- **Consider applying makeup that contrasts your skin tone.** If you have light skin, try dark colors. If you have dark skin, try light colors. Contrast, when executed properly, can look stunning. Just make sure you don't overdo it.
- **Implement hairstyles that complement your face shape.** For example, if you have a round face, stay with longer hair. This applies to a greater extent for women than men, but men can have longer hair too. This style adds length to your face and is considered the best complement to a round face. For women, if you have short to medium hair, you can flip the hair inward to make your face look less wide.

INSIGHT & INFORMATION
MAKEUP

Women often have a love-hate relationship with makeup. Some love makeup because it increases their confidence and makes them feel beautiful. Many women say that wearing makeup makes them feel prepared to interact with others and face the day. Some, including some of those who love makeup, hate makeup because they see it as a "necessary evil." Some women use it simply to avoid negative comments and attention from people. Once women start regularly wearing makeup to work, it's hard to go back. If they don't show up with makeup on, co-workers often ask about their health and become concerned for their well-being.

Many argue that there exists a sexist double standard for women in regards to makeup. If they don't wear makeup, people may begin to question their health, competence, and even sexuality. If they wear too much makeup, they're seen as overdramatic, tactless, or even promiscuous. With lots of makeup, women might avoid negative comments and attention about their appearance, but may receive unwanted attention and advances instead. The key to effective use of makeup entails a balance between too little and too much. Many makeup artists and stylists recommend using natural-looking makeup that helps highlight and accentuate existing beauty without being too over the top.

Despite mixed viewpoints regarding makeup, women can leverage makeup for good. According to Dellinger, Kirsten, and Williams's "Gender and Society, Makeup at Work: Negotiating Appearance Rules in the Workplace," makeup:

- **Challenges racial stereotypes.** Women of color can use makeup to challenge stereotypes that perpetuate the notion that they lack femininity.
- **Defies age.** Some use makeup to look older, while others use it to look younger. Defying age and fighting ageism allow women to look competent and able in the workplace and in their everyday lives.
- **Demonstrates a woman's success and credibility in the workplace.** Makeup and color are associated with health and beauty and, for better or for worse, showcasing those characteristics will help people in a professional setting. It also demonstrates one's skill at the nuances of applying makeup, as well as aesthetic sense.[4]

Some men wear makeup as well, though these men are typically found in the fashion or entertainment industry. For the most part, makeup tips and implications apply to women.

Bottom Line: Makeup remains an area of controversy, particularly because of its gendered nature, yet a large number of female professionals wear makeup to the workplace.

TACTICAL & PRACTICAL
MAKEUP

Generally, makeup advice for most professionals applies to women. Men generally use makeup in the entertainment industry or when going on camera. For the most part, these tips apply to women, but men can use this advice as well when it does relate to them. With makeup, a little bit can go a long way, but too much can prove detrimental. Used in moderation, makeup can effectively conceal flaws and accentuate positive facial features. Like with hairstyle, going natural serves as a good rule of thumb for makeup.

When putting on makeup, keep in mind that eyes are the most noticeable part of your face; lips are a close second. If you only have a few short minutes to add some extra color, make sure you accentuate these parts of your face.

What Colors Are Right for You?

To use the following chart, first determine if your skin tone is "warm" or "cool" and if it's "clear" or "muted." Warm tones often have a more reddish, yellowish, orange, and olive hues. This reflects the warmth of fire and earth. Cool tones generally have more blues and pinks, and if they do have yellow, it's very faint. Clear tones of skin are more distinguished and show contrast between the skin when compared with the hair and eyes. They show a clarity and crispness of skin, almost as if you were watching a television and turned up the "contrast" feature. That's why the skin stands out when compared to the color of hair and eyes. Muted colors have a more opaque quality and have softer colors. Think of a lowered "contrast" on television that makes images less stark and the skin blends in better with the color of one's hair and eyes. Select your two types of tones, and from there, you'll find what colors look best with your skin tone—both for makeup and attire.[5]

INSIGHT & INFORMATION
FACIAL HAIR

Facial hair is considered the ultimate statement of masculinity. So, it's not surprising that it has positive associations with men but negative connotations for women who aspire toward a more feminine look.

Researchers at Northumbria University conducted a study regarding men with five types of facial hair: clean-shaven, light stubble, heavy stubble, light beard and full beard.[6] The study found that the longer the facial hair, the more women identified the individual as masculine, dominant, and socially mature. Facial hair added age to the men as well. Light stubble added an average of three years to the man's actual age, while a full beard added five and a half years.

The perceptions of, and reactions to, women with facial hair are not so positive. One study found that unwanted facial hair carries a high psychological burden.[7] Women spent an average of almost two hours per week on managing their facial hair. Out of the 88 women surveyed in this study, 67 percent reported continually checking in mirrors while 76 percent checked on their facial hair by touch. Not surprisingly, then, that many of these women felt uncomfortable in social situations and some were clinically depressed. Double standards like this exist, which signify the gendered nature of facial hair.

Androgen overproduction causes female facial hair and can be addressed. Permanent treatment of the issue includes surgical removal of the hair follicle or electrolysis. Temporary solutions include shaving, epilation, and depilation.[8] Physicians generally don't address the problem unless the patient first requests help, so it's up to the woman to bring this issue up with her doctor.

Bottom Line: Many link facial hair with masculinity, wisdom, and maturity. Of course, you trade in your "clean-cut" image for these attributes.

TACTICAL & PRACTICAL
FACIAL HAIR

Not all of us have facial hair but for those of you who do, this one's for you. Here are some tips for both men and women on maintaining facial hair, as well as things to consider when deciding whether or not you should decorate your face with luscious locks.

Tips:

- Keep your facial hair clean and well-groomed. You should probably avoid dying, streaking, braiding, or doing anything really crazy to your facial hair. Facial hair already makes enough of a statement, so going out of your way to increase that statement could send a nonverbal "scream" from your mustache or beard.

- Women, if you have facial hair around your lips or ears, unfortunately, a double standard still exists for you. You can keep it if you're confident enough, which we praise you for. Still, most people look negatively upon women with facial hair and most who have it make strong efforts to hide or eliminate it. Think about bleaching it or seeking other types of treatments. Bleaching is a safe procedure, but we do recommend that you use high-quality bleach.

Consider This:

- Facial hair policies depend on a variety of factors such as company, industry, and geography. Make sure you understand your environment before donning your face with hair. Companies that require a more "clean-cut" image, such as those dealing with children or the food-services industry, may discourage facial hair. Companies may not overtly say so, but you can tell by looking at the dominant executives down to the most junior of staff. Pay close attention to this. Other industries, often ones that require more physical strength and stamina, may de facto encourage facial hair as a means of expressing masculinity. Take a look around you and remember that "when in Rome, do as the Romans do."

- Facial hair is usually suitable in academia, arts, marketing, and other socially involved fields. It may be less acceptable for fields such as sales, finance, and accounting, and some people may perceive you as less-polished or clean-cut.

INSIGHT & INFORMATION
EYES

Eyes are powerful. Their presence in religion, mythology, and everyday life demonstrates their dominance and pervasiveness. In religion, the omnipresence of the eye can be taken quite literally; you can see this on the one-dollar bill that we use so frequently. On the back of the bill, the Eye of Providence—an all-seeing eye—represents the eye of God keeping watch on humankind. In mythology, eyes can have different meanings. In ancient Egypt, eyes symbolized protection, destruction, offerings, goddesses, or the dead's ability to see the living world.[9] Many cultures believe in the protective quality of the eye; people wear talismans and jewelry with the evil eye—a symbol that protects them from evil spirits and misfortune.[10]

They say that the eyes are the windows to your soul. Considering that the eyeball measures approximately the same size and shape as a ping-pong ball, those are some small windows. Small as they may be, your eyes convey much about you—sometimes more than you'd expect. Here are some common meanings behind the looks you give, whether intentionally or unintentionally.[11]

- **Big eyes:** These eyes usually give the beholder a childlike look, conveying a sense of youthfulness and innocence. They also connote openness, because of their large size.
- **Looking up:** By looking up with just your eyes, you demonstrate submissiveness and evoke empathy from others. More commonly used by women, this look causes the eyes to appear bigger thereby conveying a sense of youthfulness. This often elicits a parenting reaction from the audience.
- **Sideways glance:** This glance can be used to convey interest, uncertainty, or hostility. Once you have "shifty eyes," though, you look secretive—like you're hiding something or doing something wrong.
- **Watery eyes:** This conveys a lot of emotion, though it's not always easy to tell which one. Watery eyes can result from tears of sadness or joy. This can show a weak moment of lack of logic or a powerful moment filled with emotion. It could, of course, just mean your allergies started acting up again.
- **Extended blinking:** Though you could just have a dust particle stuck in your eye, extended blinking often conveys the message that you are disinterested or no longer want to tolerate the other person. Others could view this as submissiveness or surprise. Closing your eyes for an extended period of time helps you mentally wipe the other person from your sight and mind.
- **Rolling eyes:** Another way to convey boredom, lack of interest, annoyance, and other not-so-positive thoughts.
- **Eye contact:** You've probably heard the phrase, "Look me in the eye" when someone wants to be told the truth. To some extent, eye contact is a great way to establish trust with another person. What's interesting, though, is that seasoned liars are able to look you in the eye . . . and not tell you the truth. So, just because someone's looking you in the eye doesn't necessarily mean they're being honest with you.

- **Giving the "evil eye"**: This often takes place in the form of a glare and *doesn't* help you establish trust with another person. This act generally shows disdain.
- **Eyebrow flash**: This flash acknowledges another person, especially at a distance that may be out of hearing range. It's the equivalent of a facial "what's up?"
- **Dilated pupils**: These are considered far more attractive than "beady little eyes" or "snake eyes." You can actually tell a lot from someone's pupils, since they dilate or contract as attitudes and moods change from positive to negative.
- **Winking**: Generally, this indicates flirting or that the person winking and the person winked at both know an inside joke or piece of information
- **Looking down**: This act primarily means deference or submission. It can also mean avoidance.

Bottom Line: This is by no means a comprehensive list of all of the messages you could convey with your eyes, but keep these in mind as you interact with others. Your eyes indeed reveal much more than you think. Despite the possibility of misinterpretation, people continue to believe they can understand your intentions by looking at your eyes.

TACTICAL & PRACTICAL
EYES

You've heard people say that someone has "kind eyes" or that you can "see it in her eyes." Some people even say that you can determine someone's trustworthiness by his or her eyes. Your eyes say a lot about you, so they no doubt have a big impact on your impression. If you were blessed with perfect eyes (including vision), congratulations! For those of us who lack 20/20 vision, here are some tips on how to make our eyes look great in glasses or contacts.

Glasses
- Glasses can make you look intelligent. Even if you have both glasses and contacts, you can opt to wear glasses if you think this will be advantageous in certain situations.
- Purchase glasses with thin frames and non-glare lenses for a professional look. Even if you have a strong prescription, you can usually pay a little extra for thinner lenses. Thinner lenses and frames elicit a lighter look. Thicker and darker frames project a heavier look on your face.

- Keep your glasses clean, especially before important meetings. Because glasses are located in front of your eyes, others can quickly notice any smudges or dirt you may have on the lenses. Buy some lens wipes and keep them in your pocket, briefcase, or purse.
- Keep your glasses dry. Water and sweat can get into different crevices such as the space between your lens and frames or the hinges of your frames. By wiping off the water and other liquids, you can help prevent mold from growing on your glasses.
- If you're always in a rush and running around, glasses might not be a good fit for you because they'll fog up quickly.

Contacts

- Avoid colored contact lenses or lenses with excessively eccentric designs. If you do opt for these, be aware that while they make a bold statement, others may perceive you as odd.
- Clean your contacts on a regular basis. Dirty contacts have a tendency to irritate the eyes, which may cause you to rub them more than you'd like. Red and irritated eyes can make you look ill or tired.
- If you wear your contacts for longer than the prescribed number of hours per day, make sure you re-wet your contacts. Like dirty contacts, dry contacts may lead to irritation. This may make you look tired or sick, even if you're not.
- Keep at least a small bottle of contact solution in an easily accessible location. If you have an irritant in your eye, you want to be able to deal with it immediately. At the very least, always carry around re-wetting solution.

Many people wear both glasses and contacts on different occasions. Some wear contacts throughout the day and glasses at night. Others wear glasses on a regular basis, and only wear contacts for special occasions. If you're comfortable using both, that's great! If not, use the one you're more familiar with for important situations such as interviews and meetings. You don't want unfamiliarity with your eyewear to prevent you from performing your best.

Making Eye Contact

Eye contact poses a complex interaction. In general, however, making less eye contact in the United States often conjures thoughts in an observer's mind that a person may avoid confrontation, show submission, or hide their thoughts. In contrast, staring directly into someone's eyes can result in perceptions of aggression and challenge from the observer's standpoint. To engage someone, without the extremes of looking shy or ready to pounce, you can learn to make eye contact that's not too penetrating. Here's how: When you look into a person's eyes, you can slightly and subtly move your eyes. You can slowly view their eyebrows or the areas directly around their eyes. This way, you're not constantly staring straight into their eyes, which can come off as piercing. All the while, you're making eye contact.

INSIGHT & INFORMATION
MOUTH AND TEETH

If eyes are the windows to your soul, then your mouth can be considered the door to your soul. When you meet another person, you often look at their eyes—because it's important to make eye contact—or their mouth—since it's the part of their face that's moving. Because of this, your mouth is an important part of your Impressive First Impression.

It's no surprise, then, that people spend billions of dollars on their mouths and teeth every year. Lip and mouth-related products prove fairly lucrative; the cosmetic, beauty supply, and perfume industry includes 10,000 stores with annual revenue of almost $7 billion.[12] Because the mouth is a very critical and evident part of the face, it's likely that we can attribute a high percentage of this revenue to mouth-related purchases such as lipstick and anti-wrinkle creams. Additionally, Americans spend billions upon billions of dollars on dental work that includes everything from dentistry to orthodontics and teeth whitening. Teeth whitening alone is a $14 billion industry![13]

With the popularity of orthodontic and teeth-whitening procedures, many consider straight, white teeth the norm in the United States. This standard, however, is not necessarily upheld in other developed countries throughout the world. While one of our associates worked in Japan for several months, some of the people she met (even business contacts) commented on the straightness and whiteness of her teeth. Straight teeth are somewhat of an anomaly in Japan, since the Japanese typically aren't too concerned with this trait. In fact, "yaeba" (a double tooth) is fairly common in Japan and many consider this cute and charming, especially for women. Some female celebrities and models show off their "yaeba" while smiling for photos.[14]

For better or for worse, many consider straight, white teeth the ideal in the United States. Some would say that the general American public is obsessed with these traits. According to the American Academy of Cosmetic Dentistry, teeth whitening is the country's most-requested cosmetic dental procedure.[15] A different study found that 47 percent of Americans think that crooked teeth leave a negative first impression, while 72 percent agree that people with healthy straight teeth are typically treated better in social situations than those with noticeably crooked teeth.[16]

Bottom Line: Your mouth and teeth are very important and visible parts of your body. Straight, white teeth can help boost your first impression.

TACTICAL & PRACTICAL
MOUTH AND TEETH

Your mouth serves as the origin of all of your oral communication. Additionally, it is often the point of focus on your face. As a result, you want your mouth and teeth looking great at all times. Follow these quick, easy tips to help make your lips and teeth shine.

Mouth

- Avoid licking your lips. Licking your lips cause them to dry out quickly.
- Use lip balm to moisturize your lips and make sure that your lips don't look dry or flaky.
- Create your own lip moisturizer. Add honey and sugar, and rub them on your lips. Wipe the concoction off after five minutes.
- Careful when you touch your hands to your lips and mouth. This can cause infections, such as cold sores and the common cold.

Teeth

- Practice good dental hygiene. Brush and floss your teeth regularly after every meal. Don't forget to use mouthwash after brushing your teeth.
- If you want to make those pearly whites even whiter, consider teeth whitening strips or professional teeth whitening.
- For a more natural approach, eat fruits, especially apples and pineapples, to clean and whiten your teeth.

- Stay away from sweets and sugars that will cause your teeth to decay.
- Don't drink coffee, tea, or other liquids that will yellow your teeth. If you do drink these liquids regularly, you can use a straw, so most of the liquid goes directly into your mouth rather than on your teeth. This reduces stain buildup on your nice, white chompers.
- Quit smoking.

INSIGHT & INFORMATION
NECK

Today's shirt collars are a product of medieval chemises; they descend from the ruffle created by the drawstrings at the necks of these smocks.[17] The purpose of collars has changed over the years, but they're still used for business clothing today. Though collars on dress shirts and jackets may not have an obvious functional value, they often help instill confidence and sophistication in its wearer. How? The placement of a collar around the neck prompts the wearer to keep his or her head upright, thereby encouraging good posture and helping the person look taller. When one's physical characteristics reflect confidence, this often helps the wearer become more confident as well. Additionally, collars reflect a certain level of sophistication because they're often worn in more formal occasions.

You can see the ubiquity of collars in the workplace based on the terminology we use today. Blue, white, and pink all refer to different types of "collars" that represent the various classes of the workforce. Blue collars represent the working class who perform manual labor for an hourly wage. Salaried professionals are considered white-collar workers, and do not perform manual labor as part of their jobs. Pink collar refers to jobs that are traditionally seen as female occupations, such as waitressing and nursing.

Those of you who follow recent fashion trends may be familiar with the upturned collar. Many popular hip-hop songs encouraged listeners to "pop your collar," and this action became trendy for a while with mixed reactions. Guys in fraternities often wore upturned collars, but many thought this move was too "preppy" or just downright silly. Interestingly enough, this action originally had a functional value. Rene Lacoste, the seven-time Grand Slam champion, created the tennis shirt because the existing attire for games felt uncomfortable. He designed a cotton shirt with an unstarched, flat protruding collar that could be turned up to shield the neck from the sun, preventing sunburn and hyperthermia.[18] Seeing as most professionals aren't trying to prevent sunburn in the office, we recommend against upturned collars in the workplace.

As you know, collars aren't the only things you'll often find around people's necks in a professional setting. Men wear neckties under the collars of their dress shirts, often out of tradition or obligation. Americans spend more than $1 billion to buy 100 million ties each year.[19] Regardless of your take on neckties, we have Croatian mercenaries to thank for their inception. Since then, the necktie has evolved and we have dozens of ways in which we can tie our ties. One historian told us he considers ties a form of male plumage to show individuality, confidence, and even dominance.

Unfortunately, neckties are not without risk. Some potential hazards from ties include entanglement, infection, and vascular constriction. As a result, men in occupations where a necktie can pose a safety hazard (such as law enforcement, airline pilots, etc.) often wear clip-on ties.[20] These men still opt to wear a tie, though, because neckties convey a sense of formality and prestige. Though ties are worn less frequently in the workplace thanks to Casual Fridays, you'll usually find men wearing them on every other day of the week.

Bottom Line: Collars and neckties help you convey a sense of sophistication and confidence, thanks to their neck support as well as their stylistic connotations.

TACTICAL & PRACTICAL
NECK

The one thing that's keeping that good head on your shoulders is your neck. It's hard to keep it upright and erect, because it's so much smaller than our heads. It's like holding up a bowling ball with a thin, or medium, pipe. Hold up your neck to look more confident. Because of its proximity to the head and face, the neck is an important part of making a great first impression, since it helps highlight the face, where we most express ourselves to others through our mouth and eyes. Here is some quick Q&A on how to make your neck look great.

Collars

Q: Should I wear a collared shirt in all business settings?
A: You can wear collared shirts to business functions. Button-down collared shirts alone are more appropriate for business casual, rather

than formal business, settings. Otherwise, wear a tie. You can always remove it if you feel too formal compared to others.

Q: *How far should my collar be from my neck?*
A: You should have a one-finger gap between your collar and neck.

Q: *Spread collar or point collar?*
A: Spread collars are what the name implies. The points of these collars spread more outward toward your shoulders and are popular in Europe. Point collars also are what they sound like. The points of the collars point virtually downward rather than the outward direction of the spread collar. People with narrow necks and faces should wear spread collars to widen these areas. Those with shorter necks and wider faces should don shirts with point collars, so the downward direction of the points makes your face appear narrower.

Ties

Q: *How wide should my tie be?*
A: The ideal width of ties is between 2.75 and 3.5 inches.

Q: *What about length?*
A: The tip of your tie should extend down to your belt and cover it.

Q: *What kind of fabric makes my tie look more formal?*
A: Silk.

Q: *What kind of knot suits me best?*
A: A double Windsor

Jewelry

Q: *What kind of jewelry should I wear to match my face?*
A: Use a similar logic to ties. When you have a long neck and narrower face, you can wear a choker necklace, because it accentuates your long and slender neck and face. If your neck looks wider and shorter, wear hanging jewelry to give a longer and narrower look to your neck and face.

INSIGHT & INFORMATION
SHOULDERS

From mothers to the military, we're consistently told not to hunch our shoulders forward. There's a good reason for that. Think about the common social link between shrugging your shoulders and confusion. Or it can often mean "I don't know." When people shrug their shoulders they can also convey weakness, a lack of confidence, or even fear. They may lift their shoulders up to shield themselves from cold. This act could indicate an instinctive need to protect the head or neck. Think about the old expression, "going for the jugular," which means going for the jugular vein in the neck to strike a fatal blow.

Shoulders can project a fully different air. When it comes to simple image, we think of confident, broad-shouldered heroes and heroines with V-shaped bodies. These folks usually sport pushed-back and pushed-down shoulders, while nonchalantly exposing their chest and neck without fear of attack. Although we may not all be heroes, we can try to think about them as role models for our nonverbal messages, namely those in our shoulders.

From a fashion perspective, it's no accident that many jackets, whether casual or formal, include shoulder pads. The historical era of the 1980s featured extra-large shoulder pads, but also think about some of the muscle-bound, broad-shouldered action heroes of that era—Schwarzenegger and Stallone. We had to increase the size of our shoulder pads to keep up with them.

The stark contrast to this image remains with the computer nerd stereotype. Think about how a person stares at their computer all day and hunches their shoulders while typing or cranes their neck while reading. Since this book primarily targets literate and computer-literate working professionals, it behooves us even more to watch our shoulders when we flex these skills.

Bottom Line: Shoulders speak a language beyond words, as they represent tools for the stoic and heroic.

TACTICAL & PRACTICAL
SHOULDERS

Improve Your Shoulders—Physically

Your shoulders are an important part of your body. They support your neck and head, and pain in your shoulders can literally cause headaches. As our jobs require us to be technologically savvy and hunched over the keyboard on a regular basis, make sure you follow these quick tips to ensure healthy shoulders:

- **Exercise your shoulders**. There are a variety of shoulder exercises available, both for those with shoulder problems as well as those who have never had issues in the past. Make sure you find the right exercises for you. You can do shoulder exercises at the gym or with simple free weights at home. These exercises include: lateral raises, overhead presses, and downward pushing on the pulleys. Go to a website on lifting weights and you'll see diagrams of key exercises for this.

- **When typing away at a keyboard, make sure you sit upright with your shoulders aligned with your typing hands.** If you can't find a comfortable position while using a laptop, consider using a desktop computer. Add a full-sized keyboard, as this reduces your shoulders from hunching over the tiny default screen and keyboard.

- **Invest in an ergonomic keyboard** to keep your shoulders happy. While you're at it, invest in an ergonomic mouse and mouse pad, too.

- **Elevate your monitor and/or laptop so that the screen sits at eye level.** This helps prevent back, neck, and shoulder pain from staring down too often.

Improve Your Shoulders—Visually

Besides stopping yourself from hunching over all of the time, there are other ways to improve the visual appeal of your shoulders. These are some tips for men and women that will help your shoulders look better in the workplace or formal settings:

- **Wear perfectly fitted jackets and suits.** You don't want to look too boxy or baggy in your suit jacket.

- **Beware of wearing large shoulder pads.** These are currently out of style and should be sent back to the 1980s, where they belong. Some shoulder pads are okay, as they give structure, yet these should remain small.

- **Women, cover your shoulders with a shawl if they're exposed in an evening gown.** Exposing the shoulders is considered casual, which is less appropriate for formal attire.

INSIGHT & INFORMATION
HATS

Baseball. Fedora. Gatsby. Mortarboard. Hats come in all shapes and sizes, though ultimately they're all created to fit on one's head. Headwear today can have a variety of meanings and is used as a significant symbol in religion, ceremonies, and art. Additionally, people use certain types of hats as part of uniforms to indicate social status and to demonstrate one's authority.

Hats were originally created to help protect the wearer from the elements; many people use hats for that purpose today. Baseball caps help protect their wearers from harsh sun rays. We can lose body heat through our heads, and beanies help keep us warm in inclement weather. Hard hats and other protective gear help shield the wearer from harmful, falling objects.[21]

Because one rarely encounters harsh elements in the office, we don't often see hats in the workplace. Though we sometimes wear hats on special occasions, for the most part, hats are no longer seen as appropriate business wear for the office.

Bottom Line: Originally created for protection against the elements, hats do not provide much functional value or have much relevance in today's office workplace.

TACTICAL & PRACTICAL
HATS

The general rule on wearing hats in business settings is . . . don't. Historically, people needed hats in business situations, but they're now seen as inappropriate for executives. If it's cold and you really want to wear a hat, or if hats are acceptable in your workplace, follow these rules . . .

- Make sure your hat doesn't damage your hairstyle. Your hair remains a critical part of your first impression, so you don't want hat hair when you remove your hat.
- Take off your hat when entering a building. It's bad etiquette to wear hats indoors and during meals. Most hats are made for outdoor wear, anyway.
- Out of courtesy, remove your hat if it prevents the person behind you from seeing. Also, remove your hat if it prevents someone from seeing your eyes. Many people use eye contact to establish trust and rapport.
- If you must wear a hat, consider a fedora. It shows elegance and its structure reflects the structured setting where professionals work.

NOTES

1. "Hairstyle through the Decades" *Zimbio*, http://www.zimbio.com/ Vintage+Hair/notes/1/Hairstyles+Through+the+Decades (Accessed June 3, 2009); Rachael Taylor, "Famous People and Hairstyles through the Years" *Ezine Articles* (21 October 2006), http://ezinearticles.com/?Famous-People -and-Hairstyles-through-the-Years&id=334965 (Accessed June 3, 2009).

2. Elizabeth Snead, "The Beauty of Symmetry" *USA Weekend* (1 June 2003), http://www.usaweekend.com/03_issues/030601/030601symmetry.html (Accessed June 3, 2009).

3. Stefan Anitei, "Why Attractive Faces Are Symmetric and Gender Specific" *Softpedia* (7 May 2008), http://news.softpedia.com/news/Why-Attractive-Faces-Are-Symmetric-and-Gender-Specific-84961.shtml (Accessed June 4, 2009).

4. Kristen Dellinger and Christine L. Williams, "Makeup at Work: Negotiating Appearance Rules in the Workplace" *Gender and Society* 11, no. 2 (1997), 151–177.

5. Kristin Katteringham, "Wearing the Right Color for Your Skin Tone" *Associated Content: Lifestyle* (30 July 2007), http://www.associated content.com/article/328243/wearing_the_right_color_for_your_skin.html?cat=46 (Accessed June 5, 2009).

6. Matthew Hutson, "In the Rough: The Science Behind Designer Stubble" *Psychology Today*, November/December 2008), 24.

7. Michelle G. Liptona and others, "Women Living with Facial Hair: The Psychology and Behavioral Burden" *Journal of Psychosomatic Research* 61, no. 2 (2006), 161–168.

8. Donald W. Shenenberger, "Removal of Unwanted Facial Hair" *SmartSkinCare.com* (15 November 2002), http://www.smartskincare.com/resabstracts/hair-removal_shenenberger_am-fam-physician_20021115.html (Accessed June 8, 2009).

9. Jimmy Dunn, "The Eyes Have It" *Tour Egypt!* (17 October 2005), http://www.touregypt.net/featurestories/eyeofhorusandre.htm (Accessed June 9, 2009).

10. "The Evil Eye" *Lucky Mojo*, http://www.luckymojo.com/evileye.html (Accessed June 9, 2009).

11. Allan Pease and Barbara Pease, *The Definitive Book of Body Language* (New York: Bantam Books, 2006).

12. First Research, "Cosmetics, Beauty Supply, and Perfume Stores" (20 July 2009), http://www.firstresearch.com/Industry-Research/Cosmetics-Beauty-Supply-and-Perfume-Stores.html (Accessed July 30, 2009).

13. "Customer Service Helps Whiter Image Lead in Teeth Whitening Industry" *Free Services for PR* (28 October 2008), http://www.pr-inside.com/customer-service-helps-whiter-image-lead-r884701.htm (Accessed June 12, 2009).

14. Namiko Abe, "About Japanese Teeth" *About.com: Japanese Language* (16 July 2008), http://japanese.about.com/b/2008/07/16/about-japanese-teeth.htm (Accessed June 3, 2009).

15. Linda Saether, "How White Should Your Teeth Really Be?" *CNN Health* (5 September 2008), http://www.cnn.com/2008/HEALTH/09/05/hfh.teeth.whiter/index.html (Accessed June 3, 2009).

16. "Fix Crooked Teeth with Dental Braces" *Dental Health Magazine* (16 April 2008), http://worldental.org/teeth/fix-crooked-teeth-with-dental-braces (Accessed June 3, 2009).

17. "16th Century Fashion—The Ruff, a Collar with Meaning" (31 December 2008), http://blog.aurorahistoryboutique.com/tag/history-of-the-collar/ (Accessed June 11, 2009).

18. Alex Slack, "Pop This" *The Harvard Crimson* (12 August 2005), http://www.thecrimson.com/article.aspx?ref=508376 (Accessed June 11, 2009).

19. David Johnson, "2000 Years of Necktie" *Infoplease*, http://www.infoplease.com/spot/tie1.html (Accessed June 11, 2009).

20. Michael Pollick, "What Is a Clip-On Tie?" *wiseGEEK*, http://www.wisegeek.com/what-is-a-clip-on-tie.htm (Accessed June 4, 2009).

21. Pauline Weston Thomas, "The Wearing of Hats Fashion History General Information" *Fashion Era* (2001), http://www.fashion-era.com/hats-hair/hats_hair_1_wearing_hats_fashion_history.htm (Accessed June 8, 2009).

Chapter 6

Middle Zone

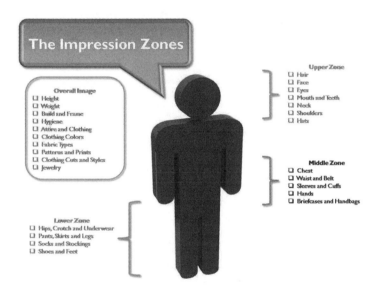

The Impression Zones

Overall Image
- ☐ Height
- ☐ Weight
- ☐ Build and Frame
- ☐ Hygiene
- ☐ Attire and Clothing
- ☐ Clothing Colors
- ☐ Fabric Types
- ☐ Patterns and Prints
- ☐ Clothing Cuts and Styles
- ☐ Jewelry

Upper Zone
- ☐ Hair
- ☐ Face
- ☐ Eyes
- ☐ Mouth and Teeth
- ☐ Neck
- ☐ Shoulders
- ☐ Hats

Middle Zone
- ☐ Chest
- ☐ Waist and Belt
- ☐ Sleeves and Cuffs
- ☐ Hands
- ☐ Briefcases and Handbags

Lower Zone
- ☐ Hips, Crotch and Underwear
- ☐ Pants, Skirts and Legs
- ☐ Socks and Stockings
- ☐ Shoes and Feet

INSIGHT & INFORMATION
CHEST

As we mentioned earlier in this book, humans are thinking animals. When it comes to displaying dominance and sexuality through chests, humans follow this school of thought.

When you look at the animal kingdom, you'll see a variety of creatures utilizing their chests to attract the opposite sex and ward off competitors. Male birds puff their chests in order to demonstrate that they would be good mates for their female counterparts.[1] Gorillas slap their chests with open-cupped hands, making a loud sound that indicates aggression or excitement.[2]

Human men use similar techniques as well. Men thrust out their chests to display their strength to members of the opposite sex, making them a more ideal candidate for mating. By "chest puffing," men make their bodies look bigger and more powerful. This also warns other men not to attack and wards off competition.

While men flaunt their chests for both women and men, women primarily use their chests to attract members of the opposite sex. When a woman thrusts her chest forward (or reveals a lot of cleavage), this is often seen as a provocative or romantic display.[3] This is why revealing attire is suitable for bars and nightclubs, where finding a mate is the primary objective, and not for the workplace. Some women use their chests as part of flirting in the workplace. According to a 2007 survey commissioned by *Harper's Bazaar*, 86 percent of women would flirt with their colleagues if it meant advancing in their careers. Be careful when flirting at work, however, because it can hurt a woman's career. According to a study by Tulane University researchers who surveyed 164 business school graduates, women who flirted more often earned only $50,000–$75,000, while those who refrained from flirting earned $75,000–$100,000. The former group only received two promotions, whereas the latter group received three.[4]

Bottom Line: The chest can show dominance and attractiveness, but in professional situations, there exists a double standard. Men's chests reflect their success in the workplace, whereas women's chests can hurt them. We cite research on flirting, because we hope that organizations will address these double standards.

TACTICAL & PRACTICAL
CHEST

Chests are often a hot topic of discussion amongst both genders. The size of female breasts and male chests link to mating, so it's no surprise that we instinctively think about this part of the anatomy. What signals does your chest give off to others? Read further to find out.

Women

By pushing your chest forward, you draw attention to it. Because men are usually aroused by the sight of breasts, this act can be interpreted as an invitation for intimate relations. As such, we highly recommend that women avoid wearing clothing that reveals too much cleavage in the workplace. Also, as the study on flirting shows, sexuality in the workplace may induce arousal but not career advancement.

Did You Know?

High heels function not only to make you look taller and showcase your legs, but they curve the spine to push out the chest and buttocks as well.[5]

Men

You can thrust out your chest to display your strength . . . and hide your gut. People use pectorals to gauge overall strength—so the bigger they look, the better you look. Plus, if you hide your gut, you'll look trimmer. As we discussed in the Weight section, you can use the illusion of trim to your advantage.

A word of caution. The rule about not revealing too much cleavage applies to men as well. Some men wear low-cut shirts or forget to fully button their button-up shirts. Most professionals don't find man-cleavage or chest hair too appealing, so we recommend that you don't flaunt this in public.

Did You Know?

You can now purchase men's girdles, also known as "mirdles," in the United States and Europe. These mirdles supposedly help sculpt and slim the male body, and improve its posture, too.[6]

If you didn't know already, it should be clear that your chest is an integral part of your impression. Use this to your advantage and make sure you send the right signals with your chest. This sometimes means not showing too much of it, whether you're a man or a woman.

INSIGHT & INFORMATION
WAIST AND BELTS

Short, long, thick, and thin. Humans come in all shapes and sizes, and this diversity applies to our waists as well.

First, let's talk about the different types of waists. If you have a short waist, your legs are longer than your torso. A long waist means that you have short legs and a long torso. A thick waist doesn't necessarily equal fat or unhealthy; as long as you have a healthy waist-to-hip ratio (WHR), which we'll talk about later, you'll be fine. Many people consider a thin waist ideal by current standards. Used appropriately, belts can complement one's waist type or draw attention away from it.

Now, about that acronym: WHR. The waist-to-hip ratio indicates levels of health as well as attractiveness. A WHR of 0.7 for women and 0.9 for men correlate with health and fertility.[7] Why are these numbers so important? For women, extremely high or low values for WHR reflect either high or low levels of body fat. These levels of body fat could increase risk for menstrual irregularity, ovulatory infertility, and life-threatening illnesses.[8] For both genders, those who have ideal WHRs are less susceptible to cardiovascular disorders, cancer, diabetes, and other diseases.[9] To figure out your WHR, simply search for "waist to hip ratio" online and you'll find websites that will help calculate this for you.

In both historical and modern cultures, society has considered a WHR of 0.7 as beautiful for women. Icons such as Audrey Hepburn, Marilyn Monroe, and even Venus de Milo all had WHRs close to 0.7. Because a WHR of 0.7 and 0.9 seem to have a strong correlation with health and fertility for women and men, respectively, those who have these ratios are viewed as more attractive. Many consider a low WHR to be attractive, so it's no surprise that both Playboy Playmates and Miss Americas have consistently had lower-than-average WHRs over the past 60 years.[10]

The WHR may at first seem to apply to standards of beauty, but like other indicators in first impressions, it reflects one's health as well. Healthier people typically prove more productive. The WHR indeed has professional implications in the workplace, because colleagues will, consciously or unconsciously, link this with your perceived health, and therefore, work effectiveness.

Bottom Line: A low WHR is more than a matter of beauty; it's a matter of health. As such, one may want to lower his/her ratio. Unfortunately, there's no easy solution. Reducing one's WHR requires a healthy diet and aerobic exercise over time. A healthy professional means a productive professional as well.

TACTICAL & PRACTICAL
WAIST AND BELTS

People come in different shapes and sizes, and those differences apply to the waist, too. See the following tips for specific waist types and general suggestions that will keep you looking good in the workplace.

If you have a short waist . . .
- Wear long tops or dropped waists.
- Don't wear outfits that change color at the waist.
- Don't wear wide belts.
- Match your belt with your top, not your bottom.
- Don't wear short jackets that end at the waist.
- Wear slacks at your hips and not your waist.
- Women, don't let your bust sag.

If you have a long waist . . .
- Sport belts that contrast with your top.
- Wear a softer and distracting top to deemphasize your long waist.
- Avoid straight, horizontal stripes on your pants.
- Men, wear a belt with big buckles and pleated pants.

If you have a thick waist . . .
- Try fabrics that draw attention away from your midsection.
- Don't wear outfits that change color at the waist.
- Avoid double-breasted suits or fitted jackets and coats.
- Women, wear pencil skirts with heels.
- Men, use medium-size belts with small to medium-size buckles.

General tips on belts:
- **Wear one-inch wide leather belts**. They can lighten up any mediocre wardrobe and enhance any great outfit.
- **Mix it up**. Like ties, belts can be used to maximize combinations of clothing.
- **Match it up**. For a slimming look, match your belt with your shirt or slacks, depending on your waist type.
- **Find the right size for you**. The perfect belt in terms of size should fasten in the second hole.
- **Use belt loops**. If you have belt loops, use them! That's what they're there for.

INSIGHT & INFORMATION
SLEEVES AND CUFFS

Though sleeves and cuff links can add a little flair to your outfit, these accessories come from humble origins. Sleeves served as snot-rags or handy handkerchiefs; they were originally intended to get dirty and help wipe up little messes.

The buttons (and now cuff links) of sleeves have interesting origins as well. One of the stories regarding their inception revolves around Frederick the Great in the 1700s. Frederick expressed concern about the appearance of his soldiers and wasn't happy about the fact that his soldiers' sleeves were dirtier than the rest of their uniforms.[11] When he found out that they used the sleeves to wipe sweat from their faces, he ordered metal buttons to be sewn on the soldiers' sleeves; if they decided to continue wiping their faces with their sleeves, they would scratch themselves. These buttons eventually made their way onto the sleeves of civilian jackets, though only for decorative purposes.

The sleeve plays such an integral role in one's outfit now that you'll often hear various expressions that address this feature. You've probably heard that someone "has something up his sleeve" or "wears his heart on his sleeve." The first expression actually corresponds with the functional value of some original sleeves, as the long-hanging sleeve (often still worn in Asian countries) used to function as a pocket.

Cuff links are not as common as sleeves, but they're quite unique in that they're one of few accessories primarily designed for men. As such, you'll often find that they come in interesting designs and shapes. One of our colleagues decided to give all of his best men cuff links as a thank-you for their participation in his wedding. These playful cuff links included nuts and bolts, Batman symbols, and ray guns.

Bottom Line: Though originally intended to get dirty, sleeves and cuffs look great if they look clean. Seriously, though, many people discount the types of sleeves on their shirts. These can give you an added flair if they have subtle touches, such as wider or narrower openings, cuff links, and interesting stitching.

TACTICAL & PRACTICAL
SLEEVES AND CUFFS

We all know that the handshake is one of the first forms of contact we have with another individual. Aside from your actual handshake and hands, sleeves and cuffs are likely the next area people notice during your handshake. Make sure your sleeves and cuffs contribute to a great first impression.

Long Sleeve? ¾ Sleeve? ½ Sleeve? Too Many to Choose From!

Not really. The answer remains pretty simple. Wear long-sleeve shirts. This rule applies to both men and women. Even if it's hot (and especially when it's hot), you want to wear long-sleeve shirts underneath your suit jacket. If you end up taking off your jacket, you don't want to be caught wearing a short-sleeve shirt.

No No-Sleeve!

Avoid wearing no-sleeve shirts underneath your suit jacket. You never know when you might take your jacket off, which can leave your arms exposed to the world. Even on Casual Fridays, wear some sleeves, please. When you wear a short-sleeve shirt with a tie, you look like a fast-food or discount-store manager. If you work in these establishments, that works fine. In many other professional contexts, tread lightly and with caution when doing so.

Elastic Is Not Your Friend

At least, elastic sleeves are not. If you have big arms, don't wear tight elastic sleeves. They'll make your arms look chunky.

How Low Should They Go?

As a general rule, sleeves should cover the wrist and should end at the top of the thumb. Some experts recommend that you show a ½ inch of your shirt below your jacket sleeve. It's okay if your shirt sleeve falls a little below that; just keep it under two inches.

And Now a Word About Cuff Links . . .

If you're wearing a French cuff shirt with cuff links, make sure you wear a jacket. Cuff links are considered formal accessories, so you'll look strange if you have cuff links with no jacket. If you want your cuff links to look really snazzy, get your links monogrammed with your initials. Try playful colors and materials as well. You can go with metals, jewels, and fabrics.

INSIGHT & INFORMATION
HANDS

Your hands say a lot about you. Take handshakes, for example. Handshakes originated in medieval Europe, where kings and knights would engage in a handshake to demonstrate that they weren't carrying a concealed weapon or intending to harm the other person.[12] Over time, the purpose of handshakes evolved and they're now used on a regular basis. Handshakes can close business deals and restore peace. A handshake can signify a greeting, an agreement, or a way to say farewell.

Handshakes aren't the only aspect of your hands that have significant meaning. Palm readers look at hands to determine futures, love lives, wealth, happiness, life span, and anything else you could possibly want to know. Whether or not you personally believe in palm reading, there's no doubt that many people do find meaning in their palms. Of course, you can literally talk with your hands, too. American Sign Language (ASL) is a natural human language one can analyze at the same level used for spoken languages.[13] Many who don't necessarily know ASL gesticulate with their hands, supplementing the words coming out of their mouths with the movement of their hands. This helps further convey their message, and allows the speaker to emphasize certain points as well.

It's not just your hand movements or the lines on your hands that have meaning. The way you take care of your hands says a lot about you, too. Manicures, along with basic grooming, can demonstrate that you have strong attention to detail and care about your image. Many link such observations with positive characteristics such as credibility and competence. Overly dry hands or hangnails, on the other hand, may send the opposite message.

Bottom Line: Your hands tell a lot about you. Encourage people to pay compliments to them by caring for them properly. Help your hands send impressive impressions by training yourself to gesture well.

TACTICAL & PRACTICAL
HANDS

Meet Clammy, Flaky, Slippery, Dusty, Soppy, Slimy, and Rough. No, these are not Snow White's seven dwarves. These are characteristics that can describe your hands if you don't take care of them properly. How can you avoid this? Simple. Maintain and care for your hands and nails so they look great.

Remember: Your hands often remain very visible to others during interactions. A handshake is one of the earliest forms of contact you have with another individual. In fact, it's usually the only form of physical contact we have with individuals we meet in the business setting (well, at least it should be). Don't ruin your first impression by having unsightly hands.

Five Easy Steps to Beautiful (or Handsome) Hands:

1. Moisturize! Take care of dry skin and rough cuticles.
2. Keep your nails groomed and not too lengthy. You don't want to accidentally claw potential business partners.
3. If you wear nail polish, stay with lighter and softer shades. They're easier to maintain and look more workplace appropriate.
4. If your nail polish starts to chip or damages your cuticles, remove the nail polish. Let your nails breathe for a bit before reapplying.
5. Manicures are a popular way to keep hands pretty, even among men!

How to Shake Hands Properly—the WWW Method

You've probably heard about how a firm handshake demonstrates confidence. Well, some people take this too far and give a death grip. Others still grab your hand in a dainty way. How do painful grips occur? Did you know that both death grippers and dainty hand shakers share responsibility for the occurrence of painful grips? When one person does not give a full grip, the other may accidentally grab a set of fingers and knuckles rather than their palms. If you squeeze these knuckles or fingers, the bones rub against one another or against rings on a person's fingers. Both lead to painful consequences. Thus, even people with dainty shakes should take some blame for painful grips because they only allow others to grip their fingers, not the webbed part between the thumb and index finger nor the palm area. You could say that they leave themselves open for a harsh grip that rubs bone to bone.

To prevent death grips, we invented a technique called the "WWW" handshake. This stands for "Web, Web, Wrap." When you shake someone's hands, make sure you properly position the "webbed" part of your hand. This webbed part is the area between the thumb and index finger. As you extend your hand, make sure your webbed area locks with their webbed area. Thus, it's "Web-to-Web." Follow this with a "Wrap." Wrap your four fingers around their hand. No need to squeeze, just wrapping here gives a firm enough handshake. Thus, you:

1. Go Web to Web, then,
2. Wrap.

"Web, Web, Wrap" will solve many faulty handshakes that lead to poor impressions.

INSIGHT & INFORMATION
BRIEFCASES AND HANDBAGS

What does your briefcase or handbag say about you? It's not just about the type of fabric it's made of or how many dollars you spend to buy the latest trend. It's about what's inside your bag. (Like they say, it's the inside that counts.) Do you have a lot of clutter? Or do you only carry around the bare essentials? Kathryn Eisman, author of *How to Tell a Woman by Her Handbag*, spent years researching what women carried in their bags. Her book lists 40 different personality types, but we've broken them down into four types that apply to both men and women. We'll also focus on the outside of your bag as well. In terms of the inside, however, some personality types include:[14]

Minimalist

Simple and clean is the way to go. This is person carries only the necessities—wallet, phone and keys—you know, the things you absolutely can't leave home without. For some men, they even forgo the wallet and use a money clip for bills and leave change in tip jars. Minimalist women can easily find their cell phones in their purse when they ring, because their purses are so organized.

Prepared and Practical

Though not as clutter-free as the Minimalist, these people demonstrate sensibility and practicality. Each and every item in their briefcase or handbag has a purpose. This includes the practical things that some of us may not necessarily think about—or carry with us—like toothbrushes, hair accessories, or phone chargers. These people are prepared for any mini-emergency or touch-up.

Busy and Hectic

The Busy and Hectic briefcase or handbag includes practically everything—from the essentials to a candy bar wrapper from a month ago. You might even be able to find a kitchen sink inside. The oversized bag trend leads to even more clutter because its carrier has more space in which to put more stuff. One British study found that an average woman's handbag weighed five pounds.[15] This isn't too surprising, given that one in four women stuff their makeup bag alone with ten or more products.[16] Though these people have almost everything in their briefcase or handbag, they might not necessarily be able to *find* everything.

The Giver

This person carries a lot of extra stuff, but not necessarily for him or herself. You name it, they probably have it. Medicine, first aid materials, gum, tissues, extra pens, and other things that others may want to borrow or use. Givers are willing to share their extra goods at a moment's notice.

The Outside of Your Bag or Briefcase

Because men don't typically wear bags, we thought we'd focus on briefcases and work bags as well. Let's start with general structure. Equate a bag or briefcase with your personality. Based on discussions with many professionals, we think a bag and briefcase indicates a person's tendencies—and whether true or not, people react in this way. For example, a structured, square, and hard-side briefcase shows your organization and desire to protect your professional documents. These hard cases exist less for your comfort than for the survival of the work inside the case. Leather bags show more style and a softer, more relaxed side. People view those carrying these bags as flexible as the bags themselves, yet still reliable. Either way, brand-new bags and briefcases tend to show a lack of experience. A slightly aged one can reveal your years of experience. Yes, we sometimes purchase new bags and briefcases, but our old companion can last us for years, so take care of them.

Bottom Line: There's no correct "handbag personality." Be sure you at least have the bare essentials inside your bag. The rest is up to you. When considering the outside, choose the one that best suits your professional style.

TACTICAL & PRACTICAL
BRIEFCASES AND HANDBAGS

When we're rushing off to meetings and events, sometimes we forget the bare essentials. Make sure you keep the following items in your briefcase and/or handbag, so you'll be prepared for (almost) any business situation.

Stationery:

- Business cards
- Business card case
- Pen
- Paper (preferably in a portfolio)
- Directions
- Invitation
- Marker for name badges

Toiletries:

- Breath mints or gum
- Toothbrush
- Toothpaste
- Dental Floss
- Hairbrush or comb
- Makeup
- Hand lotion
- Deodorant
- Eye drops
- Tissues
- Lint remover
- Stain remover
- Moist towelette
- Safety pins

Medication:

- Ibuprofen
- Non-drowsy allergy medicine

NOTES

1. Michael Furtman, *Why Birds Do That: 40 Distinctive Bird Behaviors Explained and Photographed* (Minocqua, WI: Willow Creek Press, 2004).

2. The Gorilla Foundation "Amazing Gorilla Facts" *Koko's Kids Club*, http://www.koko.org/kidsclub/learn/10facts.html (Accessed June 10, 2009).

3. "Chest Body Language" *Changingminds.org*, http://changingminds .org/techniques/body/parts_body_language/chest_body_language.htm (Accessed June 10, 2009).

4. "Does Flirting Help or Hurt Your Career?: " ABC News (9 August 2005). http://abcnews.go.com/GMA/PersonalBest/story?id=1021540&page=1

5. Chest Body Language" *Changingminds.org*, http://changingminds.org/ techniques/body/parts_body_language/chest_body_language.htm (Accessed June 10, 2009).

6. Shelley Emling, "More Men Squeezing into 'Shape-Enhancing' Garments" *PalmBeachPost.com* (6 December 2008), http://www.palm beachpost.com/search/content/business/epaper/2008/12/06/sunbiz_mensgirdles _1207.html (Accessed June 12, 2009).

7. Bjorn Carey, "The Rules of Attraction in the Game of Love" *Live-Science* (13 February 2006), http://www.livescience.com/health/060213 _attraction_rules.html (Accessed June 1, 2009).

8. Frank T. Marlowe and others, "Men's Preferences for Women's Profile Waist-to-Hip Ratio in Two Societies" *Pergamon* (December 2003), http:// www.fas.harvard.edu/~hbe-lab/acrobatfiles/profilewhr.pdf (Accessed June 12, 2009).

9. Bjorn Carey, "The Rules of Attraction in the Game of Love" *Live-Science* (13 February 2006), http://www.livescience.com/health/060213 _attraction_rules.html (Accessed June 1, 2009).

10. "Pretty Women" *Psychology Today* (1 November 1993), http:// www.psychologytoday.com/articles/pto-19931101-000002.html (Accessed January 18, 2009).

11. "Why Do Men Have Buttons on Their Jacket Sleeves?" *Big Site of Amazing Facts*, http://www.bigsiteofamazingfacts.com/why-do-men-have -buttons-on-their-jacket-sleeves (Accessed June 8, 2009).

12. Kevin Andrew, "The Handshake" *Nonverbal Communication Web Project*, http://soc302.tripod.com/soc_302rocks/id8.html (Accessed June 1, 2009).

13. "Sign Language: Historical Background" *Sign Genius*, http:// www.signgenius.com/info-sign-language-01.shtml (Accessed June 2, 2009).

14. Gill Hart, "Handbags & Your Personality Type" *Suite 101* (5 March 2008), http://handbags-luggage.suite101.com/article.cfm/handbags_and _personality_types (Accessed June 1, 2009).

15. Gill Hart, "The Oversized Bag Fashion Trend" *Suite101* (13 December 2007), http://womensaccessories.suite101.com/article.cfm/womens_bag _fashion_trends_2008 (Accessed June 1, 2009).

16. Leah Wyar, "Your Beauty Secrets, Spilled" *Fitness Magazine* (February 2009), 34.

Chapter 7

Lower Zone

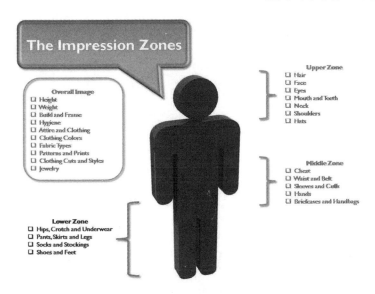

INSIGHT & INFORMATION
HIPS, CROTCH, AND UNDERWEAR

The debate of boxers versus briefs has yet to reach a point of full settlement. Though men's unmentionables used to be just that, MTV started the public discourse on men's underwear when it asked the preference of then-President Clinton back in 1994. (Clinton preferred briefs most of the time.) Since then, "boxers versus briefs" has become popular public debate with no right or wrong answer. A 2003 poll found that briefs (31%) held a slim edge over boxers (30%) among males. However, a Cotton Inc. study found that two-thirds of women preferred to see men in boxers as opposed to briefs.[1]

Of course, public interest goes beyond strictly *men's* underwear. Just how popular is women's underwear and lingerie? Let's put it this way: according to the NPD Group, Americans spent $4.4 billion on bras alone in 2003. Lingerie sales as a whole went up 5 percent—strong figures considering that the overall clothing industry was down 4 percent that year.[2] And sales keep increasing. Victoria's Secret, one of the world's largest lingerie brands, had sales that surpassed $5 billion in 2007.[3] Women see lingerie as an integral part of their daily attire. In Paris (a city some dub the "lingerie capital of the world"), 88 percent of women buy lingerie as a treat while 87 percent buy it as a necessary part of their wardrobe.[4]

In a professional context, here's a simple rule of thumb: keep your underwear exactly where it should be—*under* what you're wearing. This sounds self-explanatory and almost like common sense, but with the rise of low-rider jeans and pants, we're seeing more underwear, even in the workplace. That said, pay heed to either pulling your pants higher or purchasing low-rise underwear, which are now easy to find.

When it comes to Hips, Crotch, and Underwear, there's one other thing we'd like to mention. Pants matter. Pop-singer Jessica Simpson caused a stir in the entertainment world when she decided to don less-than-flattering high-waisted jeans and a double belt. All of that material around her waist made the then-curvy pop artist look heavier than she really was. Simpson's picture appeared all over the Internet, sparking debates on whether or not the artist was "fat," unfair standards for women, body image issues, and a whole slew of topics regarding women and weight. If you looked at the picture closely, though, the pop artist wasn't really overweight. She just made a poor choice in clothing . . . and it showed. Simpson definitely kept her underwear hidden, though, so that's more than many other men and women can say.

Bottom Line: Though not visible to the public, underwear is an integral part of our wardrobe. The way we choose to cover our hips and crotch says a lot about us.

TACTICAL & PRACTICAL
HIPS, CROTCH, AND UNDERWEAR

This section consists of a list of don'ts. When it comes to crotch and underwear, we want to convey what you *shouldn't* do in the workplace (or really anywhere).

Button Your Fly, Even on the Fly:

Before doing that, we want to provide a major tip that can save you much grief. Have you ever been caught with your zipper down? Almost everyone has at one point in their lives. Now consider this: In the morning, when you put on your pants, do you zip and then button them or do you button and then zip them? Picture yourself in the morning and think carefully.

If you answered the first choice, you're correct and should virtually never leave your home with your zipper in down position. Why? Well, when you engage in the latter choice, you button first and zip later. The zipper becomes an afterthought. Can you still hold your pants up with buttons, but no zipper? Definitely. When people button first, they can be easily distracted and forget pull up their fly and then head to work. The phone may ring or the toaster dings, so we tend to that and dash to the office. How many of us really touch our crotch at the office (unless of course we head to the restroom)? That said, buttoning and then zipping leaves you exposed to letting your zipper down.

When you zip and then button your pants, you've automatically addressed the zipper-down issue. It's difficult to hold your pants up without the button, so you'll still likely button it. Plus, the upward motion of moving your fingers from your zipper to your button will prompt you to tend to the buttons. If you read this section, you will probably never let your fly hang down again.

For the general area, don't . . .

- **Reveal your underwear.** Briefs, thongs, granny panties, boxers, tighty whities . . . whatever your underwear preferences, your colleagues really don't need to know.
- **Show your panty line.** Women, if you wear tight slacks or pants that reveal your panty line, consider wearing a thong to stop showing the world the outline of your underwear.
- **Wear pants that adorn strange pockets and/or zippers that draw attention to the region.** You don't want your colleagues inadvertently staring at that area. Also, it's best to avoid drawing attention to the midsection since it makes you look wider.

INSIGHT & INFORMATION
PANTS, SKIRTS, AND LEGS

What makes long legs so attractive? As with many things we as humans consider attractive, it has to do with evolution. Though we often hear that men find women with long legs attractive, the same holds true for women's perception of men as well. Researchers at the University of Wroclaw in Poland found that both men and women whose legs are 5 percent longer than average are considered the most attractive.[5] Past studies have found that height plays a role in sexual attraction, but it seems like leg length plays a critical role as well. In this study, participants rated the attractiveness of people who were all the same height, but different leg lengths.

What does leg length have to do with evolution? Previous research has linked shorter legs with a higher risk of cardiovascular disease, obesity, and Type 2 diabetes. According to Martin Tovee of Newcastle University, longer legs suggest good health—especially for women. Though men's legs grow beyond puberty, women's leg growth ends during this phase. Therefore, a woman's leg length serves as an indicator of childhood nutrition and overall health.[6]

Plus, think about hunters and gatherers. It's more likely that a person can sprint faster to catch prey or run from predators if they have longer legs. They could also reach further upward to gather food or stride over barriers and gaps in the wilderness. Remember that we're "thinking animals," so these preferences will instinctively carry into the workplace.

Bottom Line: Even if you don't have the longest of legs, don't fret. Pants with pinstripes or above-the-knee skirts make legs look longer.[7] Whatever you decide to showcase your legs in, though, make sure it's workplace appropriate.

TACTICAL & PRACTICAL
PANTS, SKIRTS, AND LEGS

Even though pants and skirts make up the bottom half of your ensemble, people still take notice! Here are some quick tips and how to keep your bottom half looking good:

- **Consider cuffs,** especially for men. Cuffs afford a tailored look to a pair of pants. Nowadays, some people prefer no cuffs, as society grows more casual. For those who want to stick with classics and formal tradition, cuffs prove a great choice. Ultimately, it's an individual's preference.

- **Don't reveal what should be kept under those pants.** In addition to not showing off your underwear, make sure your pants don't reveal your legs as well. That little bit of leg between the sock and the pants are unsightly for men. For women, if you wear pants, you can show skin, but try to wear stockings for a formal look. Nowadays, there's a major debate about whether true professional women should still wear stockings or not. We leave that up to your workplace, but generally, stockings are more formal.

- **Choose the right hem**—not too baggy and not too narrow. This, of course, shifts with fashion trends, but a medium hem stays classic.
- **Keep your distance from the floor.** If your pants touch the floor while you're wearing suit-appropriate shoes, consider hemming them. You don't want your pants dragging on the floor, since others will be able to see that unflattering wear and tear at the bottom of your pants. Typically, about a half-inch above the ground, with your shoes on, works fine.
- **Keep things parallel.** If you get cuffs or your pants hemmed, make sure the bottom of your pants is parallel to the floor. Sounds simple, but sometimes tailors are careless with this detail.

Of course, as a woman, if you wear a skirt in the workplace, some of your legs may show. If that's the case, keep these tips in mind when donning skirts:

- **Moisturize.** Smooth, healthy-looking skin impress more than dry skin. Plus, it's good for the overall health of your skin.
- **Shave.** It's hard for your legs to look and feel smooth when they're covered with little spurts of hair. Shave as often as you need to, particularly when wearing skirts. Europeans would have a different view, but in the United States, shaved legs for women are the norm. This is a personal choice, but there exist common preferences that favor shaved legs.

INSIGHT & INFORMATION
SOCKS AND STOCKINGS

Socks, originally made of animal skins tied around the ankles, have been around since the stone ages.[8] Since then, socks have evolved but are still used to provide warmth and comfort. Though socks seem pretty simple, they actually have multiple functions. They minimize the chafing between your foot and footwear, protect footwear from your foot's perspiration and dead skin, help prevent athlete's foot, and are (or can be) fashionable![9]

Stockings evolved from socks in Europe in the 1400s.[10] Men wore close-fitting breeches that reached from the waist to feet, like modern tights. Similarly, women wore stockings that were held up by garters.

The wealthy primarily wore these through this time period. Though it's no longer common practice for men to wear stockings (at all, but particularly in the workplace), you'll still find women donning this leg wear, particularly with skirts. Stockings and hosiery allow women to semi-comfortably slip into their heels and avoid chaffing against their heels or flats.

When it comes to socks and stockings in the workplace, subtly rules. Men commonly wear black socks, while women usually don natural-colored stockings.

Bottom Line: Though socks and stockings have changed throughout the years, their function primarily remains the same. Use them to provide comfort and protection, as they were originally intended.

TACTICAL & PRACTICAL SOCKS AND STOCKINGS

Even though they're located near the bottom of your body and aren't always visible to the naked eye, socks and stockings play an integral part of your image. The rules regarding socks and stockings are pretty simple, but if you don't follow them, you could look a little out of place. Follow these basic rules to keep up that impressive impression:

Wear socks that are . . .

- **Fitted up to your mid-calves.** They should cover the visible part of your leg when you cross your legs and your pants are rolled up.
- **Dark or neutral in color.** Socks should color-coordinate with your shoes or slacks. Don't wear white or bright socks, because they're distracting and can dominate your outfit.

Wear stockings that are . . .

- **Similar to your skin tone.** This looks more professional than dark colored stockings.
- **Monochrome and simple in design.** Your fishnet stockings (if you have any) don't really belong in the workplace.
- **Clean and neat,** which means no runs or tears. If you have a run and don't have time to buy new stockings prior to an event, dab a little clear nail polish on it to prevent it from running more.

And remember to keep an extra pair of socks or stockings at your office. You never know when you may need them.

INSIGHT & INFORMATION
SHOES AND FEET

Dress shoes. Boots. Running shoes. Sandals. Look at the ground at a mall or public area, and you'll probably see this wide variety of footwear. In fact, you probably have a couple pairs of each of these on your shoe rack at home. Footwear plays an essential role in any outfit you choose to wear—pumps with your suit, sneakers to go with your gym clothes, sandals with your swimsuit, and red heels to match that stunning red dress you just bought. Sometimes we buy shoes out of necessity, and sometimes we buy them for fun. Either way, we contribute to a multi-billion dollar industry whenever we buy shoes. Footwear sales reached nearly $42 billion in 2005. And unlike what you'd expect based on stereotypes, not all of the sales were from women's shoes. Twenty billion dollars came from women's shoes and $16 billion actually came from men's shoes.[11]

As many of us know, shoes can be fun ... but they can be painful, too. One survey by the American Academy of Orthopedic Surgeons found that eight out of ten women described their shoes as painful. This statistic isn't too surprising given that nine out of ten women actually wear shoes that are too small for their feet.[12] Finding the right-size shoe is not only critical for comfort, but for practicality as well. If you have to take off your shoes at work because they're too uncomfortable, then you lose the impressive effect you wanted from those shoes.

Pronation could affect your comfort level in shoes as well. The inward rolling motion of your foot after it touches the ground helps determine if you have neutral pronation (15-degree inward roll), underpronation (less than 15-degree inward roll) or overpronation (more than 15-degree inward roll).[13] A simple wet test, during which you step onto a sheet of paper with a wet foot, can help you determine your pronation. Based on this test—supplemented by an expert's recommendation—you can determine what insole or orthotic will make your standing and walking experience a more comfortable one.

Bottom Line: Though stylish shoes look great, comfort is key. Find the right fit for you so that you can continue sporting your shoes in style.

TACTICAL & PRACTICAL
SHOES AND FEET

Though shoes rest at the bottom of your ensemble, people often notice them. If someone quickly glances over you from head to toe, your shoes stand in full view at the end of the full-length glance. Great looking shoes add that final touch to your outfit.

How Can I Keep My Shoes Looking Good?

Keep your shoes looking sharp by doing something as simple as polishing them. A little bit of buffing and polishing can go a long way. If you buff and polish, but your shoes still look scratched up, maybe it's time for a new pair.

Should I Wear Uncomfortable Shoes for the Sake of Looking Fashionable?

You don't have to sacrifice comfort for appearance. If you're on your feet all day, or even for a few hours, you want shoes that are comfortable. If you end up awkwardly shifting your weight around or tripping because of the lack of comfort or functionality of your shoe, you won't look great or fashionable.

What Types of Shoes Are Appropriate for Women?

This depends on your workplace, of course. We assume here that you work in a professional office. If so, flats might look a little too casual in the workplace, so stick with some heel. Not too much heel, though. Etiquette and business experts agree that heels for the workplace should stand 2 to 3 inches high. As far as heel thickness goes, keep in mind your ability to balance and wear what's comfortable for you.

As for type of shoe, we recommend traditional pumps. Fashion sandals or shoes that have open toes or backs are not always perceived as professional enough for the workplace.

What Types of Shoes Are Appropriate for Men?

Generally, black or brown leather shoes should serve as your staple. Shoes with laces tend to be more formal than shoes without, so for that extra bit of polish, laces can do the trick. Suede shoes lean toward more casual footwear. Buckles, tassels, and other non-lace styles add flair for a more business casual look.

Can I Wear Stand-Out Shoes?

Yes. You can wear stand-out shoes in terms of quality, but not necessarily in design. Shoes should complement your outfit, but not overpower it.

If I Have Different-Sized Feet, What Should I Do?

About 90 percent of people have different-sized feet, so you are not alone. To maximize comfort, buy shoes that fit your larger foot. But don't buy shoes that are too big. You don't want to have boats on your feet!

NOTES

1. Brett Johnson, "Getting to the Bottom of It" *Freshpair* (21 September 2003), http://www.freshpair.com/in_the_news/ventura_county_star_20030921.html (Accessed June 1, 2009).

2. Arlene Martell, "How Sexy Lingerie Works—Going Undercover" *HowItWorks* (25 August 2008) http://www.howitworks.net/how-sexy-lingerie-works.html (Accessed June 1, 2009).

3. Limited Brands, "Limited Brands 2007 Annual Report" (2008), http://ww3.ics.adp.com/streetlink_data/dirLPD/annual/HTML1/default.htm (Accessed June 1, 2009).

4. Arlene Martell, "How Sexy Lingerie Works—Going Undercover" *HowItWorks* (25 August 2008), http://www.howitworks.net/how-sexy-lingerie-works.html (Accessed June 1, 2009).

5. Ian Sample, "Why Men and Women Find Longer Legs More Attractive" *The Guardian* (17 January 2008), http://www.guardian.co.uk/science/2008/jan/17/humanbehaviour.psychology (Accessed June 5, 2009).

6. Ian Sample, "Why Men and Women Find Longer Legs More Attractive" *The Guardian* (17 January 2008), http://www.guardian.co.uk/science/2008/jan/17/humanbehaviour.psychology (Accessed June 5, 2009).

7. "Figure Fixers: Make Your Legs Look Their Best with the Right Skirts" *Marie Claire* (1 July 2006), http://www.accessmylibrary.com/coms2/summary_0286-17346175_ITM (Accessed June 5, 2009).

8. Jerry Smith, "History of Socks Timeline" (11 February 2006), http://www.articlealley.com/article_28545_27.html (Accessed June 8, 2009).

9. "History of Socks" *Holeproof*,http://www.holeproof.com.au/About-Holeproof/Study-Centre/History-of-Socks.asp (Accessed June 8, 2009).

10. Jerry Smith, "History of Socks Timeline" (11 February 2006), http://www.articlealley.com/article_28545_27.html (Accessed June 8, 2009).

11. "NPD Reports U.S. Footwear Industry Takes a Big Step Forward in 2005" *Business Wire* (10 February 2006), http://www.allbusiness.com/company-activities-management/sales-selling-sales-figures/5370035-1.html (Accessed June 9, 2009).

12. "Shoe Tips and Facts" *Designer Shoe Salon*, http://www.designershoesalon.com/tipsfacts.htm (Accessed June 9, 2009).

13. "Understanding Pronation" *Asics Running*, http://www.asics.co.uk/running/knowledge/understanding-pronation (Accessed June 9, 2009).

PART III

Advanced Strategies
Powerful Tools for Impressive First Impressions

MASTER YOUR CULTURAL CONTEXT AND PHYSICAL SURROUNDINGS

Audience. Culture. Environment. What do these three elements have in common when learning to create Impressive First Impressions? They echo and draw from the foundation of *Golden Virtue No. 3: Impressive First Impressions Are About More Than the Individual.* We call these three elements ACE and want you to learn the advanced strategies of Impressive First Impressions as you *Embrace your ACE* (Audience, Culture, and Environment).

Why do we place these strategies under the "Advanced" category? Some readers may scratch their heads and wonder, "What's so advanced about knowing an audience? I automatically have an audience when I make an impression." Others may ask, "I want to put my best foot forward and impress others; why do I need a lesson on culture?" Still others may question why knowing an environment can help with a personal Impressive First Impression. Many people limit the value of first impressions as an individual action, whether based on dress or behavior. We regard these as very important, but want to take the notion of first impressions to the next level by shifting the focus to others.

Ever consider how television and film directors make their stars look stellar to viewers? These film makers even apply these concepts in more modest productions like documentaries. When the History Channel or Discovery Channel interviews experts for documentaries, what usually accompanies these experts? You may see a prominent historian commenting on a major event while sitting in front of her bookshelf of history books. Audiences associate the historians with having read these books as part of their extensive research and training. Forget whether or not they've actually read every single one of these books. We often make the assumption that they have. For instance, when visitors come to our office and see many shelves overflowing with books, we often get comments like, "Wow, you've read so many books." Yes, we've read numerous books, but of course, sometimes we purchase books that we have yet to start or complete. Still, people often make the assumption that we've read them all.

Similarly, consider the audience and expectations of those viewers who watch a wildlife expert on the Discovery Channel. They want knowledge of raw wildlife and the facts behind animal behaviors. Think about what would look more convincing about this expert:

A. If that expert sat on an armchair, in a suit and tie, surrounded by volumes of books, or

B. If they wore rugged safari clothing and handled reptiles in the wilderness

Of course, choice B makes more sense in this second scenario. No wonder Steve Irwin, the Crocodile Hunter, proved so alluring to audiences! Choice B embodies experts like him, and he showed his prowess and knowledge by embracing the wild animals that he wanted viewers to embrace as well. Even when chefs on the Food Network cook or just talk about food, ever notice that instead of bookshelves or the wilderness, they have shelves and pantries behind them filled with cooking tools and ingredients?

All of these people project the impression of their expertise by both leveraging their image and interactions that reinforce their impressions. They know what their *audience* wants to see and deliver on that. They understand the *culture* of their viewers, whether it be a scholarly culture for the historian, the wildlife culture for Steve Irwin, or the food culture for the television chef. Third, they truly master and wield their *environments*, be it an office, jungle, or kitchen.

When reading these advanced strategies, we want you to think of your impression as an entire media production. The first parts of this book provided you with a multitude of advice and strategies to master your own impression. Now we expand the emphasis to your cultural context and physical surroundings. We want you to truly Embrace Your ACE.

This concept distinguishes our approach, because we elevate the term "impression" as one that goes beyond *image*, since we also include *interactions*. Most authors, readers, and practitioners focus on the concept of image—how people project themselves. We return to what we discussed at the beginning of this book about the crucial concept of interactions. Recall the *Impressions Diamond Model*, which takes into account both image and interactions. More so, Impressive First Impressions account for both the intention of the individual conveying the impression and the interpretation that results from that individual's image and interactions.

Simply stated, how can you truly make an Impressive First Impression on others if you fail to understand what they want? We stress the importance of the three ACE elements, because they constitute your cultural context and physical surroundings. Your context and surroundings consist of those often invisible and intangible factors that underpin human interaction. These include understanding your audience, having basic cultural competence and leveraging your environment. In chapters 8, 9, and 10, we'll give you useful frameworks and practical strategies for implementing ACE in your impressions. By the end, you should Embrace Your ACE.

VIRTUAL VIRTUOSO

The advent of the Internet and various technological advancements profoundly changed the work environment. We no longer have to work within the walls of a cubicle or conduct meetings at the office. In fact, we don't even need to be in the same country as our colleagues and clients in order to conduct business with them. Thanks to the Internet and technology, the world is literally at our fingertips.

This new environment led to significant changes in work culture and attitudes as well. The dot-com boom of the 1990s allowed for a more relaxed work atmosphere in some technological and web-based companies, where young 20-somethings would roll into the office at 11 AM with an ensemble of a t-shirt, shorts, and flip-flops. Though the dot-com bubble didn't stick around, some of the casual workplace attitudes did.

As Internet use became more commonplace in the workplace, this casual culture continued. The Internet provides a forum for individuals to broadcast their thoughts and provide minute-by-minute updates regarding their daily activities. Because many websites focus so much on the user himself, he may forget to seriously consider his audience before sending a Twitter update or creating a Facebook wall post. The Internet, as well as other forms of technology, provides us with opportunities to create virtual impressions on a regular basis. We provide you with some of the tools you need to ensure that the virtual impression you create is an impressive one.

_____ Chapter 8

Embrace Your ACE—
Audience Attraction

AUDIENCE AND EMPATHY

We believe it's actually very difficult to embrace others when making an excellent impression. Researchers found that managers tend to overestimate their ability to understand what motivates their employees.[1] This shows that managers may not know their "audience" of employees as well as they think. So, before you think you're great at gauging your audience, pause and read on (or risk misunderstanding your audience). You must focus your mental, emotional, and physical energy simultaneously on yourself and others. It's much easier to think only about your own motivations and actions. Place these actions in external contexts and the stakes grow much higher, while the energy needed to process these external surroundings increases dramatically.

When it comes to your audience, understand them as much as possible and you can appeal to them better. We can't stress enough the level of difficulty in getting to this point of understanding. For example, in terms of culture, keep in mind that cultural differences exist so abundantly that what you consider "best" may prove worse for someone with different cultural values and perceptions. With environment, you also can leverage and alter your external environment to enhance your impression even further. Still, influencing your surroundings, let alone dramatically altering them, takes much effort. Even reaching a level of awareness about our environment remains challenging. Picture, then, the major task of changing and leveraging your context.

Let's start with the foundations of how to *Embrace Your ACE*. Understand empathy. In fields that study emotional intelligence, empathy remains a cornerstone of social interactions, from adapting to daily relationships with others to growing into successful professionals and leaders. On one level, researchers show that empathy prevents us from hurting others, because we feel and understand their pain. It allows us to comprehend others' viewpoints. At its best, it affords us the opportunity to help others and advance social relationships through acts of generosity.

According to researchers, empathy includes three active functions. First, cognitive empathy allows humans to look beyond their own perspectives and understand others. It allows us to take educated guesses on how others feel and even predict the actions from these feelings. Empathy manifests in our daily actions that allow us communicate better with others. Those with high levels of empathy seem like mind readers by hearing the tone in our voices, paying heed to our word choices, and reading our body language. The second, affective empathy, treats emotions as contagious. Very empathetic people will "catch" others' emotions by both consciously and unconsciously mirroring others' emotional expressions. For instance, if an empathetic person interacts with a friend who expresses sadness, then the empathetic person will also tend to show facial expressions or voice tones of sadness. Third, sympathy comes about in a much more escalated fashion. This occurs when an empathetic person relates to another so much that they'll act on it to improve the situation. Think of sympathy as a form of empathy in action.[2]

How does this relate to your own impression? If you empathize with others at a high level, then you'll create a sympathetic action that will appeal to them. When you incorporate your own needs and wants with theirs, then you will strive toward creating a mutually beneficial impression. Embracing the value of empathy and your impressions will generally prove favorable in your dealings with others.

Indeed, we fail to consider our surroundings and audience on a daily basis. For example, why do so many of us engage in subtle, yet rude behaviors? We cut people off in our cars. We ignore or roll our eyes at certain people who annoy us at work, even if we have to collaborate with them. We dress in what pleases us, whether in regards to aesthetics or comfort, rather than pay heed to how our management dresses or wants us to dress. (Keep in mind that they determine our raises and promotions, yet many people still bypass these management recommendations!) In other words, do we understand one another across cultures, including our work culture? Do we take heed of the environment of our surroundings in professional settings? Or do we just act as we please, because it's easier and reflects what we know and want?

Ever notice how people say that women tend to "be in touch with their feelings" better than men? How is it that most mothers tend to nurture their children, while fathers tend to say "suck it up, buttercup" to them? Scholars have shown consistently that women tend to communicate and exhibit more empathy than men. Girls, even from the age of 1, show more expressions of concern than boys. Women are also more adept at interpreting nonverbal communication than men. Research has also found that girls tend to share much more than boys. Boys are as much as 50 times more competitive than girls, according to one study.[3] It's no accident that we've evolved into a society comprised of males with more dominant and competitive personalities than females. These attitudes even embed themselves into placing orders. Ever notice how men in a restaurant tend to say, "I'll have the steak," while a woman may say, "Can I please have the steak?"

How does this gendered empathy relate to impressions? You'll notice that females tend to dress better and carry themselves in a more-nuanced fashion and that people perceive them as better listeners than men. All of these actions contribute to an Impressive First Impression—and they all involve empathy.

On the other hand, lack of empathy can lead to serious consequences. One engineer we trained recounted how a fellow engineer lost his job because of an unimpressive first impression. As this fellow engineer began to exit the employee parking lot at the end of the day, he immediately turned on the one-lane road and drove behind a sedan cruising along at slightly below the speed limit. Frustrated and anxious to get to an appointment, the fellow engineer went around the sedan and raised his hand to give an obscene finger gesture to the female driver. The next day, he discovered that the sedan driver was a director at an adjacent unit within his own company. His supervisor found out and this engineer no longer remained an engineer at that company. In focusing on his own frustrations, the fellow engineer acted as he pleased rather than considering others. He clearly lacked empathy and it cost him. Considering others will function as a major part of Impressive First Impressions.

How and when should you consider others? In the above case, some would say that common wisdom states that one should avoid making obscene gestures to drivers within a mile of work or home, because these could be your co-workers and neighbors. We find that wisdom somewhat limited, because does it really serve a purpose to make an obscene gesture to anyone, regardless of distance to work or home? Does anyone really want to receive an obscene gesture for anything they've done, even if you believe they deserve it? Even the common wisdom of linking proximity to obscenity only captures a small part of considering others when managing your impression. Would you want an obscene gesture made at you, no matter where you are? Of course, there exist exceptions (we're sure if you were filming a movie or making a point in certain contexts, obscene gestures may come in handy). Understand your audience and you'll move closer to effectively practicing Impressive First Impressions.

Relate these rude behaviors with your childhood classroom experiences. If you sit in most mixed-gender classrooms, boys tend to get in trouble more often than girls. They tend to poke fun at one another much more loudly and publicly than girls. Boys certainly speak their minds and may even make mean-spirited comments more often than girls. They show less empathy, and instead, exhibit more stoicism ("Boys don't cry") and competitive behaviors. As a result, we tend to see boys who are less polished and clean. They tend to be less well-behaved than girls, meaning that they're not considering others and even offending them. They tend to show less concern for their audience. Despite gender, knowing your audience proves beneficial in crafting your impression.

AUDIENCE AND MARKETING: SUPER MARKETING AT SUPERMARKETS

Picture in your mind a supermarket within a traditional supermarket chain. Focus less on boutique and specialty stores (including Trader Joe's), mini-marts, warehouse discount stores (such as Costco and Sam's Club) as well as discount retailer megastores that offer groceries (such as Wal-Mart and Target). We mean major chain supermarkets where most people purchase groceries. Picture this type of traditional chain supermarket.

When you enter from the parking lot, how many entrances do you typically walk through? Most have two entrances, one on the left and one on the right. This distributes traffic flow as shoppers enter. It also allows people to park either toward the left or right sides of the store, so that they're not too far from any entrance. It also means that when you enter through one side, you'll likely have to traverse the store to the other side if you plan to purchase multiple items. You'll open yourself to more temptations and reminders to buy other items as you walk across the store.

Ever take notice of where these retailers place their cash registers? They often place them between the two entrances, but seldom directly in front of the entrances. When you see registers and witness transactions, what comes to mind? For most people we've asked, money comes to mind. Specifically, spending money and watching these cashiers take your money. How many consumers would want to think about spending as they've just entered a store? Most of us want a good experience, from a pleasant shopping layout and friendly staff to saving money and convenience. Take note of how supermarkets steer your attention away from the registers initially.

Instead, they tend to place more-appealing visual elements either near the left and right entrances. Generally speaking, these sides host either the produce or the bakery/deli sections. Consider how these displays of produce appeal to consumers. They signal thoughts of freshness and life. Produce comes in all types of visually vibrant colors and shapes. The bright colors stimulate appetites and excite us about buying. If you enter on the other side, you'll notice that the bakery/deli section typically occupies that space. Again, these displays conjure freshness in our minds, from freshly baked bread and cookies to appetizing deli meats and prepared salads. They speak to our need for convenience and buying prepared foods, or they furnish us with ideas to cook our own versions of these dishes. Ever notice how some stores place recipes around their shelves? You'll need to purchase multiple ingredients to execute each recipe successfully.

As companion features to these produce and deli/bakery areas, you'll notice that some stores will place fresh flowers and balloons as soon as you enter. These items also encourage you to think about freshness, vibrant colors, and festive moods. The more festive we grow, the more we likely eat and spend. Think about when we go on vacation, we often say to ourselves, "It's okay, I'm on vacation," so we eat more and spend more than we do on a daily basis. Bring these celebratory components into a store and alter a person's mood from frugal to festive—they'll spend more. You may also encounter the stand with their weekly advertised specials. This reminds you to go through different aisles to take advantage of these specials. As you comb the many aisles, searching for these items, you'll need to look at other items along the way. This can tempt you to purchase more than you originally planned.

What do we typically see in the rear of the market? Meat and dairy, which constitute the protein that acts as one of life's staples, reside there. Most of us already know that they place these items in the back of stores so that we'll pass other temptations as we head back there to get our life's necessities. Why not, then, place produce and bakery/deli areas back there? That's because meat and dairy generally remain unattractive commodities. Meat concisely signifies a less-pleasant reality of what it really is: bloody raw flesh, sliced and diced. We're not making any claims for animal rights or vegetarianism. We're just reminding you of the true nature of meat. More so, plain, white gallons of milk give little appeal to shoppers compared to the more-colorful items available throughout the store. Plus, these refrigerated areas emit cold air; few people would want to enter a cold store. A cool store works fine, but a cold one may repel some shoppers.

Knowing what you know about the perimeters of these supermarkets, you'll realize that all four major food groups reside in their outskirts. The four major food groups consist of meat, milk and dairy, fruits and vegetables, and breads and grains. If you shopped only at the perimeter of a supermarket and virtually ignored the aisles in the center, you'd probably lead healthier lives (if you don't make *all* of your purchases from the bakery). Short of items such as sugar, spices, and oils, this perimeter covers our basic needs. So what do these grocery stores place in the dozens of aisles within this healthier perimeter? Mostly processed and frozen foods, household products, hygiene items, and bottled liquids. Even knowing this, do you think you and others would give up the ice cream, cookies, cereals, soda, and bottled water that inhabit these aisles? Almost all of the people we've surveyed and trained gave the direct answer that they wouldn't relinquish their consumption of these items. Supermarkets give people what they want, so they'll continue to shop this way, even knowing that many of these products are not healthy.

The aisles also cater to the height of the shopper. Generally speaking, items that appeal the least to customers or are commodities tend to occupy the less-premium shelf space at the bottom or top shelves. Sugar and flour often occupy the bottom shelves and stores stack less-popular items on the very top shelves. The eye-level shelves represent premium real estate for products and most adults will look here first. A child's lower eye level will likely prompt him or her to look at the second-most bottom shelf. That's where you will find more children's items, such as children's cereals and snacks. The markets know their audience by addressing their physical height and correlating that with their age-based wants.

Ever notice how bright and white many supermarkets appear? These dimensions stimulate our senses and prompt us to act in a more-alert fashion. We'll want to observe more items and labels. We may get excited to look at items we may normally pass over. The bright colors keep our senses sharp and awake, so a necessary act of purchasing food can stir excitement in a subtle way.

As you can see, supermarkets give you what you want and enhance your shopping experience so that you choose to spend there. They go beyond strictly thinking about their bottom line and coaxing you into buying multiple items. Instead, they give you what you desire so that you'll choose to spend on your own. Emulate and exceed the supermarket strategies and you will move toward generating an Impressive First Impression. It's more than about you, the individual. Give people what they want and they will give you what you want.

As with any Impressive First Impression, if your favorite grocery store reflects and projects what you want, then you'll keep coming back. They need to display a consistent message and impression. Of course, a great retailer continues to adapt and cater their impression to what you want. They refuse to remain static, but instead continually evolve to the tastes of their audience. That's how many of these stores survive and thrive for so many decades. As your career evolves, so should your impression and personal brand. Your audience's tastes will evolve as well, so make sure to adapt to these fluid factors. Consider implementing this strategy into your own impression as well.

AUDIENCE AND FOCUS: FIRST IMPRESSIONS AS FILTERS

You can also leverage Impressive First Impressions to filter a more-targeted audience. Luxury retailers, for example, do this quite well. When most people walk into an indoor mall, as they pass a high-end, luxury clothing store front, you'll notice that very few step into these particular stores. Somehow, these stores seem to display some sort of unseen social barrier that prevents most from entering. It seems like they display an invisible "keep out" sign. A select few enter these stores without hesitation and receive royal treatment. How do retailers accomplish this? They construct an Impressive First Impression.

Like grocery stores, when we take the time to dissect what these luxury retailers do, it seems more apparent. Let's assume that most mall shoppers rarely, if ever, purchase these extravagant and expensive goods. As we walk by their stores, we notice that they display very few items rather than cluttered shelves or racks. This reflects and projects an air of limited supply and exclusivity. It practically screams "limited edition" and "expensive." When we go in to look, there's very little inventory to examine, so this subtly makes us feel self-conscious about whether we should consider seriously buying, guilty if we handle the merchandise without buying, or bad about wasting the sales associate's time without buying. Given the few racks and shelves to browse items, we stand out and immediately fall upon the eyes of the sales associate who can instantly approach to assist us. Further, some sport such great service that as soon as you enter, they ask you if you need help. Many of us feel so self-conscious and guilty that we can't fade behind racks to examine items semi-anonymously without someone approaching to help us.

This impression creates a social barrier to entry that sends delicate messages of exclusivity. Impressions can thus act as filters and barriers that limit interactions. We can employ impressions to encourage selective interactions rather than open ourselves to others. Remember the earlier example of the mountain lion and how we can create an impression to intimidate it into leaving? This approach reflects that mode of thinking.

AUDIENCE AND SELF-MARKETING: TREAT YOURSELF LIKE A BUSINESS

How can you apply this discussion of audience and business to you? In one phrase: Treat yourself and your impression like a business. According to Reid Hoffman, the founder, chairman and CEO of LinkedIn, he created the online social networking site because he realized that individuals are in a major transformation process: individuals are becoming small businesses. He likens us to businesslike and professional organisms that compete with other organisms in an ecosystem.[4]

Taking from Hoffman's view, we believe that you should treat yourself like a business and should learn from other businesses. Like the supermarket or the luxury retailer, you're vying to stand out and catch the eyes of others in the professional realm. Businesses gain customers based on their impression. They can attract or repel customers with physical elements such as signage, logos, colors, and layout. Their behaviors, such as customer service and sales, can likewise appeal to or turn off customers. These businesses need to understand their customers' needs and wants. This knowledge means the difference between survival and extinction.

Treat your colleagues as your customers. You're a business and the customer can come from anywhere in your professional world. They can be your management, direct supervisor, lateral peers, team members, and clients. Treat your management and supervisor poorly and risk your job, or even career. Treat your lateral peers and team members poorly and they make your next few months or years miserable. Treat your clients poorly and the entire business could go under as you bite the hand that feeds you. This last group represents the lifeblood of your organization. That idea leads you to the necessity of treating everyone like a customer. When you view and deal with everyone from a customer-satisfaction (and happiness) standpoint, your work relationships improve. You'll make a more Impressive First Impression. Remember that the Impressive First Impression resets all the time, so you can even make new impressions on existing colleagues.

HOW TO GAUGE YOUR AUDIENCE: IMPRESSIONS ARE NOT ONE-SIZE-FITS-ALL

Like supermarket and luxury retailers who understand audience preferences and how to appeal to their needs, you too can take the time to understand your audience when crafting your Impressive First Impression. We do want to stress that great impressions go far beyond a one-size-fits-all approach. You'll need to take the time and make the effort to grasp the nuances of your audience, from their expectations and motivations to their actions and reactions.

In a professional context, it means more than simply dressing formally. It also means distinguishing yourself from your colleagues. Think of it as a spectrum between the extremes of appearing unabashedly "over-the-top" or excessively conforming so your impression drowns in a sea of sameness.

For instance, a colleague of yours would do more than stand out if she wore a formal business suit to a company beach barbecue. If the company's staff generally sport t-shirts, flip-flop sandals, shorts, and jeans to this type of event, the formally dressed colleague would appear stiff, unwilling to frolic in the sand and water, as well as possibly arrogant and standoffish. Shift the scenario to the company's office. She may look more appropriate if she wore the suit there, especially when the company hosts clients. If she wore t-shirts and jeans, finished off with flip-flop sandals, there's a good chance the company management would send her home to change. Of course, some organizations allow casual clothing, but most would frown upon sandals in the workplace, because it sends an unprofessional impression. That, and sandals bring up safety concerns due to their floppy and open-toed nature. If you think this sandal-sporting staffer seems exaggerated, start looking at media articles about employers growing increasingly concerned because they see this phenomena much more frequently than before.

What strategies and practical techniques can you use to gauge your audience? This subject ranges from learning the intricacies of body language to categorizing your audience, but we certainly believe that you will benefit from a few fundamental tips. You can immediately benefit from these pieces of advice if you practice them and put them to action in your professional life. We begin by looking at your audience at a broad level, whether with an individual or a large number people. We then shift as we provide nuances for reading individuals.

Know the Audience's Motivations: The word "motivation" comes from the Latin *motivus*, which means "to move." Each person possesses her own motivations and wants to move toward her goal. Stated another way, some say that motivation mainly means "goal-oriented actions and behaviors." You can prepare your Impressive First Impression by taking the time to know your audience's motivations beforehand. This way, you can influence their behavior by thoroughly grasping what will get them to act or "move." Before you engage with others, ask yourself some simple but very key questions. What does the other individual or group want from their interaction with you? What will they likely expect from you? Many people come into an interaction armed with much more clarity about what they want than what the other person wants. You will gain the upper hand if you take time to understand what motivates your audience.

This notion of discovering others' motivations seems deceptively simple, yet the nuances take time to sift through and embrace. For instance, most would assume similar motivators that would interest business students and business practitioners, yet one study demonstrated very different motivators. Motivating someone can mean more than understanding what incentivizes them; it can derive from understanding the barriers of why they block out your messages. If you remove the barriers, you can motivate someone more easily. Business students expressed that their top-three listening barriers stemmed from:

1. Lack of interest in the subject
2. Distractions, such as hunger and headaches
3. Daydreaming

Business practitioners, on the other hand, reported that their top-three barriers to listening resulted from:

1. External distractions, such as ringing phones and others talking
2. Distractions, such as hunger and headaches
3. Desire to form counterarguments before others are finished speaking and stating their thoughts[5]

As you can see, motivations will shift depending on the audience. It takes attention to detail and substantial effort to gain awareness of your audience's motivations.

Know How Your Motivations Interact with Your Audience's: When interacting with others, some think about how they want to appear to their audience, while some focus too much on others' motivations. Making an Impressive First Impression requires that you navigate both. Sometimes, this means giving them what they want, while other times, it means withholding what they want for a period of time, so that you can increase their interest in your own motivations. This way, you can move them closer toward your goal and theirs. Keep in mind the word *"motivus"* and that you want to "move" your audience toward both their goal and your goal.

Leverage Hot Buttons and Pique Interest: Delving into the motivations of others provides a strong foundation when you want to craft the proper impression. With their motivations in mind, ask yourself how you plan to leverage these so that your audience acts in your favor. Certain hot buttons will either repel them or pique their interest.

Listen Actively: With two ears and one mouth, why do many professionals find it so difficult to listen and have others listen to them?

When you place your audience first, listening grows easier. Besides, it's two-to-one odds that your ears will overcome your mouth. Still, don't just stop at listening. Make sure that you listen actively. Active listening takes a lot of effort and can be much more complex than most of us realize. We furnish you with several key techniques for active listening that you can apply immediately:

1. Reflect and refine the speaker's content
2. Mirror their emotions and body language
3. Ask thoughtful questions

As you *reflect and refine content*, you'll start realizing that you will surpass simply listening to what a speaker says, because you will actively take their point and help them improve it. What better way to express generosity than to think beyond yourself and give the speaker a leg up? The speaker may articulate an idea and provide additional contextual information to clarify his point. This takes more verbiage, but the context sometimes remains necessary for showing the importance and meaning of his point. A great communicator can listen actively to those points and somehow process and summarize the main points in a concise and impactful manner. That action demonstrates to the speaker that the person has taken the time to listen. No need to summarize every single point the speaker makes, but when it's your turn to talk, you may allude to what the previous speaker just said. This shows respect, first of all. Second, it shows that you've listened to the nuances and key points.

The nonverbal aspects of communication can greatly influence the content of a message, so subtly *mirror a speaker's emotions and body language*. As demonstrated earlier by the importance of empathy, this conscious or unconscious act of reflecting on the speaker's emotions and body language creates a rapport. No need to overdramatize your mirroring. In addition, you need not immediately mirror. Your reflection of expression could grow during the course of the conversation rather than immediately after the speaker's statements. If you mirror too quickly or dramatically, you might come off as mocking or not genuine.

Third, *ask thoughtful questions* by incorporating their content and emotions into your questions. This could start with a general question that involves who, what, when, where, why, or how. We believe that it can go beyond asking general questions, though, because you can incorporate the previous speaker's content and emotions into your question. For example, you could say, "You very passionately stated your point about [insert topic]. Could you further elaborate on [insert specific point or nuance]?" This allows you to gather more data and truly show that you're listening. You've truly presented an engaged impression.

On the other end of the spectrum, some people disagree with the previous speaker and will start their reply with "I disagree." This can serve a purpose, which is to strongly assert a point and initiate a confrontation. In many cases, however, this places the previous speaker in defensive mode and undermines what he's been trying to say. On top of that, there exist many instances when the person replying often does not completely disagree with a point. A more productive alternative lies in asking questions for further clarification. You could say, "If I'm understanding you correctly, are you saying that . . . " Starting a statement like this shows that you're actively listening enough to recapitulate and reply to their statement. It also gives them a chance to further clarify and fine-tune their point. Sometimes, it may not always take undermining the previous speaker to prove your point. You could offer an alternative view by stating, "An alternative idea is to . . . " or "What if we took this in a different direction by . . . " These examples demonstrate that sometimes a disagreement need not escalate into a confrontation, but can function as an alternative or negotiation.

GIVE TO GET: KNOW YOUR AUDIENCE, WOW YOUR AUDIENCE

The audience is the first and most important part as you Embrace Your ACE. It's more than about you, so pay close attention to the expectations and motivations of your audience. Understanding your audience will facilitate a better impression, because you will align your image and interactions with those who are interpreting what you project.

NOTES

1. Morse Gardiner, "Why We Misread Motives" *Harvard Business Review* (1 January 2003).

2. Daniel Goleman, "Empathy—Who's Got It, Who Does Not" *The Huffington Post* (2 May 2009), http://www.huffingtonpost.com/

dan-goleman/empathy—whos-got-it-who_b_195178.html (Accessed June 13, 2009)

3. Bhismadev Chakrabarti and Simon Baron-Cohen, "The Biology of Mind Reading" *First Impressions* (New York: Guilford, 2008), 57–86

4. Mark Lacter, "How I Did It: Reid Hoffman of Linkedln" *Inc Magazine* (May 2009), 83–84.

5. Kittie Watson and Larry R. Smeltzer, "Barriers to Listening: Comparison between Students and Practitioners" *Communication Research Reports* 1, no. 1 (1984), 82–87.

Chapter 9

Embrace Your ACE—Captivate with Cultural Competence

DEFINING CULTURE: THE LENS OF YOUR WORLD

Many associate culture with ethnic and national connotations. For instance, many people conjure images of China or Mexico upon hearing the word "culture." Yes, these examples both constitute different cultures, but we want to apply a broader definition of culture. We define "culture" as a set of attitudes, behaviors, and values within a certain group. Think of it as a lens through which different groups view the world. One culture's lens may see the world as green, while another views it as purple. The objects and actions in this world remain the same, but the lens colors these perceptions differently. We want you to keep your lens constantly flexible, moving and operating so that you can truly understand and interact effectively with your audience. This effective interaction will in turn allow you to create an Impressive First Impression.

Culture with a capital "C" has a different meaning than our use of it here. This capital "C" culture is associated with being of a higher class or level of sophistication. We use culture with a lowercase "c" to represent the attitudes, behaviors, and values of a particular group. This group could be generational cultures. For instance, Baby Boomers (born between 1946 and 1964) possess different cultural norms than those of Generation Y (born between 1978 and 1995). Organizations feature very different cultures as well. The work culture within Google differs dramatically from that of Raytheon. Working within the U.S. Army will differ tremendously in terms of culture when compared to working for the Red Cross.

Culture directly affects how you will craft your impression. Cultural barriers and filters will impact how others interpret the image you project and your interactions with them. Most writing on first impressions and image spend little or no time on culture, which we believe is critical to the success of your impression. For instance, if you sport white at an event, it may mean purity in one culture but death in another. One culture may deem it appropriate for weddings, while another may find it more suitable for funerals. Your intention may be celebratory, but the interpretation could end up offending your audience. Fret not, because in this chapter, we'll go through the major factors behind these cultural differences and some strategies to consider that will boost the effectiveness of your impression.

One way to understand your audience is to understand the cultural differences and similarities between you and your audience. These are the differences in the underlying values that you hold, as compared to those of your audience. These values may exist invisibly and intangibly, but they directly dictate people's behaviors. For instance, if you slurp soup in one culture, it could make you look (and sound) rude. In a different culture, it signifies that you love the soup. If you're part of the latter culture, you've probably grown up learning that you should slurp when you consume soup. Therefore, your values dictate your behaviors. The interpretation by others, however, may result in their thinking that you're behaving in an impolite manner. How can you know that if you don't know the underlying values? How can you learn all of these cultural subtleties?

It's virtually impossible to know every nuance of every culture, so we're not going to focus on these vast quantities of differences. Instead, let's look at a different way of learning tools of cross-cultural competence. We do this by broadening common definitions of culture. Another way to understand culture lies in the barriers to cultural understanding. Understand these barriers and you'll at least have an advantage in recognizing cultural differences and how to navigate them. We also cover how to leverage cultural patterns, as contrasted with stereotyping. Yes, you will need to understand the norms of a particular culture, yet we also distinguish between discerning patterns versus discriminating based on stereotypes. From there, you can modify your impression to suit the values and perceptions of your audience.

BROADENING CULTURAL DEFINITIONS AND LEVERAGING DIVERSITY

As we started to lay out the explanation of culture, we stated that it covers the attitudes, behaviors, and values of a particular group. There exist numerous ways to divide cultures and subcultures; this wide gamut of cultures reflects how we break down and categorize these cultures. Taking these differences into account, we can look at a multitude of them. We call this vast array of differences *diversity*. Some argue that diversity can encompass politics and economics. For ease of understanding, we place politics and economics within the definition of culture, because one can even divide political and economic systems into groups with their own distinct attitudes, behaviors, and values.

Take for example, the case of Capitalists and Marxists. Capitalists hold dear very different values from Marxists. Capitalists, for instance, believe in the free market and Marxists believe in distribution of resources according to each person's needs. Similarly, Democrats and Republicans advocate for their positions, which in turn affect U.S. politics. They each struggle to push forward different values, which underpin their attitudes toward politics. For this reason, even economic and political systems fit with certain cultural norms. To truly cultivate an Impressive First Impression, you'll need to gain cultural competence and understand diversity. Otherwise, you'll look at the world through a limited lens. When you do engage different cultures, this will allow you to more strategically adapt your impression to a broader spectrum of audiences.

Culture, of course, changes over time. When people claim to have one true, authentic culture, they often overlook the reality that culture changes. Take a look at the word and concept of Chinese culture. There exist many scattered groups who all represent a part of the Chinese culture. These can include formal nations that feature a strong ethnic Chinese presence, such as Taiwan, Malaysia, Singapore, as well as Hong Kong (both before and after China reclaimed it from the British). Ethnic Chinese exist everywhere, from Chinese Americans and Chinese Canadians to Chinese French and Chinese Peruvians. Even China itself represents a very diverse landmass of regional subcultures. These include rural versus industrial, northern versus southern, as well as rich versus poor. As a cultural group spreads and interacts with those from other cultures, these actions change how we define that particular culture.

When people hear culture, many people define it by ethnicity and race. Even a word ostensibly as diverse as "diversity" can remain confined to narrower definitions. Many diversity practitioners discuss how people relegate diversity to the trio of ethnicity/race, gender, and age. It's often the differences we can see with our eyes that encompass our definitions of diversity. As we broaden culture, we also need to move beyond narrow definitions of diversity. Diversity can represent all types of differences, which can include:

- Geography
- Language
- Economic Status
- Religion
- Education Level
- Race
- Gender
- Age and Generation
- Intelligence
- Physical Appearance
- Disabilities
- Personal Preferences

We can apply culture and diversity, then, to a very broad range of concepts. These two concepts, taken together, form *cultural diversity*, which we define as the numerous differences and varieties of groups that each possess certain distinct attitudes, behaviors, and values.

Truly *Embrace Your ACE* when it comes to cultural diversity. Embracing cultural diversity opens your mind toward continuously learning about the nuances of different groups. This in and of itself will allow your lens of the world to operate in a more flexible and strategic way. You can quickly shift the lens, too. Embracing cultural diversity takes you out of complacency and into lifelong, open-minded learning about others. What better way to understand your audience than to go to the core of your lens and keep it open to new and different observations? Cultural diversity represents the oil that allows your lens to continually move and operate.

BARRIERS TO INTERCULTURAL COMMUNICATION

Intercultural Communication scholars examine all types of barriers to communicating across cultures. Here we identify and provide explanations of six major barriers, which according to Fred Jandt, include:

1. Assumptions of Similarity
2. Stereotypes and Prejudice
3. Ethnocentrism
4. Nonverbal Misinterpretations
5. Language
6. Anxiety[1]

Assumptions of Similarity: Ethan, a former investment banker, leaves his job to work at an Information Technology (IT) startup. Throughout the morning of his first day, Ethan spends time at his various colleagues' desks and takes time to get to know them, because he values building trust and social bonds. By the end of the day, however, his colleagues actually trust him less and view him as a lower performer. They question his sincerity at wanting to further the company and perceive him as a distraction.

What happened? Ethan engaged in assumptions of similarity. He assumed that his IT colleagues value trust as primarily social bonding and equated his mingling as team-building. His colleagues, on the other hand, tended to be mostly software programmers who are task-oriented and more introverted. Although social bonds are an important part of building trust to them, they also primarily evaluate performance as accomplishing detailed tasks. Excess socializing to them can result in distracting peers and wasting others' time. Equally vital, they viewed Ethan as not doing his job, and how can they trust a team member who doesn't do his job?

This first barrier to communicating across cultures can initially seem like an asset. When we meet people from different cultures, we tend to gravitate toward similarities that we have with them. This helps us to create more rapid rapport with these culturally different strangers. Often, however, this tendency manifests as an assumption of similarity. Assuming that other cultures are similar to ours blocks us from seeing these differences. This then prevents us from under-standing them, and thus hinders us from forming a great impression that also aligns with our audience.

Another workplace example happens often at lunch hour. Some employees may socialize in the lunch room or go out for lunch with a group of peers as a nice break and to get better acquainted. They may view other employees who take lunch at their desks as less social or not team players. These lunch socialites assume that the desk din-ers are antisocial or lack team spirit. They may fail to see that the desk diners value task-oriented work or take shorter lunches so that they can leave earlier to pick up their kids from school. Assumptions of similarity over a simple act of lunch can cause workplace tensions.

Stereotypes and Prejudice: A stereotype forms when someone applies a perception or experience to *every single person in a group without exception*. When a person, for example, sees several Middle Eastern Muslim terrorists on television, they indeed do witness that there are some terrorists who happen to be of Middle Eastern descent and Muslim. These are facts. Stereotyping occurs when the individual begins to assume that all Middle Eastern Muslims are terrorists. Yes, there are some who could be terrorists, but we know that terrorists can come from any region or religion. Stereotypes about a group often form as a result of someone having personal experiences inter-acting with people from that group. What escalates them from a per-sonal experience to a stereotype is when that individual applies these experiences to everyone in the group, even complete strangers.

Prejudice occurs when a person acts on those stereotypes and treats people from a certain group differently as a result. So if the individual we discussed began to fear and avoid all Muslims from the Middle East, then they have acted on these stereotypes. These actions demon-strate a form of prejudice.

Relating this to Impressive First Impressions, how can someone possibly form an effective one if they automatically write off people from a group as behaving or thinking a certain way? If this stereotyp-ing and prejudice happens, then those holding them would always treat people from a certain group the same way. As stated previously, first impressions are not one-size-fits-all and this person has just neglected their audience's wants or needs.

Ethnocentrism: When a person negatively judges others' cultures when compared to her own, that's ethnocentrism. When a person believes that his own culture is superior to another culture, that's ethnocentrism. One man from China asked a friend of ours, "Why do you Americans eat so many raw vegetables?" and went on to talk about how these raw vegetables were rough on the body and didn't taste as good as cooked vegetables that many Chinese tended to eat. This Chinese gentleman believed in the superiority of his culture's cooking.

Our friend grinned and simply replied, "Why do Chinese eat so many cooked vegetables that lose nutrients and taste so greasy or soggy?" Our friend went on to discuss differences rather than try to demonstrate that his practices were better than those of the Chinese. This case teaches us to seriously consider cultural relativism. Cultural relativism means that we should take time to understand someone else's culture before we judge it. It does not mean that all cultures are perceived equally, since some people favor certain cultures or cultural aspects over others.

How can overcoming ethnocentrism and embracing cultural relativism improve our impressions? It may allow us to grow beyond our comfort zones and become less complacent. If we, for example, have been working in the casual culture of an engineering firm, we may say to ourselves, "I'm so glad I don't have to work in that law firm that makes its lawyers all wear stuffy and ridiculously expensive suits." That comment assumes that suits are financially wasteful and show rigid attitudes. To the lawyer and her clients, the suit may simply show more professionalism and polish. The so-called financial "waste" may be investment in clients, because the lawyers go out of their way to dress well and demonstrate the highest regard for their clients. High-billing lawyers know that clients equate this polish and investment with competence and success. Each work culture has its value, but before writing off your cultural perspective as best, take the time to weigh the value of the other person's cultural values and practices.

Nonverbal Misinterpretations: Most people are visual learners, so nonverbal behaviors dramatically shape our daily interactions. Unfortunately, we often misinterpret these physical nuances. For example, many people interpret folding one's arms across his chest as a sign of mental resistance and that the person either has stopped listening or disagrees with the speaker. Many body language books state this, but folding one's arms can actually mean the exact opposite at times. Some people fold their arms to think more about what the speaker has said. The act of folding the arms inward can actually mean that they listener has taken the time to internalize and process the speaker's message more carefully. In this case, many people misinterpret this nonverbal action.

Nonverbal communication needs to be viewed in context of factors such as one's culture and setting and amidst multiple body-language cues. What if, for instance, the listener folds his arms, but then points one arm upward and touches his finger to his chin? This could reflect a classic "thinker's pose" where the listener looks slightly like Rodin's *The Thinker*—this famous statue rests his chin on his fist to think. Also, the listener could nod in acknowledgement. These other nonverbal cues can show that the initial arm-folding means the opposite of resistance but instead signifies acknowledgement and pensive behavior.

Social space presents an ongoing issue when it comes to nonverbal misinterpretations, and this directly impacts your impression. In the United States, if you "keep someone at an arm's length," this usually means that you're keeping a formal physical distance in face-to-face social interactions. This distance means a length that's not too intimate and not too stand-offish. You can usually measure acceptable social space as an arm's length in mainstream American culture, but this distance varies based on culture.

We can partially understand these nonverbal cues by addressing the intercultural communication concepts of high-context and low-context communication preferences. Though typically complex and rich concepts, we simplify them for you here so that you can quickly apply them to your interactions with different audiences. High-context cultures generally rely more on the surrounding context than specific individuals to read how they communicate. In other words, people from these cultures tend to act in a more-reserved, seemingly introverted way. Their motions and words tend to be more subtle. They tend to emphasize others more than themselves. Low-context cultures tend to place more emphasis on individuals than their surroundings. They tend to function in a way that seems more extroverted and open. Their surroundings matter less in what they say, because they call more attention to themselves.

Tie in social space and you'll notice that people of high-context cultures tend to take up less physical space during interactions and act more reserved. Someone from a low-context culture may seem loud and aggressive to an individual from a high-context culture. The low-context person may speak with what they deem confidence and assertiveness, but this perception is magnified when applied to a low-context person. In contrast, when a low-context person engages the high-context one, the latter may seem less responsive and shy. The high-context person may see himself as respectful by placing others first, but the low-context person may view him as passive. The high-context person may actually be very receptive, but may just express himself with less-noticeable facial and bodily nuances.

Think of these extremes as low-volume and high-volume settings on a radio, with a "1" being very high-context, while a "10" represents very low-context. A high-context person may move with smaller and subtler motions that she thinks is an average of "5" on how she perceives her scale. The low-context person may interpret this as a "2" on his scale. Both people simply use different scales.

With this in mind, as you forge your Impressive First Impression, consider how someone with a different cultural lens will view your nonverbal behaviors. If you're low-context culturally and tend to move more assertively and with wider, harder movements, consider softening and slowing them when dealing with a high-context person. If you're high-context and engage a low-context person, you may need to speak with more vigor and what you may consider flat-out bravado or loudness.

Understanding nonverbal misinterpretations can improve our impressions. When we can learn how others view body language, we can then adapt our body language to "speak" what our audience understands and send the best message that suits both parties.

Language: On a very fundamental level, if two people cannot understand one another because of language barriers, this prevents very complex communication. Even if two people can communicate in a common language, chances are that one or both are not engaging in their native tongue. This inherently prevents the use of sophisticated vocabulary and concepts. Also, a speaker's body language and verbal language may be misaligned. First impressions also largely depend on verbal language, not just body language or other physical characteristics such as dress or physique. When language acts as a barrier, you can simply spend more time observing the other person more carefully. Of course, there is a loss of opportunity to project your message and impression more strongly in the short term, but the result is more long-term understanding that you can use later.

There exist many intricacies related to intercultural communication and language, but we wanted to provide you with a very practical direction: listen and observe actively. Of course, you can study a particular culture before dealing with someone from that culture, but that's a more-robust and detailed time commitment. When you're interacting and trying to impress a person spontaneously, active and thoughtful observation are actions that many people neglect. This will at least help you survive, if not thrive, in this foreign interaction.

Anxiety: When two people of different cultures communicate, this creates anxiety and even frustration. These emotional barriers can then hinder accurate communication. Arms may flail more widely or quickly. They could also perhaps move less than when the person speaks their usual native tongue. Anxiety leads to a higher likelihood of misunderstandings as well. For example, one study surveyed a cross-national team of Japanese and American colleagues. When asked how often they were understood when communicating in English, the Japanese colleagues believed that they were only understood by their American counterparts two-thirds as often as their American counterparts actually understood them. The Japanese had more anxiety about being understood because they were communicating in their nonnative language and in a foreign country, the United States.

Understanding the barriers to intercultural communication provides you with a different way to broaden your lens than with embracing cultural diversity. Cultural diversity keeps your lens open, while knowing the barriers allows you to break down the rigidness of your lens. Whereas cultural diversity allows you to move your lens, constantly breaking cultural barriers parallels cleaning out the dust and debris that blocks your lens.

CULTURAL CONSCIENCE: PATTERNING VERSUS STEREOTYPING

We've been discussing the notion of knowing your audience and understanding their cultural patterns. We also defined stereotypes as blanket assumptions about a particular group, without exception. These two ideas represent extremes. Although we may strive to understand our audience, we can never truly understand our audience, on one hand, because we're not them. On the other hand, once we relegate a group to a stereotype, we claim to truly understand them—and that's impossible without being them. Just because you're part of a group doesn't mean that you can't still stereotype them. A member of one group can still generalize and stereotype about behaviors within their group. These two extremes also reflect very different attitudes. We hope you opt for the first attitude. That said, if it's impossible to 100 percent understand our audience, we can pattern them. We advocate that you employ patterns in helping you to shape your impression.

Patterning assumes some margin for error, which differentiates it from blanket stereotyping. It's a form of inductive reasoning (remember that from school?). In short, inductive reasoning states that if it rains every day for 1,000 days, then it's likely to rain on day 1,001. Although there's no guarantee that it will actually rain, precipitation remains very likely. Recall the chapter where we explained how the supermarkets and other retailers try to understand what you think and feel. They engage in a form of patterning your behaviors. Also recall how we discussed empathy earlier as well. When people empathize with you, they can virtually read your mind and your heart. The next step leads to sympathizing, or acting on the empathy to satisfy your needs, whether it's eliminating a craving or a sad emotion. This act of empathy, called sympathy, forms a bond with you. They impressed on you that they exist to help you.

All of this stems from their motivation to both benefit you and benefit from you. It's a win-win that comes from understanding the patterns behind your thinking. Can they ever 100 percent accurately guess your motivations, needs and wants? Not at all, but understanding what you want influences the Impressive First Impression they give to you. This potent combination of image and interactions can sway you toward giving them, in turn, what they want. You can do the same to and for others. Of course, patterns may shift based on how accurately they reflect a group, but you can certainly use them to your advantage in crafting your impression.

CULTIVATING CULTURE COMPETENCE

As you can see, the complexities of culture can furnish you with quite powerful tools for cultivating your Impressive First Impression. When you Embrace the ACE of culture, you understand how the lens of culture shapes your world. More so, you can couple it with diversity to continually broaden your cultural definitions. Your lens remains well-oiled and grows flexible. When further combined with an awareness, and breaking, of cultural barriers, you constantly clean the lens and ensure that its powers of observation stay sharp. Most important, leverage these tools to craft your impression and you'll increase your professional effectiveness.

NOTE

1. Fred E. Jandt, *Intercultural Communication: An Introduction* (Thousand Oaks, CA: Sage Publications, 2001).

Chapter 10

Embrace Your ACE—
Leverage Your Environment

FROM NASTY INTERROGATIONS TO HOLLYWOOD SET
PRODUCTIONS: KNOW YOUR SURROUNDINGS

The vast majority of writing and research on first impressions and image management focuses on improving you as the individual. We take a different focus by bringing your attention to the ground that you walk on and the space that you occupy. Emerging fields, such as Design Psychology, leverage psychology in the service of designing spaces, such as homes and offices, so people react more favorably toward that particular space. You may have heard of people "staging" their homes to attract more buyers and fetch a higher price for their homes. The emphasis in this field rests on the designed space itself and how people react to it. We take a different focus, because we train you on how to leverage these spaces to focus on you as the individual. The space improves how others perceive you. In other words, this chapter trains you on how to leverage your environment to improve your individual impression.

Simple tools such as lights and pens can influence your credibility. What do your professional accessories and environment say about you? How can you select the best combination of these for your needs? More so, we discuss how to leverage the people around you as resources to boost your impression. Yes, you can get help from people in this sense, but we also advocate making it a win-win. Our accompanying practical strategies reinforce this point about giving and acting generously to others while enhancing your impression. That's where this chapter should change your thinking on how to observe, analyze, and utilize your context. In this chapter, we focus on how to improve your impression by utilizing your environment, specific tools, and props, as well as working with other people. As you change the physical landscape around you, people change their perception of you.

In the movies, or even in real-life, police cruisers use flood lights that can wake the dead. How do these create Impressive First Impressions on those pulled over? Imagine the bright and near-blinding glare of these spotlights pounding on you as you squint in disorientation. The lights inhibit your vision of the police officers, yet give them full view of you. They appear as more than people, but silhouettes with no face and obscured details. You and your details, in contrast, remain exposed. This light of justice induces intimidation and illuminates you, the possible threat. Now that you feel this emotion the police officers themselves look more fearful and intimidating than if you saw them in a donut shop, which only reinforces that stereotype of the officer on break. The scenario of flood lights suddenly shifts your perception of the police officer.

Flash to Hollywood sets that replicate entirely different eras. From fantasy-like pasts to science-fiction simulated futures, these sets create drastically different environments. These environments evoke all types of emotions, from historical nostalgia to post-apocalyptic possibilities. The colors, textures, props, and lighting intertwine and establish a certain mood and ambience. These sets transport people into a different world. A knight in shining armor looks majestic and noble when placed in an open field in front of his stately castle. Place this same knight in modern New York City and he suddenly looks out of place and probably insane. Place him in a scene out of *Star Trek* and he looks like a flat-out antique. Shift his setting and you shift how people view him. The impression you have of him dramatically transforms when you transform his terrain.

In some ways, these sets are like much-more detailed and strategic counterparts to staging your home in a real estate sale. The sets prove vastly more elaborate and their return on investment can also prove equally immense. These sets prove effective when people buy more movie tickets or when television viewership increases. Home staging also draws buyers and dollars. If you apply these same principles of synergizing with your surroundings, but to boost your own impression, imagine the positive possibilities.

Shift to daily interactions, such as in restaurants. When you dine at a fine establishment, the multitudes of subtle touches appeal to the senses. You may notice only some of the details initially, before they whisk you to your table and pamper you with great service. Those subtle touches contribute to the broader ambience of the restaurant. Start with the materials. Does the restaurant sport rich dark woods and classic leather on the walls and trim that convey heartiness and class? Or maybe the place emphasizes clean, modern steel and glass that sends a message of openness and innovation?

The selected colors then stimulate the senses when you carefully consider a restaurant's design. The dark brown woods may accompany the beige-colored glass and slight reddish hue of the trim. These elements conjure thoughts of chocolate, caramel, and cinnamon. Hungry for dessert? Another restaurant may feature glass and steel that they color with fire-engine red to show bold, cutting-edge looks and recipes. The red incites passion and hunger. Ready to savor your food, while engaging in a loud, vigorous discussion? The restaurant designers complement these touches with all types of other nuances, from shape designs and patterns to fixtures and paintings. The list goes on and on. Ever notice how the people you're with also change their mood and how they perceive you? Ever notice how it affects your perception of them? For instance, a romantic candlelit dinner in a dim restaurant can soften someone's facial features, making his face look more gentle and attractive. The soft cloth dinner napkins also soften others' view of that person, as does a little bit of wine to lighten the mood. Surround that same person with harsh, fluorescent lighting, loud patrons, cheap plastic tables, and uncomfortable seating. Wouldn't factors such as these change how you interface and view that other person?

Envision your cubicle or office, as well as entire workplace, as your miniature Hollywood set or retail establishment. What possibilities do you see arising from your space in terms of improving your impression? You'll learn how to go beyond your office and leverage any environment to transform your impression and increase its effectiveness. Remember the Golden Virtue that first impressions are about more than the individual. Even if you master many individual tactics for your impression, you can augment this significantly by utilizing your environment to create the ambience that aligns with your goals. Better yet, when you try to influence others with your impression, they may notice the improved aspects of your individual impression that you've altered. When you employ your environment, however, these same people may not even realize that you've done so. With first impressions forming within microseconds, all of these details may seem imperceptible to others, but you can plan them carefully with thoughtful consideration before any encounter.

THE SPACE SURROUNDING YOU

When we ask people to describe the physical landscape of their cubicles, offices, and office buildings, we often hear very common words. These include adjectives such as sterile, drab, dull, beige, gray, impersonal, lifeless, and cold. Nicknames even come to mind, such as cube colony, cubeville, and *Office Space* (yes, taken from the movie). Occasionally, we hear bright and cheerful descriptions, such as "my second home" or "a warm place with friends and colleagues." Of course, these more-pleasant descriptions fall under the shadow of the more "lifeless" ones.

First, we'll show you how these landscapes can actually serve a purpose and how professionals underutilize them. Second, many professionals underestimate their own ability to transform their work places into a different atmosphere with more soul, passion, and artfulness. We'll help you transform these spaces into ones that will increase the impressiveness of your impression.

UNDERSTAND THE MEANINGS BEHIND YOUR SURROUNDINGS

You can benefit from common associations between images and what they mean. First, you'll need to thoughtfully ponder what various surroundings connote. As we continually advocate throughout this book, consider your audience carefully. Think about what you and others commonly think about when you view certain spaces, such as:

- Blue skies
- Green, grassy fields
- Narrow, dimly lit office hallways
- Boardroom with a wood table, projector, and screen

Take a moment to imagine and reflect upon what initially comes to mind for each of these environments. For instance, when we say blue skies, what do you immediately think about? When we show these images to people we train and speak with, most of them associate this image with freedom, dreams, calm, beauty, peace, serenity, openness, and escape. When we present an image of a green, grassy field, it elicits similar, yet different words: freshness, nature, vacation, fun, sun, relaxation, community, calm, safety, laughter, and friendliness. Did these words, or variations of them, initially enter your mind?

Contrast this with the latter two settings. Pause for a moment and think about which words first popped in your head before you read further. Let's take a closer look at these settings. The narrow, dimly lit office hallways usually evoke words such as creepiness, confinement, tightness, claustrophobia, sterility, trap, narrowness, and cold. The boardroom triggers words such as power, authority, structure, politics, struggle, decisions, control, forcefulness, sophistication, and refinement.

What do these four settings have in common with your professional work space? You can probably access all of them at work or the areas surrounding work. Each of these settings likely exist in or near your office and you can use these common associations to your advantage when crafting your impression. The meanings associated with these places will help you to set the mood. We'll delve into how to use these places in the upcoming sections, but we want to stress the importance of understanding the common meanings of each place. Ask your friends, colleagues, and family members what they associate with these four settings. That way, you'll get a broader pulse of "what" people think of in regards to each space.

Making associations may not seem so difficult once you use common sense and common perceptions. The operative word here is "common," since most people will perceive different images in different ways. Not everyone will perceive each space in the same way, but there clearly exist patterns on how people view each of these areas. You can't 100 percent predict how others will react to a particular place, but if you understand frequent reactions, that will at least serve as a strong starting point, and you can move on to leveraging them.

FROM OUTDOOR TO INDOOR: LEVERAGE THE SPACE THAT'S ALREADY THERE

Starbucks considers itself the "Third Place," between home and work. The company's CEO, Howard Schultz, helped establish this culture and environment for the company's stores. Customers come to feel comfortable and can hang out for hours. These same customers want to work productively, but with the ambience and energy of people around them. The coffee shops encourage conversation and the consistent influx of customers who want to stay. This adds more human warmth and lively energy. The company often furnishes its shops with nice tile and/or carpet, armchairs, sofas and dark-colored small tables suited ideally for intimate conversation in a public place. This atmosphere further induces people to make themselves at home, yet still behave with public decency. The human energy draws further human energy as it forms an increasing gravity of people. Customers may come to converse and/or work, so they purchase coffee as their unwritten, unspoken way of bartering for this space.

Many customers like the customization of beverages that also helps make it feel like home, because they receive the comforts of items tailored to their tastes. In addition, the professional baristas craft drinks with deft skill and friendly service—a reminder of how a workplace should function. This "Third Place" marketing strategy built a community of customers by offering an alternative to home and work that still retains elements from both spaces. Starbucks engages in more than selling coffee—they leverage space to attract buyers. They influence their customers to buy through their space.

Think beyond your office. Where can you find this "Third Place" that can help you influence others? There's no need to create a new "Third Place." Instead, look to the areas that already exist around you. What's one of the most wonderful benefits about leveraging your existing space? It's already there and all around. Another benefit: it's more than just about you, so you avoid most perceptions of you acting in a self-centered manner. In essence, you can reap the benefits for yourself without necessarily focusing on yourself. We provide you with some settings that you can likely access around your office building. From outdoor openness to office organization, we've got you covered.

The Great Outdoors: Next time you want to influence a colleague, supervisor, employee, or friend to engage in open and relaxed dialogue, lead them to a park. Pause for a moment and imagine yourself in this verdant and vibrant place. What images do you conjure in your mind when you think of a park with grass, trees, and benches? Most people we ask associate this space with variations of the following: children playing, fun, laughter, recreation, relaxation, reading, peace, sharing, nature, openness, activity, and living. Occasionally, someone plays wise guy or gal and links this setting with drug deals. Yes, those happen, but generally speaking, parks represent positive places.

You can employ this setting to your advantage in the workplace as well.

How do you use the park to your advantage in a professional setting? Take people there when you want to bond with them or have an honest conversation with them, as well as help them relax and share. A park allows for a public shared space, yet affords privacy as the sound of your conversation diffuses away into the vast space around you. It simultaneously allows a sense of openness from its locale in a public sphere, yet anonymity as it affords a sense of being amidst others. It may sound counterintuitive, but the outdoor space of parks makes them in some ways seem more private than offices, because the open-air atmosphere makes people feel open to speak. Others will often associate the freedom of the outdoor space with you and this enhances your impression.

You need not necessarily journey to a nearby park, but likely have a nice bench or table nearby your office. Find one that features park-like qualities, such as grass and trees, as well as nice statues and possibly playful elements. An outdoor café presents another nice alternative to the park and can foster more open dialogue, since it blends privacy amidst a public space. Like other outdoor settings, outdoor cafés usually allow noise to spread, yet still are located within public spaces. The privacy found in a public space further fosters open dialogue that you can find outside of the office. The beverages and food also bring a sense of comfort and help build rapport. People generally "break bread" with those that they respect, so talking over food and drink adds another factor into broadening the channels of dialogue.

The outdoors can create a stronger impression, because others associate this open, relaxed environment with you. They may likely not know why they feel more at ease with you, but you'll notice a difference in how they interact with you. This underlying link between you and this open space will help you create an impressive impression to others in a nuanced way.

Restaurants and the Bar during Happy Hour: Speaking of partaking of food and drinks during your conversations, you can employ indoor dining and social spaces to bolster your impression as well. As stated, food and drinks facilitate relaxation and people tend to associate these with taking breaks. Ever wonder why so many organizations interview job candidates over lunch or dinner? Most people act on their best behavior during job interviews. It's difficult to tell how they would really behave day to day once they're hired.

You generally don't know from just a few interviews, and not until they start working for you do some of their undesirable habits emerge. Meals often disarm these candidates by relaxing them.

When using food to create an impression, you can factor in traditional comfort foods that may reflect a person's childhood. Once you find out this information, you can take someone out for this meal. Remember it's the "A" in ACE that represents audience, so if you understand their favorite foods from their childhood, you can try to arrange to take them to a restaurant that serves that particular dish. If it's mashed potatoes and meatloaf, find a place that serves this dish. Maybe they're an immigrant from a region of China who loves dumplings served during dim sum. Perhaps their parents served them baguettes with butter or pâté, a French favorite. Watch as nostalgia softens them and they reminisce about pleasant childhood experiences. Their perception of you changes.

In addition, eating in a more relaxed way (read: not at your desk) helps facilitate better digestion. According to the Institute for the Psychology of Eating, this boosts the digestion and changes your relationship with food.[1] Yes, it advocates for altering the way you view and interface with your meals. So as the food comforts and relaxes you and others, eating in a relaxed environment optimizes digestion of the food. This creates a truly virtuous cycle!

Turn from the table toward a bar and you now further change the impression. Ever notice how people gossip more and drink more liberally during happy hour? They let their guard down and feel at ease. And, as the title states, it's a time when people act happily! Cater to a colleague during happy hour at a friendly bar, pub, or restaurant, and you will instantly notice that he or she tends to relax even further. As he unwinds, fills his belly with cheap (or even free) food, sips on tasty drinks, and hears fun-filled music in the background, he will view you in an equally at-ease fashion. Your impression changes in his mind. At a base level, many people call that "beer goggles." We go beyond the simple notion of "beer goggles" and assert that you can use this spatial situation more strategically by shifting your entire context to a bar (and not just rely on trying to inebriate someone into looking at you favorably with a liquored lens).

Food and drink accompany certain social spaces, such as restaurants and bars. What if you must remain in the office? Why not bring someone edibles and drinkables? When you're visiting someone, whether within your organization or outside, bring a small food or drink offering. This could be as simple as a box of chocolates or candies, a tin of tea or bag of coffee, or even a fresh batch of cookies or donuts. We've consistently observed that with such positive actions, people tend to treat you better, remain more open to dialogue and generally react happier. Besides, how could you possibly treat someone poorly if they've just gifted you with some love in the form of food? Of course, make sure that the recipient likes or isn't allergic to what you've offered as a gift.

On a more toned-down scale, you can also spend time in the lunch or break room. Most employees gather here at one time or another throughout the day. Privacy diminishes in these areas, but the odds increase of you bumping into someone with whom you'd like to chat and impress. Ideally, you should directly invite the person you want to impress to a meal or happy hour, but the lunch or break room offers one alternative. Plus, you know the area will almost always feature food and drinks.

Food, drink, and the terrain that goes with these items can thoroughly change the way someone views you. Of course, the impression you convey here takes the form of a more relaxed one. As long as you remain professionally appropriate and ethical, however, there's plenty of value in applying these settings to your advantage.

A Conference Room: Swing the environment pendulum toward the other end of the spectrum and you walk into the conference room. For more serious and "roll-up-your-sleeves" efficiency, move your meeting to this haven of productivity A conference room generally connotes structure and serious meetings, as well as other exchanges. The open tables allow you to spread out and work, so this room can enable serious, task-oriented progress. The bare, or near-bare, walls of conference rooms scream "let's work" rather than focus on aesthetics. The conference setting sends a strong message of accomplishing tasks. It also increases your psychological orientation toward thinking actively about time. The room also connotes a sense of formality, because it's typically a dedicated work area.

This works even for just two people and can increase productivity in the short term, because most people would not occupy a conference room and waste time in there. When you take only one or two people to occupy an entire room that's shared space, you tend to all feel responsible for taking up such a large area. Watch as the sense of responsibility compels you all to get the task done. This room may not represent social bonding, with its Spartan nature, but it instead sends a message of formality and productivity. If your goal rests in having others shine a more serious light on you, then a conference room will aid you in arriving closer to achieving it.

Your Office Space—From Desk to Wall: We now return to your regularly scheduled office or cubicle. Yes, this daily staple really can prove a great way to make an impressive impression every day. (If you telecommute, you can read the chapter on virtual impressions.) You can leverage either cubicle or office to make your impression more impressive if you take the time to examine the nooks and crannies of your space. From the details on your desk to the words on your walls, this space serves as your daily stronghold at work. When people come to you, they will view this area as the inanimate version of your impression. Inanimate need not mean lifeless. You can breathe life into your gray and beige work space. We provide advice to move beyond the Dilbert-like dead zone, where many plow away daily as dreaded drones. That's a mouthful, so pay close attention.

Start with your desk. What impression do you want to project about yourself, as represented through your desk? Some people argue that a clean and organized desk creates the ideal professional impression. Others stress the need to have some clutter, which truly reflects a busy professional in action. What works best? Go back to the *Impressions Diamond Model* that we discussed earlier in this book. It all depends on what impression you, the sender, want to convey (Intention). Of course, you have to juggle your Intention with the Interpretation, or how others will process your message. Accomplishing that takes the willingness to Embrace the "A" in Your ACE, which entails understanding your audience. Looking further at the application of the Impressions Diamond Model to your desk, the main emphasis here rests on the image rather than interaction. We'll discuss strategies for your desk to appeal to both goals.

Let's begin with the notion of clean versus cluttered. Many argue that the former connotes a clear, organized thinker, as well as someone who can manage their own time and space well. They usually deride the latter for deficiencies such as lacking organization, efficiency, and mental clarity. Authors Eric Abrahamson and David Freedman suggest through numerous cases that a moderate amount of messiness can actually lead to more productivity. In their book *A Perfect Mess: The Hidden Benefits of Disorder—How Crammed Closets, Cluttered Offices and On-the-Fly Planning Make the World a Better Place*, they unearth examples of how slightly disorganized spaces can lead to more innovation and efficiency.[2] They also provide examples of the time it takes to maintain an organized environment, which can lead to more inefficiency and less overall productivity. Whatever side you take, make sure that either a clear or cluttered desk aligns with the impression you wish to convey.

For those who wish to send a more-organized impression, a clear desk definitely does you justice. This includes keeping a clear space in the center and edges closest to you. The areas farthest from you would likely host items that would normally obstruct your daily work, yet still allow these items to stay within an arm's reach. These other items should appear practical to show that you're an organized and efficient person. This would include items that send the message of your optimized organizational capabilities. You could sport a desk clock and desk pen set to show that things are in order, yet you're ready. A nice, large desk writing pad with a calendar on your desk shows that you simultaneously keep track of dates and like to write on your desk with this soft pad. These configurations provide the impression of a tidy, organized, and punctual person who cares about her space so that she can interact with others more easily.

Going beyond your desk, if you want to show organization, you should keep your walls fairly bare. This shows a minimalist approach and that you maintain such an organized professional life, you don't even need to rely on the walls. If you do keep any objects on your wall, they should prove functional, such as wall clocks or a hanging calendar.

For those of you who want to exhibit how busy you truly are at work, you should think about organized piles and clutter. A truly messy and cluttered desk generally sends the impression of a sloppy person. Controlled clutter can send the impression that benefits you more—that you're busy, innovative, and willing to roll up your sleeves and get your hands into your work. Stackable bins with files represent one way to effectively leverage this. A similar item could be a basket with hanging file folders. These types of items show "in" boxes and "out" boxes for projects in which you currently are engaging. A multi-boxed organizer of paper clips, rubber bands and post-its may show that you keep your items in one place, but like to leave them scrambled in these mini-bins on your desk and ready to go. Dry-erase markers, multiple sizes of Post-It pads and a rainbow of colored markers complement this inventor's and innovator's work-shop. Some people who project this impression sport puzzles and playful trinkets to keep themselves mentally flexible—and to share this fun with others. Still, it's tough to function in both an innovative and an organized way. A study of more than 240 presidents, CEOs, and chief operating officers' behavioral profiles found that CEOs actually are more creative, but less organized."[3]

Moving beyond your desk, if you want to show your innovation and "perfect mess," you should consider white boards where you can draw process flows and diagrams, as well as to-do lists. Some people have walls covered with dry-erase wallpaper, so they can utilize the full space. Others tape printed charts and papers on the walls. Either way, this shows a little bit of messiness, from drawings to tape, but also features your sense of creativity and free-flowing thoughts. These tactics generally emit the impression of a creative, innovative, busy, and experimental person.

Either clean or cluttered, another consideration for your desk rests with your computer. You should have your computer screen facing the rear of your office, so that when you view it, you can see visitors coming. This also protects the privacy of your work on the screen, since visitors will only see the back of your monitor. Of course, this also obstructs the view of visitors from seeing you directly and can feel less welcoming. You should consider how either option sends the impression of privacy and preparedness, as compared with openness and easiness.

The walls present another key area of office space that we began to discuss. Whether you're Mr. Clean Organizer or Ms. Cluttered Inventor, personalized and warm touches can truly present a different image that welcomes others. You could hang photos of family and/or pets on the walls, or of course, place them on your desk to add heart and soul to your cubicle or office. Recognition frames and plaques also show your hard-earned achievements. If you want to add humor, hang up a cartoon clipping or fun calendar. This sends a message that you're more relaxed and have a good sense of humor. A painting or art piece can sport your creative side and appreciation for the arts. Choose these objects wisely, since the real estate on your walls limits your ability to depict a personal touch. Too many items on the walls make your office resemble a garage sale, so avoid over-zealous decorating. How you leverage your cubicle or office walls will shape your individual impression.

Even the placement of these objects proves vital. For instance, if you place a clock on the wall behind you, it keeps visitors conscious of time. This tends to prevent them from lingering. It can also make them feel less comfortable talking with you, because it may indicate to them that you're time conscious. Conversely, if you place the clock over the door behind them, they will feel more relaxed and not as pressed for time, but may hang out at your office longer than you'd like. Similarly, do your family and pet photos face at an angle where visitors can see them or are they more turned so that only you can see them? Either way, you display warmth and a personal feel, but this shows that you're either sharing these with visitors or that you want to focus on your loved ones more for yourself. Either way, the placement of photos also poses an important factor.

Plants afford one more category of office possibilities. Plants add life and balance the harsh electric cords and buzzing from computers. They show your nurturing side and your desire to nurture more life, even within the office. The type of plant you choose also sends a certain message. Is it the more-resilient and low-maintenance cactus that exudes practicality? Will it come in the form of the greener indoor waxy plants that take more time, but reflect your nurturing attitude and actions? Either way, one or two plants can truly breathe life into a sterile office environment.

As you can see, your individual office space projects an impression of you. It can enhance or balance a certain impression you wish to convey. Carefully consider what impression you want others to form of you and then you can match office configurations and décor to match this goal.

USING PROPS

Even the tiniest of what we'll call professional props (going with the Hollywood theme) can alter your impression. These props range from pens and pins to tools and electronic devices. As you present, carrying a pen in hand can make you look more erudite and ready to engage others by taking notes or expressing ideas. When we present a Power-Point deck, we try to use a USB advancer in the shape of a pen, which enhances others' perceptions of our expertise. This pen-shaped advancer looks better than carrying a square or rectangular advancer to move our PowerPoint forward. Even the type of pen you carry can reflect the type of person you are. A cheap, stick pen that comes in a box of a dozen shows that you just write, but with less attention to your writing tool. Key nuances, such as the type of pen, can make a big difference in how others view you. A fountain pen adds class.

The pen's color should complement your message. Most pens are conservative and stately black and metallic. You can add flair with a color pen, such as one with purple metallic colors or fancy trims.

Pins also signal to others your affiliations. Some sport cancer-awareness or other pins that show they support a certain cause. Rotary International provides pins to identify you as a member and instantly bond with others. Of course, you want to avoid looking like a Friday-night waiter with too many pins—you may have to wear suspenders to complement this weekend waiter look. Wear pins with care, as they symbolize certain causes or groups that may have loaded connotations, such as political partisanship. Overall, one pin can help you to bond with others and send a cause-based message with your impression. Certain pins, however, may not indicate a group affiliation, so these lay more in the realm of individual tastes.

You can employ your mobile phone as another major prop, since almost every professional uses one. Now companies make so many customizable designs and features for phones that you can stand out from the crowd or send the impression you really want. These include everything from color covers and flashy sequin stick-ons to visual applications and ring tones. You can arm yourself with these audio and visual props to further carve out your impression to others. Just make sure to carefully consider what these sights and sounds on your phone mean. The ring tone can represent a great talking piece or an annoying sound that turns people off as you forget to turn it off. Colors can distract or attract clients, depending on your choice and their preference. In the end, you should select custom elements of a mobile phone that best send the impression of who you are. You can also err on the side of caution by adhering to the default phone colors or cases and rings or vibrations.

THE CONTEXT CHECKLIST

We can't predict every single scenario about your surrounding space that will influence your impression, so we crafted a checklist of key items to think about when you leverage your context. We call it the *Context Checklist*. Some key factors to consider when leveraging your environment include:

1. Who is your audience? (*Embrace Your ACE*, of course)
2. What impression would you like to convey to them?

3. What is your ultimate goal when interacting with your audience?
4. What mood would you like to set?
5. Indoor vs. outdoor?
6. Casual or formal?
7. Bright vs. dim?
8. Spacious or cozy?
9. Private or public?
10. Loud or quiet?
11. Natural or human-made?
12. Can you leverage scents?
13. Can you employ sounds?
14. Can you alter your environment or is it fixed?

If you can address just a fraction of these questions, you've really embraced your ACE. It takes time, effort, and skill to master your individual impression—how many of these factors does it take to master your environment in crafting your impression? We presented some practical and detailed ideas, but ultimately, if you can answer the questions above, you're far more planned and advanced than most when it comes to creating an Impressive First Impression.

THE HALO STRATEGY

Now that we've discussed how to leverage inanimate objects in your environment to improve your impression, let's move to a much more difficult skill to cultivate: working with other humans to accomplish the same goal. People generally feel more relaxed and comfortable when they talk about others instead of themselves. This fact rings particularly true when it comes to praise, because people can more easily extol the virtues of others than of themselves. Trumpeting the talents of others presents an easy way to show that you go beyond wanting to help others, because you're making a positive impression for them. We call this the "Halo Strategy." The Halo Strategy encourages you to leverage others by exhibiting social generosity. Simply stated, if you make others look good, you look good, too. Like a halo, these partners stand close to you, but make you shine. That's the reasoning behind the Halo Strategy when it comes to forming an Impressive First Impression.

Perhaps the most memorable use of the Halo Strategy (although not for professional purposes) occurred in the movie *Top Gun*, where the character Maverick (played by Tom Cruise) wants to meet an alluring woman at a bar. Rather than "crash and burn" by approaching her solo, he enlists the aid of his wingman "Goose" (played by Anthony Edwards). They sing a duet to her and virtually the whole bar joins in on the song. This introduction by Maverick escalated from one wingman to a bar full of wingmen. They all make Maverick shine, while elevating the mood of the entire room. A win-win scenario, where both make an Impressive First Impression. (Unfortunately, Maverick "crashes and burns" in his follow-through impression, but that's another story.)

How does this dating scenario relate to a professional one? The pair supported each other to meet someone new. They may have held romantic motives, but if you keep in mind that you can partner with your trusted friend and colleague to meet people in a professional context, then you can apply their tactic to your own situation. Will, a colleague of ours, took to heart our Halo Strategy at a reception. Within minutes after arriving at this event, he accidentally spilled red wine on his nice white shirt and tie. With a gracious sense of humor, he met Ophelia, a nice young lady whose company he enjoyed. He got to know her and discovered that she loved cooking and exploring fusion recipes. The conversation shifted to how these cooking preferences reflected her passion for her work and exploring new, innovative concepts in her office. Will knew he had a glaring wine stain on his shirt and tie, so he jokingly told her that he really loved trying new wines and thought he'd give his shirt a taste, too. She laughed, thus starting their new friendship.

Will explained our so-called Halo Strategy and asked her to join him in meeting new people. As an explorer, she instantly caught on and they met and engaged in lively discussions with multiple people that night. Will lauded Ophelia's willingness to explore and this served as a reason for meeting new people. Ophelia transformed Will's love of wine into a topic of conversation, while Will chimed in that he loved wine so much that he wore it on his shirt! Will transformed the stain into a chance to meet a new Halo and implement the strategy. He served as Ophelia's halo and she served as his. Thus, thinking about others and acts of social generosity can truly benefit both parties toward forming that Impressive First Impression.

DONNING THE HALO: APPLY IT PROFESSIONALLY

Now imagine if you were Will and that Ophelia was more than a recent acquaintance, but a good friend and colleague. That should make it easier to speak about her to new acquaintances. You can implement the Halo Strategy with ease if you consider the following steps:

1. **Attitude**: Keep in mind that the vast majority of us find it easier to talk about and praise others than ourselves. This attitude will enhance your success with all of the subsequent steps.

2. **Seek Trusted Partners**: One of the best ways to practice the Halo Strategy is to get to know a colleague or friend with whom you go to networking events. Make sure you know and trust her. You both should also have some alignment with adding value to your organization, team, or just each other. Paramount to this relationship is trust—trust that your partner will make you shine and that you'll make her shine.

3. **Communicate Common Cause**: If you both attend an event for a particular purpose, such as to represent your company or meet others within your own organization, make sure that you both clearly communicate what you want to share before the event. This way, you can align what you're both stating. For example, do you want to show how your organization values telecommuting? If so, then talk to your partner beforehand about the different telecommuting benefits in your organization, as well as how the management looks favorably upon that practice. Does your organization pride itself on innovation? Then you can both plan key talking points about how your organization encourages this type of thinking and what they do to reward it.

4. **Praise Produces Halos**: Even better, if you want to mutually elevate the status of your organization, or at least each other, this strategy is for you. Talk about how telecommuting has allowed you to save gas and the environment, while attracting top talent. If you focus on innovation, then make sure to comment about how innovation leads to new product pipelines at your organization or how it allows employees there to use it as an outlet for their creativity. You are like public relations agents in a sense, so believe in what you do, believe in your halo, and you can believably speak about each other or your organization. Either way, view it as an act of generosity and it will result in a win-win for everyone involved in the conversation.

5. **Spontaneous Scripting**: Next, come up with some talking points for each other, but try not to sound too "canned" when introducing each

other to other people. These points should reflect their positive
behaviors or a praiseworthy part of their character. Again, this comes
from having a great relationship with your halo that you've truly
developed. We call this Spontaneous Scripting, because it partly
comes from preparation, but mostly comes from what you feel at that
moment—it comes from the heart. These thoughts should primarily
come from what you truly believe and feel about your trusted
partner. Thoughts that come from your sincere belief in the other
person will add that extra, spontaneous tone of passion in your voice,
nuances in your praise, and desire to help your partner. When you
meet others at a mixer or meeting, you can talk about them and
introduce them to a person you've newly met. You can praise one or
two of your partner's good qualities (from your prepared talking
points). Give concrete examples to accompany the praise, which
makes it easier to understand why you admire your partner. Most
important, the part that comes from the heart makes this truly
spontaneous and warm.

The upshot? Implementing this halo strategy makes you look good
and feel proud, because you speak highly of others rather than talking
about yourself. Plus, it's often easier to speak about others than about
ourselves anyway. This builds confidence, positions your halo in a
favorable way and creates a great mood with those you've just met.
This action establishes a halo effect that makes you seem like a positive person who builds great relationships. Now isn't that an Impressive First Impression?

Think about it in reverse. If a person you've just met negatively gos-
sips about someone else that isn't present, would you trust this new
acquaintance? What if they gossip about you next? If instead,
you proudly use the Halo Strategy, it will benefit all involved.

If you don't have a Halo buddy yet, who should you partner with?
When choosing a partner, mix it up! Try to network with someone of
a different background, because it can add diverse perspectives to
conversations. Also, pair and surround yourself with people of high
quality and caliber, as they will create a halo effect for you. Again, if
they look good, you look good by association. Go beyond "if you
don't have anything nice to say, don't say it at all." Take the initiative
and say something nice about someone. Be a halo and the halo effect
will shine in crafting a mutual impressive impression.

The three keys to perfecting the Halo Strategy are practice, more
practice, and even more practice. We've met a number of people
who love the strategy, but had a difficult time actually implementing

it in mock scenarios. Practice the Halo Strategy and over time you'll develop a chemistry that will allow you to effectively praise one another without going over the top. Once you develop that chemistry and skill, it will become second nature. We truly encourage this as another act of social generosity with a potential payoff.

NOTES

1. Cindy Sutter, "Food for Thought: Boulder's Institute for the Psychology of Eating Wants You to Think Differently about What You Eat" *Your Daily Camera Online* (23 February 2003), http://www.dailycamera.com/news/2009/feb/23/Boulder-Institute-for-the-Psychology-of-Eating (Accessed June 13, 2009).

2. Eric Abrahamson and David H. Freedman, *A Perfect Mess: The Hidden Benefits of Disorder* (New York: Little, Brown and Company, 2006).

3. Kate Lorenz. "Is a Messier Desk Better?" *CareerBuilder.com* (24 September 2007), http://www.careerbuilder.com/Article/CB-646-The-Workplace-Is-a-Messier-Desk-Better/?ArticleID=646&cbRecursionCnt=1&cbsid=720eac70a7814d348a18f09772251d22-302820270-wb-6&ns_siteid=ns_us_g_PsyMax_Solutions_orga_ (Accessed on October 20, 2008).

Chapter 11

Virtual Impressions

IMPRESSIVE VIRTUAL IMPRESSIONS

With the technological advances of our time, it grows increasingly critical to make an Impressive First Impression before even meeting someone. With the proliferation of telecommunication, we now communicate virtually more than ever, making our virtual impression more important than ever. This can occur as a result of intentional virtual communication such as phone calls, faxes, e-mails, instant messages, and texts. It can also happen unintentionally via social networking sites like Facebook and LinkedIn, and search engines like Google.

A recent case study in the *Harvard Business Review* entitled "We Googled You" addressed this very issue.[1] A firm's vice president of human resources red-flagged a very qualified interviewee because of a Google search. Why? According to page 9 of the search engine's results, the candidate served as the leader of a nonviolent but vocal protest group shortly after college. It gets even more serious. A few more clicks through this link revealed a picture of this candidate protesting outside of China's San Francisco consulate. Because the firm wanted someone to head its company's flagship store in Shanghai, the company internally expressed hesitation toward hiring this strong candidate because of her Google search results.

In light of this study, an important question to ask yourself is: "How appropriately (or inappropriately) do you portray yourself on the Internet?" This proves very critical when looking for a job as well as dealing with colleagues and clients. More than a quarter of hiring managers use Internet search engines and more than 10 percent use social networking sites to research potential employees. So, those pictures you posted on your Facebook account showing you taking shots of tequila at your friend's birthday party could land you in trouble. Complaining about how much you hate your job on your blog could lead to the loss of that very job. Wisdom suggests that you avoid complaining about work in general, yet some throw wisdom out the window. Even if you've already landed a job, be aware of how you present yourself on the World Wide Web. As the name states, it's worldwide! You never know who may Google you.

Virtual impressions apply to more than the impression you make on the Internet. These impressions can even impact in-person meetings. Virtual also comes in the form of paper. For instance, when someone sees your résumé, they instantly form a virtual impression. Studies have shown that people display prejudice against certain ethnic-sounding names when viewing a résumé. They form judgments prior to even meeting the person. Your grammar, style, and spelling all contribute to this impression. Virtual impressions also entail the impressions you make in phone conversations, fax messages, and texting. Because virtual communication has become more common in recent years, virtual impressions have yet to be discussed in most first impression literature. We hope that you gain some valuable insight from this groundbreaking take on first impressions.

VIRTUAL ETIQUETTE AND THE GOLDEN RULE

Before delving into the details and nuances of virtual impressions and virtual etiquette, we provide you with a single tool that works as their foundation. It's one of the greatest tools of all time: the Golden Rule. Like gold, the rule shines and endures because it works. It basically advises, "treat others as you would want them to treat you." This rule exists across many cultures and time periods. It spans religions across continents and in writings that people continue to read now. This rule is actually a tool that will guide you through the workplace—both physical and virtual—and help to catapult you in your career. It will help you build those lasting relationships, gain that stellar reputation, and create that amazing first impression. Now we raise the bar with the Platinum Rule, which states, "treat others as they want to be treated." This rule takes even more effort as you should more carefully contemplate what others may want. Think of it as bartering: you give others what they want and they may give you what you want.

How do you apply these rules (and tools) in your daily work? If the Golden and Platinum Rules serve as major philosophies and ways of life, then virtual etiquette functions as their means of day-to-day implementation. To some, "virtual etiquette" may sound like a bunch of frumpy rules that stifles people from being free to behave how they truly want when communicating electronically. But take virtual etiquette seriously, as it can help improve, and even save, your career.

Take a common work scenario where virtual etiquette, as well as the Golden and Platinum Rules, applies. When a person sends text messages during a boring presentation where he feels he's not learning much, how can the Golden Rule apply? Let's think about why the texter texts and how this impacts others. The texter may feel that he can get more work done by tending to messages rather than "wasting" his time listening to a speaker that may add little or no value. Well, value becomes a moot point, because the texter didn't even pay further attention to that speaker. Even if the speaker only made one valuable point, it could have occurred during the text messaging, but either way, the texter won't know. The texter dismisses the speaker and the speaker feels dismissed by the texter. The other audience members either may perceive the texter as rude or question whether the speaker is indeed truly boring. This results in a lose-lose scenario. These impacts can have unnecessarily negative consequences. The sender of text messages should be courteous enough to know that he may have to attend an important meeting where he can't reply immediately. If people employ the Golden and Platinum Rules and respect one another in this scenario, they can prevent many misunderstandings and negative consequences.

More so, following etiquette leads to efficiency. As two people follow the same rules of etiquette, they prevent the time and emotional frustrations that result from miscommunication. Even without the emotional aspects, it takes time to sort through the different actions and perceptions that result when two people each follow different sets of rules. If you think about etiquette as a means of efficiency and time savings, it's no wonder we have so many processes, protocols, and guidelines at work. They do save time and increase productivity if people all follow them. That's a big if, since people often view themselves as the exception to the rule.

Speaking of exceptions, of course, you could receive an emergency message, but that can come at any time. Does it take many long minutes to scan our smart phones for emergency messages? We're not advocating that you never check messages during interactions, but rather ask you to think about how you want to be treated by others and do the same. The texter could quickly scan e-mail or texts messages for a brief few seconds to catch emergencies. Even then, does the texter need to do this more than a couple of times an hour? How many emergencies happen to a person on a daily, let alone hourly, basis? If absolutely necessary during a true emergency, texters can excuse themselves and leave the room and really take care of the situation. Virtual etiquette, as well as the Golden and Platinum Rules, means thinking about others, which can lead to a win-win.

Virtual etiquette actually has a larger function and isn't just a set of frumpy rules. The age-old Golden and Platinum Rules underpin virtual etiquette, so if you want others to engage and respect you, you should first engage and respect them. Even if they don't require this of you, life would be easier if people interacted with this rule in mind.

The advice that follows will help you with nuts-and-bolts of how to apply the Golden and Platinum Rules via virtual etiquette. Apply them to create a stellar virtual impression. We divide this chapter into common professional environments, meetings, and messages, where they will boost your development most.

TELEPHONE

Phone Messages

Some people intend ironic, deadpan, and sarcastic messages to elicit humor in others. Other people can easily misinterpret these messages. They may miss the nuances of your humor and irony. They may also miss qualifiers. What are qualifiers? Here's a simple example: When someone says, "I think you're a nice person, but...," all people hear is what comes after the "but." When we hear on a date, "I think you're a nice person, but..." Most of us only hear the negative that we think will follow the "but." These qualifiers won't save you at all times. Unfortunately, we can't get others to appreciate your humor and savvy message nuances at all times, but we do include tactics for improving messages, and how they function, in the workplace. These tactics will help you succeed in your professional life and improve your virtual impression.

Phone Impressions: Treat Phone Calls Like In-Person Meetings

Even though you might think you're the politest person in the world, keep in mind that sometimes people's etiquette goes flying out the door when talking on the phone. And given that over two-thirds of business professionals engage in some form of virtual work, chances are you'll have to engage your colleagues over the phone, not to mention you're probably already communicating with your clients via phone on a regular basis. Remember, they can read telltale signs about you through a variety of factors, such as your voice. They can hear the tone, gauge the speed, note the pitch, and observe the volume of your voice. Just because the other person can't see us doesn't mean he can't hear the distractions in the background or sense that we're not engaged in the conversation. The best way to talk on the phone is to pretend that you're at an in-person meeting with the other person.

What does this mean? You should avoid the following while on the phone: talking to other people, eating, heating something up in the microwave, washing your hands, using the restroom, doing other work, etc. Yes, people do use their cell phones in the restroom, and a majority of Americans used to think this was perfectly fine! In a survey released by Let's Talk, in 2003, 62 percent of respondents said it was fine to use the cell phone in the bathroom.[2] That shocked us too, but it obviously doesn't shock most people. At least progress prevails: In 2006, this figure dropped down to 38 percent, so we recommend that you listen to the wise opinion of the majority and keep your cell phones away from the bathroom.[3]

These seemingly minor mistakes will dramatically destroy any impressive virtual impression you want to project. Make sure that you focus on the call. Would you talk to someone in person that you're trying to impress while engaging in these other activities? Then why would you behave in these inappropriate ways when the person can't see you? Even if you focus on the call, but convey seriously negative tones in your voice, listeners will surely pick up on these cues.

If you want to take this one step further, you can even dress for your call. This may help your positive physical impression translate to your virtual impression. Some people find that they take calls much more seriously if they're dressed in a suit when they take a call. Think about how this works in person. When you, or someone you know, dons formal wear, ever notice how they behave more formally as well? They pay more close attention to the details of their movements, so as to not stain their nice outfit. Likewise, you'll pay more attention to these nuances when you dress more formally for calls. You need not wear a suit, but at least ponder the possibility of ditching your pajamas (or better, put on pajamas if you take calls in your underwear . . .). Even if you don't want to wear a suit, be sure to wear a smile across your face. People can hear smiles, which is critical to carrying a positive tone throughout the conversation. You can also stand up and move around while conversing, so that others can hear energy in your voice. For the most part, people enjoy talking to others who sound friendly and energetic during a phone conversation.

Conference Calls

Seventy percent of all virtual teams have used audio conferencing to communicate with other team members.[4] Ever been on a ten-person conference call and couldn't tell who was saying what? That's probably because the person didn't state his name before speaking. Save others the headache and don't make the same mistake. Identify yourself. If no one else is doing it, start a trend! Or you could just opt to get lost among the other voices if you don't want to take that risk. Forming that virtual impression means that they can't see you, as they could during an in-person meeting, so you'll need to identify yourself to stand out from the crowd.

Speaking of headaches, have you ever sat in on a very long conference call where one individual decides to babble on and on for what seems like forever? (On what, you don't quite remember, because you zoned out after the first five minutes of his yapping.) If you have, you may have pressed mute so that you can carry on a side conversation or get a little work done without being detected by the other conference call participants. If you choose to do this, make sure the mute button works. And as tempting as it is to bad-mouth the soliloquist, don't. If for some reason you're not muted, your comment will be heard by all. How embarrassing would *that* be? Employ some virtual etiquette and keep negative thoughts to yourself. Honestly, would it help you to speak negatively of a person in a sidebar conversation when they're present? You would probably look like a real jerk. Why would you create that virtual impression of yourself on the phone?

Last, try to avoid using speakerphones because they have an impersonal touch. If you were put on speakerphone during a conversation, you might be hesitant to say certain things because you don't know who could be listening. If you do need to use the speakerphone during a conference call, make sure you ask the other party's permission to put them on speakerphone and be sure to identify everyone in the room with you. Take special precautions while using the speakerphone. You're basically broadcasting a loud conversation, so make sure that others around can't hear. Your call will suddenly morph to one of public knowledge and will disrupt your office neighbors as well. Also, it's tough for two people to speak at once on a speaker-phone, so it's easy for you to accidentally cut off the other speaker when you're simply just saying "Okay" or "I agree." Also, road noise or other background ambient noise from one caller can drown out the other speaker's words. Engaging in a speakerphone conversation can help you access other materials, so this type of conversation certainly adds value in certain cases—just use it judiciously.

Virtually Prepare Yourself

Preparing yourself for phone calls is just as important as preparing for in-person meetings. And here's the added advantage—you can have all of your materials sprawled out in front of you *and* multiple documents open on your computer. Since other callers can't see you, this presents one advantage of speaking via phone. You can look more polished and prepared because your materials can support you readily, which creates one major advantage in a virtual impression. In addition to having your documents, you can prepare the following:

Tip No. 1: Prepare any questions you need to have answered. Also, make sure you have pen and paper (or a computer to type notes on), your calendar for setting appointments, and other information from previous contact with the person on the other line. You'll project a virtual impression of an organized person.

Even before you go through all this preparation for the phone call, ask yourself this question: Do you really need to call someone for this information or can you look it up yourself? Before picking up the phone to ask a basic question, try to find your answers elsewhere. When you do make the call, know exactly what you want and how you're going to ask for it.

Tip No. 2: Script your message and rehearse it out loud. This may sound ridiculous to you, but it'll help ensure a smooth conversation and strong virtual impression. You can draft key speaking points, so you sound prepared, poised, and orderly.

When you finally make the call, make it easy for the other person to remember who you are so she isn't spending five minutes flipping through her mental Rolodex trying to recall who you are. State your name, the name of your company, and how you met. Then, go into your conversation.

Overall, the phone allows you more flexibility and benefits in crafting your virtual impression than if you met in-person. Many people do not leverage this to their advantage, so employ these strategies to boost how others perceive you.

How to Get Your Calls Answered

Everyone's busy and sometimes it's difficult for people to take calls. According to an AT&T study, 75 percent of all business calls are not completed on the first attempt.[5] Use some of the following tips to help you become part of the 25 percent that get their calls answered the first time. When you meet someone while networking, ask him if it would be alright if you followed up with him. Find out if he prefers phone calls to other means of communication as well as if he has preferred days/times to take calls. You can also ask for the name of his assistant. That way, you'll either get a hold of him directly or at least you increase the chance that your message will get to him.

Here's another tip to make your life easier. Ever get cut off during a phone conversation and then you both try to call each other back immediately only to reach each other's voicemail over and over again? It just never ends! Think of it as if two people kept physically bumping into each other and interrupting each other when trying to talk. Well, here's an easy way to stop the madness. Create communication protocol with your friends and colleagues. Whoever initiated the last call should call the other person back. That way, you won't both end up spending five minutes playing phone tag. Virtual etiquette indeed can lead to efficiency that prevents voicemail limbo from trapping both callers.

How to Receive Calls

When the phone rings, what should you do? Answer it, of course! But, before you pick up, make sure you're prepared to take the call and make a strong virtual impression. Try not to take the call if someone's in your office, unless it's urgent. If you don't have any major distractions (like another person) in your office and have pen and paper in hand, then you're ready to take the call.

Answer incoming calls by the third ring and identify yourself by first and last name. Make sure you write down the other person's name and jot down some notes while you're at it. If you weren't able to pick up the phone and the other person left a message in your voicemail, try to return the call within 24 hours. There's no hard and fast rule for this, but a little common courtesy can go a long way.

A note on holds. Before putting the other person on hold, ask him if he's able to do so. And do him a favor; don't leave him on hold for more than a minute. When you return, make sure you thank him for waiting. If you stood in front of that person physically, imagine how rude your would look if you kept him waiting for a long period of time. Your virtual impression works in a similar way.

Voicemail Greetings

Does it annoy you when you get a generic automated voicemail greeting and you have no idea if you're leaving a message for the person you're trying to reach? So does everyone else. Don't get caught with a nondescript voicemail greeting. Create a strong virtual impression with a personalized greeting today!

How can you do this? Simple. Include your name, title, and company name in your message so people can know for sure that they're leaving a voicemail with the right person. And make sure it's current. If you're going out of town, say so, and let others know when you'll be back. Let them know how to contact you in case of an emergency or, if you're vacationing on a remote desert island and have no access to any form of technology, whom to contact in your absence. Fifty-eight percent of adults believe that voicemail makes life easier, so make life easier for everyone so they know how to reach you.[6]

A personalized greeting should be just that . . . *personalized*. Do it yourself. Having someone else record a greeting for you makes it seem like you're "too good" to leave your own greetings. If you're nervous, script out your message before you record it. When you finally do record it, make sure you speak slowly and spell out unusual words. Personalized greetings mean you care.

Leaving Voicemail Messages

First of all, if you get someone's voicemail, don't be afraid to leave a message. It's pretty standard for people to leave messages, as research shows that nearly 60 percent of people prefer leaving voicemail messages to messages with administrative assistants and receptionists, and 78 percent of people prefer leaving voicemail messages over waiting for an operator or calling back later.[7] Besides, 40 percent of workers check their voicemail messages when they're not working so you may hear back from the person you're trying to contact even if he or she isn't working at the time.[8]

When leaving messages, keep them short and sweet. We once had an intern who left a five-minute message about why she couldn't attend a meeting. Truth is, no one wants to be accosted by your life story when he's innocently checking his voicemails. Try to keep your voicemail message under 30 seconds without talking too fast. Mention the following: your name, phone number and/or e-mail address, who referred you, the purpose of your call, the best way/time to reach you, and your name and phone number (again). Piece of cake. This way, you'll leave not only a great message but also the virtual impression of a crisp, polished, and efficient person.

TECHNOLOGY DURING IN-PERSON MEETINGS

Although we focus on how technology can leave a virtual impression, we haven't yet addressed how technology can affect in-person meetings. This brief section allows us to cross technology with physical meetings. As you're trying to manage your virtual impression, you may start to harm your physical impression. Even if you're attending a low-tech, in-person meeting, technology can still play a major role in this presentation or conversation. Here's some advice to help you leverage technology while keeping its distractions to a minimum.

Tip No. 1: Wear a watch, even if you have a mobile phone. Really, this simple piece of "old-school" technology can work wonders. Let's assume that you have two identical clones, but one person wears a watch and one doesn't. All things being equal, think about how others perceive the watch wearer—generally as more punctual and aware of time. Given that there's an advantage with this perception, there's virtually no downside to wearing a watch.

You may ask "Why even wear a watch when my mobile phone already has a clock?" You certainly can pull out your mobile phone from your pocket or bag under the table, but how does that look? People may think that you're being rude and checking your messages during the meeting. Further, what if you're sitting at a meeting in a room without a clock and need to watch your time so that you can finish punctually? You can ask others the time, but that makes you appear unprepared and lacking a time piece. As you rely on technology and how it relates to your virtual impression, don't discount how reliance on it can erode the quality of your physical impression.

Okay, so you say that you can leave your phone on the table to tell the time, well this leads to why we have Tip No. 2.

Tip No. 2: Keep your mobile device off the table. If a message appears, the phone will either vibrate or flash. As this distracts you or others, it shows a lack of courtesy for the person speaking.

To prevent any kind of mobile phone distraction, turn it off or silence it during the duration of the meeting. If you've sat in on any meetings recently, it's highly likely that some sort of electronic device has disrupted the flow of conversation. A recent study found that 91 percent of people regularly encounter public displays of insensitivity caused by personal digital assistants.[9] There are 3.5 billion mobile phones circulating the world today.[10] Imagine if even an extremely small percentage of phones went off during meetings. That's a lot of wasted time. So, avoid texting, instant messaging, checking e-mails, or browsing the Internet on your handy device while others are talking. You wouldn't want others instant messaging their friends while you're holding the floor, would you? Of course, there may be those occasional instances in which you're expecting a very important call during your meeting. What should you do then?

Tip No. 3: Before the meeting even starts, let everyone know that you must take an important call during the meeting. That way, when your phone vibrates and you have to step out to take the call, you don't appear rude to others.

These tools for using technology during a physical meeting will help with your impression, so that you avoid losing sight of your physical impression.

FAXING 101

Always use a cover page. Your cover page is your virtual impression when it comes to faxes. This may sound pretty elementary, but you'd be surprised by the number of faxes people send out that don't include cover pages. Plus, it helps to prevent people from receiving mistaken faxes. Like a cover letter, it shows what the fax pages entail and why you've sent them. Plus, your company logo will appear on the fax cover sheet, so this helps increase the value of your brand. Here's a quick checklist of things you should have on a clear, preprinted page:

- Your name
- Your contact number

- Number of pages being sent, including cover sheet
- Name of intended recipient
- Fax number of intended recipient
- Message with clear instructions on how you want the recipient to respond

Fax Etiquette: Follow-Up

If you don't fully trust modern technology, chances are you stand by the fax machine until it beeps that your fax has been sent. But even then, you're still not 100 percent sure that your fax went through and into the right hands. Yes, virtual impressions can disappear into a black hole, whereas physical ones won't. Still, if that's the case, it's appropriate to call the intended recipient before or after you've sent the fax. Call beforehand if you're sending confidential or potentially sensitive information so that he'll be ready. It's also a good idea to call after you've sent the fax to make sure the recipient received it, just in case everything didn't go through.

When Not to Use Fax

With the advent of e-mail, faxes may not necessarily be the best way to transmit messages. And for those of us who hate the loud-pitch beeping noises of fax machines, this may come as a relief. You may want to use e-mail, phone calls, or even "snail mail" instead of faxes when:

- You have tons of information to send. Try using e-mail, overnight mail, or U.S. mail instead. Avoid wasting others' paper and toner ink. Remember that they pay for this transmission more than you do. If you choose to ignore this, then congratulations, you've created a very negative virtual impression.
- You need confirmation that the recipient received the message or you need written record of the communication. E-mail keeps records of this.
- You want the message forwarded to others. E-mail allows for this function.
- You're sending sensitive or confidential information. Phone calls leave less trace of the communication.
- You want to send something in the middle of the night. If someone has a home office, they will not want the fax machine screeching at three in the morning.

- You want to send a thank-you card or congratulatory note. If you want to send a card, send one via mail. Don't fax it. Faxing in this case establishes a virtual impression that you're rushed, sloppy, or impersonal.

THE INTERNET

It can be your friend. It can be your enemy. A "frienemy," if you will. It's the Internet. If you're like most people, you probably spend some time on the Internet for non-work-related activities while you're at work. Surveys found that 61 percent of workers do just that. "One-third of time spent online at work is not work related."[11] Internet misuse is a huge issue at the workplace, seeing as such activities are costing American corporations more than $85 billion annually in lost productivity.[12]

As you can imagine, companies aren't too thrilled about this. So, it's no surprise that a good number of them are monitoring web use and firing employees for Internet misuse. According to a survey by the American Management Association, over three-fourths of companies monitor employee Internet use and 26 percent of employers have fired workers for misusing the Internet at work.[13] What kind of Internet misuse can get you fired? Keep these statistics in mind—of the 30 percent of employees who were fired for Internet misuse, 84 percent downloaded, viewed, or uploaded inappropriate or offensive content; 48 percent was violated company policy; and 34 percent engaged in excessive personal use.[14] In this case, not abiding by basic virtual etiquette could cost someone his job.

Your Internet Impression

Even if you don't get caught or engage in any unethical acts, how you carry yourself online will determine the Internet impression that you make. As stated in the *Impressions Diamond Model*, the person receiving the message may not interpret your message as you intend. In fact, one study demonstrated that the impression a person receives from a sender's e-mail depends on that receiver's personality. E-mail messages, although static words on a page, will leave an impression. Like any other impression, it's subject to interpretation.

And what's more, it's difficult to tell how others perceive you online, because unlike a physical meeting, you typically can't read their body language. That said, prevent a negative virtual impression by watching your basics: diction, spelling, grammar, tone, punctuation, and word choice. Some people write in low-caps and this may lead others to judge these senders as having equally low standards of language use. Misspellings grow increasingly common as we write more and more quickly via e-mail and mobile messages. Try to use a spell checker when possible. Most of us rush so much that we forget that simple tool.

You can use emoticons to add emotions to your message. Still, emoticons could serve as a salvation, or simply stink, as a tool for your Internet impression. Emoticons convey a sender's facial expressions created by using combinations of certain symbols. They can add emotional value to your message or simply make it look childish. In a positive vein, research does corroborate the value of emoticons toward intensifying a message. Emoticons can even help express sarcasm.[15]

E-MAIL

E-mail Content

The cardinal rule of e-mail is to remember that it can potentially go very public very quickly. So, try to make an impressive virtual impression, especially when sending out communication that could potentially go out to a mass audience. Make an effort to sound professional in your e-mails, which means don't use e-mail as a forum to chastise or criticize someone. We don't condone negativity but if you really need to express your displeasure, do it over the phone or in-person. That way, there's no written record of the conversation. How else can you sound professional?

Tip No. 1: Keep your e-mails free of grammar, spelling, punctuation, and capitalization errors. As you've probably heard before, don't use all caps. And, you may not have heard this one as often, but use upper and lower case letters when writing. It looks like very childish if you don't.

Speaking of childish, because e-mail is a relatively casual forum, we often let ourselves go and carry an overly friendly tone when communicating with others. How can you avoid being too casual?

Tip No. 2: Be mindful of your expressions. Don't be sloppy with your words. It's yes, not yeah. You, not you guys. All right, not okey dokey. Humor and sarcasm may also not translate well via e-mail, so use them sparingly. Last, although we discussed the value of emoticons, don't overuse them. You can tell people in words that you're happy instead of drawing it out for them like this (=^_^=).

In addition to being formal, be informative.

Tip No. 3: Write clear and concise e-mails with a call to action at the end. To make your e-mail easier to read, try using bullets. If you're responding to an e-mail, be sure to respond to all of their questions. Bullets can make you look more organized and provide a checklist for your readers to follow.

The last tip is very important, but often not followed. You'd be surprised at the number of e-mails we receive where people just don't respond to all (or sometimes any) of the questions we asked in previous communiqué. By answering all questions the first time around, you don't waste time by forcing the recipient and yourself to engage in another round of follow-ups. You can answer all questions and still be concise about it. Make your e-mails short and sweet, but don't forget your manners either.

Tip No. 4: Be polite. Use appropriate salutations, and write "please" and "thank you" even on the shortest of e-mails.

The moral of this section is to be wise about e-mail usage. A quarter of the companies surveyed by the American Management Association terminated employees for e-mail misuse. Basically, don't do anything that will get you fired.

E-mail Nuances

As we all know, e-mail involves more than just the text you type into the white box on your screen. It entails subject headings, copies, replies, flags, attachments, and all the works. Here's a little cheat sheet to make sure you know how to use all of them properly.

- **Subject Heading**. Give the reader a reason to read your e-mail. Be concise but informative, even in your subject heading. Sometimes you can communicate the entire message in the heading.

- **Copies**. Use CC if everyone on the list knows everyone else. Use BCC if you're sending an e-mail to a large group and they don't want their names broadcast over e-mail. That's basically the only time you should use BCC, though. Typically, if you're sending a pertinent e-mail to a few people, they have a right to know who else is receiving the message. Don't send an e-mail to an individual recipient and BCC others. This act is tantamount to online gossiping. Would you want to be viewed as a virtual gossiper?

- **Replies**. Hit reply to all only if *everyone* on the list needs to hear your reply. If not, just reply to the sender and anyone else who needs to know the information. In one case, someone hit "reply to all" on a message. An annoyed recipient responded to everyone by stating "please do not hit 'reply to all' when it should be sent privately." A third person responded to the annoyed sender, "You hit 'reply to all' yourself, so please practice what you preach." This exchange led to several more group exchanges and escalated out of control to the point where the original sender had to step in and resolve the conflict.

- **High Importance Flags.** Use these only when necessary. If you flag everything as important, you'll be the boy who cried "important" and no one will believe you anymore. And remember . . . just because you consider something important doesn't mean the person on the receiving end will.

- **Attachments.** Know what you're sending. It's pretty annoying when you get two e-mails because someone forgot to add the attachment the first time. Make sure you add the attachment and, more importantly, make sure you're sending the *correct* attachment. For a really large file, give the other person a heads up before you e-mail it.

Realities of E-mail

The recipients of your e-mail may be so busy that they may not respond right away. With a flood of e-mails overwhelming many of us, it sometimes takes longer to respond. Don't expect an answer right away. Sending your message several times in one week will not necessarily guarantee you a timely response, but it will likely annoy the recipient. If you want to increase the chances of someone reading your email, give the recipient a call.

While we're on the subject of answering e-mails, try to respond to incoming e-mails within 24 to 48 hours. This will give you good e-mail karma, and hopefully others will send you replies within the same time frame. If you're unable to answer e-mails, set up an out-of-office auto-reply but be sure to take it down as soon as you're back in the office.

Remember, e-mail functions as an impersonal form of communication, so don't use it as the sole means of communicating with others. Twenty percent of workers use e-mail specifically to avoid speaking with someone in person.[16] Don't be part of that petty 20 percent. If someone sits ten feet away from you, try talking to him (gasp) in person rather than sending him many e-mails a day. More so, talking face-to-face helps us bond through body language and talking about non-business topics. We seldom send private messages or too much detail about our personal lives via e-mail, particularly company e-mail that can get us in trouble. Although creating a virtual impression can serve a great value, don't substitute it for personalized, physical communication.

E-mail Names

Create an e-mail address that represents who you are. It's best if you embed your name into your e-mail address for lack of confusion. If you already have a set e-mail address that doesn't include your name, try setting up your account so that the receiver can see your name.

If you already have a set e-mail address that includes the following characteristics, though, you might want to consider changing it:

- **Anything blatantly vulgar or inappropriate,** because it gives insight to an aspect of your personality that you may not immediately want to share with others. BigDaddy696699@yahoo.com is not an appropriate e-mail address.

- **Anything that may be misconstrued as vulgar or inappropriate.** Just because you absolutely love your energetic cat doesn't mean that your e-mail address should be xoxofeistyfelinexoxo@hotmail.com.

- **Combined personal and professional e-mail addresses.** If you must keep your xxbustybombshellxx@gmail.com e-mail address, then make sure that you use it for personal reasons *only*.

- **References to sexual orientation, religion, race, cultural acronyms, or neighborhood.** AZNricerider5@aol.com isn't work-appropriate.

People and organizations judge others based on their ability to wield this powerful communication tool. The virtual impression professionals convey with e-mails, both in name and content, affect how others treat you. An e-mail often serves as the equivalent of one's name and association. E-mail is usually the first, if not only, form of virtual contact that you have with others. In other words, your e-mail address is your virtual first impression. People will judge you on this even before they've met you.

One of our colleagues learned the significance of appropriate e-mail addresses firsthand while trying to communicate with one of her advisors. Though she did not intend to offend anyone, her e-mail address was misconstrued as inappropriate and her advisor did not respond to her messages. After not hearing back from him for a couple of weeks, she had a chance to talk to him in person. It was only then that she found out that her advisor had indeed received her messages, but had deleted them thinking they were inappropriate solicitations. This misunderstanding wasted time for both individuals and temporarily strained their relationship. Though things improved with her advisor over time, our colleague learned her lesson. Based on this experience, she immediately changed her e-mail address to the basics—her first initial and last name. Since then, she hasn't had many problems receiving responses to her e-mails.

Be smart about e-mail. Research shows that roughly 25 to 40 percent of North American firms monitor employee e-mail in some capacity.[17] Don't use your current work e-mail address to apply for jobs. And if you want people to know who you are beyond an e-mail address, create an e-mail signature that includes your name, title, company name, and alternative ways of contacting you.

TITLES

The titles you use to identify yourself can prove just as powerful as your e-mail address—both virtually and in person. Many individuals include their titles in their e-mail signatures, and give out business cards with their titles on them at networking events. The few letters that reflect your educational background (i.e., MD, JD, PhD) or the few words that demonstrate what you do (i.e., Chief Financial Officer, Executive Vice President) can carry and convey a lot of power. Anecdotally, many authors state that statistics presented by an individual with a doctoral degree often carry more weight with an audience than those same facts presented by a "layperson." Wield titles as a powerful tool to make an impactful first impression.

Titles come in all shapes and sizes, and each individual can have a multitude of titles. Even though you're only one person, you can be a father, brother, Ivy League graduate, PhD, Executive Vice President, supervisor, employee, board member of a nonprofit organization, and active community volunteer. We all wear different hats, both in the professional world as well as in our personal lives. Some of our greatest accomplishments are evident in our professional and educational titles, and these accolades may have taken years to achieve. Despite how proud we may be of our own achievements, here we present two rules of thumb about titles:

1. **Don't flaunt it.** You have every right to be proud of your PhD or the fact that your CEO recently promoted you. However, the entire world probably doesn't need to know these facts about you. It's one thing when your wife and best friend know about your accomplishments; it's another thing when you share this unsolicited information with your child's kindergarten teacher's cousin. You can

write it on your business card, but avoid overstating it, whether spoken or written, during interactions.

2. **Respect it.** If people did take the time to share this information with you, then respect it. If they have a PhD, call them "Dr." instead of by their first names, unless they tell you otherwise. If individuals are proud of their academic or professional accolades, don't fault them for it. Celebrate their accomplishment with them.

WORKING AND INSTANT MESSAGING—CAN THE TWO COEXIST?

Instant messaging (also known as IM-ing) poses certain issues. Over 43 million people use consumer instant messaging programs at work.[18] It's common practice at some companies and completely unacceptable at others. Know the rules at yours and act accordingly.

Even if your company allows you to use instant messaging programs at your desk, it isn't a carte blanche to do whatever you want online. Follow some basic rules of virtual etiquette. For instance, try not to instant message a colleague until you know that the recipient is at her desk. If you type something personal to the recipient while she isn't at her desk, her colleagues or boss might walk by and see the message. On the same token, don't leave your instant message program running at all hours of the day. You wouldn't want your friend inadvertently announcing the details of your recent breakup to your boss and colleagues while you're away from your desk.

When you're actually using instant messaging for work purposes, prioritize the messages you answer by gauging their importance and choosing whether or not to respond. And don't feign interest because that just wastes everyone's time. Address the issue as soon as possible, or just tell the other person that you can't respond immediately but will try to get to it later.

IM Etiquette

Do you find it rude when others bombard you with instant messages without taking the time to give a quick greeting first? Even if you don't take offense at this, some people find it pretty rude. So, make sure you start off your conversations with a friendly greeting. Your important news flash can wait two seconds for a quick "hello." Make others feel loved by making sure they don't feel ignored. Seventy-eight percent of instant messagers like the faster responses they get from IM-ing versus e-mail, so don't leave people hanging. If you're taking a while to respond to an inquiry, let them know that you're working on it so that they know you'll get back to them soon.

TEXTING

Text messaging has become an increasingly popular mode of communication. A study conducted in June 2008 showed that over 75 billion text messages are sent every month.[19] You can apply a lot of the basic rules of e-mailing etiquette can be applied to text messaging— keep your texts short and sweet, go easy on the emoticons and think before you send. But some of the rules change for text messaging. In reality, text messaging is not as widely accepted in the workplace as e-mailing, so you should keep your texting to a minimum. If you text too much, it looks like you're not doing your work and just playing with your phone. And because text messages link to your phone, make sure you keep your phone on vibrate or silent so that your colleagues don't have to hear you receive a text every five minutes.

People have begun to report interviewees who send thank-you notes via text messages. One interviewer commented on how wonderful one of the interviewees performed during their time together. This all came crashing down when the interviewee texted her minutes after their interview. She reacted unfavorably and was appalled because he used text abbreviations and didn't take the time to at least draft an e-mail thank-you note that could have contained more thoughtful and tailored comments. Texting generally belongs in a more casual relationship.

INTERNET SOCIAL NETWORKING

Social networking sites have boomed in recent years. With the growth of these sites comes a myriad of possibilities to meet and mingle with people. Geographic boundaries virtually melt in this world and you can connect with friends 24/7 in all types of groups. We present some advice for the adventurous, as well as some virtual etiquette for the online social networker.

Start with an interesting profile, since this serves as your public virtual impression. Go beyond answering the questions. You now hold at your fingertips opportunities to showcase your passion, flaunt your wit, and share with the world. Just parallel it with a billboard or magazine advertisement. With so many of these advertisements flooding our senses, we gravitate toward the catchiest and most exciting ones. Given today's media sensory overload, you only have a short time frame to draw in a reader, so showcase yourself in a creative but concise manner.

Read the profiles of others. You can learn a lot about others on these profiles, from their communication styles and personal preferences to their friends and groups. If you reach out to folks through this medium, make comments about the elements on their profiles. You can also get to know acquaintances better if you take the time to read their profile and then engage them about their interests. It's easy to write what you want on your profile, but it takes effort to get to know the many people you may have claimed as "friends" within your social network.

Join groups that express your interests, because this action can speak louder than words. Of course, more than making a statement about your preferences, a group can allow you to find others with common interests as well. This may make it easier to network than going to an event. People in groups automatically convey that they share common interests with you and you can sometimes further delve into their profiles or writings to see if there are even more common interests (if the profiles are public, that is).

Just be aware that others may view your involvement in these groups as an extension of you. Of course, you can't control what other group members state on that group page, so most will be forgiving enough to know that those groups do not necessarily reflect your true views. If you don't agree with the direction of that group, though, you can always leave.

Some people boast thousands of friends, which can show how vast your network stretches. If you dig a little deeper and ask some simple questions, those thousands of friends listed on your page may prove more liability than asset. For instance, some may wonder:

- Even if this person spends 5 minutes a week with their 3,000 friends, how can she possibly maintain meaningful relationships? Do they prioritize quantity over quality?
- How close is this person to his or her friends? Are these really friends or just mere acquaintances?
- Isn't this person just like a typical "name dropper" who claims to know everyone but knows no one well?

Avoid nagging and poking others excessively. Virtual nags aren't too much different from real ones. People can still get annoyed with too many of them, if these acts are unsolicited. One major difference:

you can't see how annoyed they may really be at you. In general, however, would you want an office colleague to nag or poke you in person? This would normally result in a sexual harassment filing. Even though this would probably not prove so online, avoid this anyway.

People frequently post messages on profiles rather than sending private messages. Everyone could know where you'll be at a particular time if you announce it that way. Does it help you if everyone in your network knows that you engaged in a particular activity? You may want to mask your whereabouts or actions from your colleagues, because it may impair your career if you don't. For instance, we have seen employees who post on their social networking profiles or state their current status *before* they've answered their boss' messages—and the time stamps on the profiles prove it! This is a sure way to receive a reprimand or warrant a potential firing. Worse, some complain about their job or supervisor with these wall or status updates. The consequences here go without saying.

BACK TO BASICS

Thanks to technological advancements, there are now hundreds of ways for us to communicate with one another without actually having to be in the same physical space as the other person. Such advances are particularly useful for international and mass communication. The benefits of telecommuting can be alluring, especially since it's always nice to work from home in one's pajamas. However, when considering the option of telecommuting, one should weigh its convenience against the potential opportunity costs. Though telecommuting may save you time and money by eliminating your commute, it will also reduce opportunities for you to directly network and interface with others in your company. If you think about it from a manager's perspective, all things being equal, should she promote the telecommuter that she never sees or someone that she regularly interacts with at the office? With the relationship and trust that she builds over time, she will likely view the in-person candidate more favorably than the telecommuter. A physical impression generally trumps a virtual one.

As one executive at a Fortune 100 company put it, "Never turn down an in-person meeting." Throughout the years and developments in technology, this executive consistently showed up for in-person meetings whenever possible. He attributes some of his success to these interactions, since they help him build strong networks and relationships.

We understand that sometimes virtual communication and tele-commuting can't be avoided. In those situations, we advise you to seriously consider virtual etiquette and the virtual impression you make. When you do have an opportunity to meet in person, though, we strongly suggest that you go with the "old-fashioned" route and meet with others directly. There's just something about in-person contact that we can't really replace with teleconferences, e-mail conversations, or any other type of virtual communication.

NOTES

1. Diane Coutu and others, "We Googled You" *Harvard Business Review* (1 June 2007), http://harvardbusinessonline.com/flatmm/ics/HBR InteractiveCaseStudy.pdf (Accessed June 12, 2009).

2. Let's Talk, "New Survey of American Wireless Phone Etiquette Says Bathroom Calls Now 'OK' " *Let'sTalk.com* (28 October 2003), http://www.letstalk.com/company/release_102803.htm (Accessed October 20, 2008)

3. Let's Talk, "Let's Talk Annual Cell Phone Etiquette Survey" *Let's Talk.com* (14 March 2006), http://www.letstalk.com/company/release_031406.htm (Accessed October 20, 2008).

4. WorldCom Incorporated, "MIA3.pdf" *Verizon Conferencing* (2001), https://e-meetings.verizonbusiness.com/meetingsinamerica/pdf/MIA3.pdf (Accessed October, 20, 2008).

5. "Google Answers: Voicemail Usage Stats" *Google Answers*,http:// answers.google.com/answers/threadview/id/144377.html (Accessed October 20, 2008).

6. Massachusetts Institute of Technology, *News: Press Releases* (21 January 2004), http://web.mit.edu/invent/n-pressreleases/n-press-04index.html (Accessed October 20, 2008).

7. "Google Answers: Voicemail Usage Stats" *Google Answers*, http://answers.google.com/answers/threadview/id/144377.html (Accessed October 20, 2008).

8. Andrew Gilman, *Managing the Trend toward Increasing Use of Electronic Messaging Tools* (June 1999), http://www.opengroup.org/comm/the_message/magazine/mmv5n3/managing.htm (Accessed October 20, 2008).

9. Rachel Zubek, "Six Ways to Deal with Digital Bad Manners" *CareerBuilder Jobs* (17 January 2008), http://www.careerbuilder.com/JobSeeker/careerbytes/CBArticle.aspx?articleID=702 (Accessed October 20, 2008).

10. MobileActive.org, *About MobileActive.org*, http://mobileactive.org/about (Accessed October 20, 2008).

11. Rachel Zubek, "What Do You Do When the Boss Isn't Looking?" *CareerBuilder Jobs* (6 June 2008), http://www.careerbuilder.com/

JobSeeker/careerbytes/CBArticle.aspx?articleID=866 (Accessed October 20, 2008); Websense Incorporated, *Key Internet Usage Statistics* (2003), http://www.3w.net/lan/internet-use-statistics.html (Accessed October 20, 2008).

12. Websense Incorporated, *Key Internet Usage Statistics* (2003), http://www.3w.net/lan/internet-use-statistics.html (Accessed October 20, 2008).

13. Rosemary Haefner, "Job Searching on Company Time?" *Career Builder.com Jobs* (24 September 2007), http://www.careerbuilder.com/JobSeeker/careerbytes/CBArticle.aspx?articleID=480 (Accessed October 20, 2008).

14. Rachel Zubek, "What Do You Do When the Boss Isn't Looking?" *CareerBuilder Jobs* (6 June 2008), http://www.careerbuilder.com/Job Seeker/careerbytes/CBArticle.aspx?articleID=866 (Accessed October 20, 2008)

15. Daantje Derks and others, "Emoticons and Online Message Interpretation" *Social Science Computer Review* 26, No. 3 (2008), 379–388.

16. Andrew Gilman, *Managing the Trend toward Increasing Use of Electronic Messaging Tools* (June 1999), http://www.opengroup.org/comm/the _message/magazine/mmv5n3/managing.htm (Accessed October 20, 2008)

17. Marc Saltzman, "Should You Monitor Employee E-Mail?" *Business Tech News*, http://technology.inc.com/managing/articles/200610/email monitoring.html (Accessed October 20, 2008)

18. Websense Incorporated, *Key Internet Usage Statistics* (2003), http://www.3w.net/lan/internet-use-statistics.html (Accessed October 20, 2008).

19. CellSigns Incorporated. *CellSigns—Company :: Mobile Statistics* (December 2006), http://www.cellsigns.com/industry.shtml (Accessed October 20, 2008)

Conclusion

We originally thought to end this book with the words: "You never get a second chance to make a first impression." This would definitely not do justice to our premise that first impressions reset and that you can leverage subsequent impressions to change the minds of others and even craft a personal brand. That said, how about several alternate conclusions to the book, since we do advocate for resetting our impressions and addressing different audiences. If a DVD can feature multiple alternate endings, then why can't a book contain conclusions for each audience?

Alternate Conclusion No. 1: For Our Past Participants and Supporters

Does the book live up to your expectations based on what you've seen when we've delivered our presentation to you live? We truly hope that this book complements the Impressive First Impression we made on you in-person. As you advance in this journey, realize that *Impressive First Impressions* really embodies a *framework, philosophy*, and *lifestyle*. The book presents all of these, from theoretical to practical. As those who have seen in-person and book impressions, you wield the ability to make truly transformative change. Change for more than yourselves—for others as well. Leverage what you've learned from our interactions with you, boost it with this book—and live Impressive First Impressions every day.

Alternate Conclusion No. 2: For Those New to Impressive First Impressions

Congratulations, you've made it to the last section of this book, which means that you can embark on the first step beyond these pages and practice Impressive First Impressions. If you've applied these learnings along the way, you know what we mean by how understanding and practicing Impressive First Impressions can change your career.

Alternate Conclusion No. 3: For the Skeptics

We hope you can see the link between the milliseconds it takes to form first impressions to the lifelong career benefits of attuning yourself to these initial impressions. As in the term "Embrace Your ACE," we hope that you do believe and embrace your audience. You're our audience, so we embrace you with this conclusion and hope that you embrace what this book offers, both philosophically and practically.

Alternate Conclusion No. 4: For Those Who Already Live Impressive First Impressions

You truly understand that you needed to complete this book, among many others, in your journey toward continuous improvement. You're the type who would read this book multiple times and digest different nuances each time. We aspire to reach your level, which fuels our drive to continually form an Impressive First Impression.

Alternate Conclusion No. 5: For the Ones Who Want a Concise and Poignant Conclusion, But Probably Don't Get One in Most Books

Don't just understand Impressive First Impressions—live them.

Acknowledgments

Creating an Impressive First Impression takes extensive diligence, discipline, and dedication. This book took much of the same, but more so, it took a significantly more important element: devotion from others. Words can only do some justice to their devotion, but these words are a start.

We extend our deep gratitude to Dr. Asad Madni, for writing our foreword with passion and precision. Our agent, Stan Wakefield, for being an awesome agent. Larry Harrington, who's supported us in so many different ways professionally. A hearty thanks to all of our staff and interns who helped us with the extensive research and editing processes of this book: Daniel Duan, Josephine Han, Kyle Herbertz, Seiko Holland, Amy Huang, Vivian June, Vu Nguyen, Kini Shyu, Ashley Sun, Irena Wang, and Petra Zavala.

We also sincerely appreciate the support of and thank the many client organizations and the thousands of individual participants who have attended our presentations and trainings. You breathe life and dynamism into this book.

From Lisa Miyake: Many thanks to my parents for always encouraging me to pursue my passions. And to Greg—thank you for all of your love and support.

From Vu H. Pham: To my loving wife, Siu, for giving me your heart. I can now say that this book truly has a "heart and soul." And to my parents, you are that and more—you're also my truest mentors. This book may be different from the one you thought I'd write, but I hope it's a lot better.

Bibliography

Abe, Namiko. "About Japanese Teeth." *About.com: Japanese Language* 16 July 2008. 3 June 2009 http://japanese.about.com/b/2008/07/16/about-japanese-teeth.htm.

"About Face Shape." *eHow* 3 June 2009 http://www.ehow.com/about_4565826_face-shape.html.

Abrahamson, Eric, and David H. Freedman. *A Perfect Mess: The Hidden Benefits of Disorder.* New York: Little, Brown and Company: 2006.

Accountemps. "Dressing the Part: Office Attire." *Careermag.com* 10 June 2009 http://www.careermag.com/articles/dressing-the-part-office-attire-1669-article.html.

American Society for Aesthetic Plastic Surgery. 2005. 4 June 2009 http://www.surgery.org/download/2005stats.pdf.

American Society for Aesthetic Plastic Surgery. "Cosmetic Plastic Surgery Statistics." *Plastic Surgery Research* 12 June 2009 http://www.cosmeticplasticsurgerystatistics.com/statistics.html.

Andrew, Kevin. "The Handshake." *Nonverbal Communication Web Project* 1 June 2009 http://soc302.tripod.com/soc_302rocks/id8.html.

Angier, Natalie. "Powerhouse of Senses, Smell, at Last Gets it Due." *The New York Times* 14 February 1995. 13 June 2009 http://www.nytimes.com/1995/02/14/science/powerhouse-of-senses-smell-at-last-gets-its-due.html.

Anitei, Stefan. "Why Attractive Faces are Symmetric and Gender Specific." *Softpedia* 7 May, 2008. 4 June 2009 http://news.softpedia.com/news/Why-Attractive-Faces-Are-Symmetric-and-Gender-Specific-84961.shtml.

Bar, Moshe, Maital Neta, and Heather Linz. "Very First Impressions." *Emotion* 6.2 (2006): 269–278.

Bareiss, Seth. "Tessellations." *Tessellations*. 9 June 2009 http://www.tessel
    lations.org.
"Beautiful Bangs for Your Face Shape, Part II: Square." *Bellasugar* 31 October
    2007. 3 June 2009 http://www.bellasugar.com/746894.
"Beauty and Makeup Tips." *Pioneer Thinking* 3 June 2009 http://www
    .pioneerthinking.com/rmt7.html.
Bixler, Susan, and Nancy Nix-Rice. *The New Professional Image: From
    Business Casual to the Ultimate Power Look*. Cincinnati: Adams
    Media, 1997.
Bragg, Shirley. "How to Look Taller." *About.com: Beauty* 8 June 2009
    http://beauty.about.com/cs/basics4men/a/howlooktaller.htm.
Bryner, Michelle. "Sports Psych." *Psychology Today* 1 September 2005.
    4 June 2009 http://www.psychologytoday.com/articles/pto-20050831
    -000017.html.
Byron, Kristin, and David C. Baldridge. "E-mail Recipients' Impressions
    of Senders' Likability: The Interactive Effect of Nonverbal Cues and
    Recipients' Personality." *Journal of Business Communication* 44.2 (2007):
    137–160.
Carey, Bjorn. "The Rules of Attraction in the Game of Love." *LiveScience*
    13 February 2006. 1 June 2009 http://www.livescience.com/health/
    060213_attraction_rules.html.
Casperson, Dana M. *Power Etiquette: What You Don't Know Can Kill
    Your Career*. New York: AMA Publications, 1999.
CellSigns Incorporated. *CellSigns—Company: Mobile Statistics* December
    2006. 20 October 2008 http://www.cellsigns.com/industry.shtml.
Chakrabarti, Bhismadev, and Simon Baron-Cohen. "The Biology of Mind
    Reading." *First Impressions*. Ed. Nalini Ambady and John J. Skowronski.
    New York: Guilford, 2008. 57–86.
"Chest Body Language." *Changingminds.org* 10 June 2009 http://
    changingminds.org/techniques/body/parts_body_language/chest_body
    _language.htm.
Collins, Anne. "How to Look Thinner Without Dieting!" 5 June 2009
    http://www.annecollins.com/leaner-shape-without-dieting.htm.
Coutu, Diane, and others. "We Googled You." *Harvard Business Review*
    1 June 2007. 12 June 2009 http://harvardbusinessonline.com/flatmm/
    ics/HBRInteractiveCaseStudy.pdf.
"Customer Service Helps Whiter Image Lead in Teeth Whitening Industry."
    Free Services for PR 28 October 2008. 12 June 2009 http://www
    .pr-inside.com/customer-service-helps-whiter-image-lead-r884701.htm.
Davis, Jeanie L. "Boxers vs. Briefs: Increasing Sperm Court." *WebMD* 2004.
    1 June 2009 http://www.webmd.com/infertility-and-reproduction/
    features/boxers-vs-briefs-increasing-sperm-count.
"Decade Profiles." Oracle ThinkQuest site 4 June 2009 http://library
    .thinkquest.org/19760/menudec.html.

Dellinger, Kirsten, and Christine L. Williams. "Makeup at Work: Negotiating Appearance Rules in the Workplace." *Gender and Society* 11.2 (1997):151–177.

Derks, Daantje, Arjan E. R. Bos, and Jasper Von Grumbkow. "Emoticons and Online Message Interpretation." *Social Science Computer Review* 26.3 (2008): 379–388.

"Does Flirting Help or Hurt Your Career?" ABC News 9 August 2005. http://abcnews.go.com/GMA/PersonalBest/story?id=1021540&page=1.

Dougherty, Thomas W., and Daniel B. Turban. "Behavioral Confirmation of Interviewer Expectations." *The Employment Interview Handbook* Ed. Robert W. Eder and Michael M. Harris. Thousand Oaks, CA: Sage, 1999. 259–278.

Dougherty, Thomas W., Daniel B. Turban, and John C. Callender. "Confirming First Impressions in the Employment Interview: A Field Study of Interviewer Behavior." *Journal of Applied Psychology* 79.5 (1994): 659–665.

Dunn, Jimmy. "The Eyes Have It." *Tour Egypt!* 17 October 2005. 9 June 2009 http://www.touregypt.net/featurestories/eyeofhorusandre.htm.

Edmonds Wickman, Lindsay. "On the Hunt for Talent," *Talent Management* 4.3 (March 2008). 12 June 2009 http://www.talentmgt.com/recruitment_retention/2008/March/572/index.php.

Einhorn, Thomas. "Brain, Bone, and Body Mass: Fat Is Beautiful Again." *The Journal of Bone and Joint Surgery* 83.12 (2001): 1782.

Emery, Mike. "Men's Bodybuilding: A Short History." 10 June 2009 http://bodybuildingreviews.net/Bodybuilding.html.

Emling, Shelley. "More Men Squeezing into 'Shape-Enhancing' Garments." *PalmBeachPost.com* 6 December 2008. 12 June 2009 http://www.palmbeachpost.com/search/content/business/epaper/2008/12/06/sunbiz_mensgirdles_1207.html.

"The Evil Eye." *Lucky Mojo* 9 June 2009 http://www.luckymojo.com/evileye.html.

Faist, Sandra. "How to Look Thin When You're Not." *Ezine Articles* 5 September 2008. 8 June 2009 http://ezinearticles.com/?How-to-Look-Thin-When-Youre-Not&id=295358.

"Fashion through the Decades: 1900–1990." 4 June 2009 http://www.angelfire.com/ok5/coenfashionfiles/faafiles/faaunit1/fashionthroughthedecades.pdf.

"Fashion through the Decades: A Crash Course on the History of Fashion." *Belle de Four* 22 October 2007. 4 June 2009 http://fashionbella.blogspot.com/2007/10/fashion-through-decades-crash-course-on.html.

"Figure Fixers: Make Your Legs Look Their Best with the Right Skirts." *Marie Claire* 1 July 2006. 5 June 2009 http://www.accessmylibrary.com/coms2/summary_0286-17346175_ITM.

First Research. "Cosmetics, Beauty Supply, and Perfume Stores."
    20 July 2009. 30 July 2009 http://www.firstresearch.com/Industry
    -Research/Cosmetics-Beauty-Supply-and-Perfume-Stores.html.
"Fix Crooked Teeth with Dental Braces." *Dental Health Magazine* 16 April
    2008. 3 June 2009 http://worldental.org/teeth/fix-crooked-teeth-with-
    dental-braces/.
Flick, Mallory. "The Best Hair Styles for Your Face Shape." 4 June 2009
    http://www.getbeautytips.com/Articles/HairStyles2.php.
Frank, Mark G., and Thomas Gilovich. "The Dark Side of Self- and Social
    Perception: Black Uniforms and Aggression in Professional Sports,"
    Journal of Personality and Social Psychology 54.1 (1988): 74–85.
French, Michael T., et al. "Effects of Physical Attractiveness, Personality
    and Grooming on Academic Performance in High School." *Labour Eco-
    nomics* 16.4 (2009): 373–382.
Furtman, Michael. *Why Birds Do That: 40 Distinctive Bird Behaviors
    Explained and Photographed* Minocqua, WI: Willow Creek Press, 2004.
Gallagher, Jenny. "A Brief Look at the Fashions of the Twentieth Century
    from the 1920's–1990's." *Fashion Through the Decades* 10 June 2009
    http://drake.marin.k12.ca.us/students/gallaghj/fashion/fash_thru_decade
    .html.
Garza, Kimberly. "Secrets of Chillaxation." *Spirit Magazine* June 2009.
Gilman, Andrew. *Managing the Trend toward Increasing Use of Electronic
    Messaging Tools* June 1999. 20 October 2008 http://www.opengroup
    .org/comm/the_message/magazine/mmv5n3/managing.htm.
Gladwell, Malcolm. *Blink: The Power of Thinking Without Thinking*.
    New York: Little Brown and Company, 2005.
Goldman, Lynda. *How to Make a Million Dollar First Impression*.
    St-Laurent, Quebec: GSBC, 2001.
Goleman, Daniel. "Empathy—Who's Got It, Who Does Not." *The Huffing-
    ton Post* 2 May 2009. 13 June 2009 http://www.huffingtonpost.com/
    dan-goleman/empathy—whos-got-it-who_b_195178.html.
"Google Answers: Voicemail Usage Stats." *Google Answers* 20 October
    2008 http://answers.google.com/answers/threadview/id/144377.html.
The Gorilla Foundation. "Amazing Gorilla Facts." *Koko's Kids Club*
    10 June 2009 http://www.koko.org/kidsclub/learn/10facts.html.
Haefner, Rosemary. "The Internet vs. Your Professional Image." *Career
    Builder.com Jobs* 24 September 2007. 20 October 2008 http://www
    .careerbuilder.com/JobSeeker/careerbytes/CBArticle.aspx?articleID=573.
Haefner, Rosemary. "Job Searching on Company Time?" *Career-
    Builder.com Jobs* 24 September 2007. 20 October 2008 http://www
    .careerbuilder.com/JobSeeker/careerbytes/CBArticle.aspx?articleID
    =480.
"Hairstyle through the Decades." *Zimbio* 3 June 2009 http://www
    .zimbio.com/Vintage+Hair/notes/1/Hairstyles+Through+the+Decades.

Hall, Gregg. "How to Make Yourself Look Thin By Just Changing Your Clothes." *Ezine Articles* 26 August 2006. 8 June 2009 http://ezine articles.com/?How-To-Make-Yourself-Look-Thin-By-Just-Changing -Your-Clothes&id=283457.

Hart, Gill. "Handbags & Your Personality Type." *Suite101* 5 March 2008. 1 June 2009 http://handbags-luggage.suite101.com/article.cfm/hand bags_and_personality_types.

Hart, Gill. "The Oversized Bag Fashion Trend." *Suite101* 13 December 2007. 1 June 2009 http://womensaccessories.suite101.com/article.cfm/ womens_bag_fashion_trends_2008.

"Hats Glossary." *About.com: Accessories* 8 June 2009 http://accessories .about.com/od/hatglossary/Hat_Glossary_Hat_Styles.htm.

Hemphill, Michael. "A Note on Adults' Color-Emotion Associations." *Journal of Genetic Psychology* 157.3 (1996): 275–280.

Herman, Katie. "Presidential Candidates Have Large Height Difference." *The Fed* 22 October 2004. 15 June 2009 http://www.the-fed.org/ articles/volume20/issue2/presheight.html.

Hernandez, Natalie. "How to Know the Best Hairstyles for Round Face Shapes." *eHow* 3 June 2009 http://www.ehow.com/how_2231827 _best-hairstyles-round-face-shapes.html.

"History of Socks." *Holeproof* 8 June 2009 http://www.holeproof.com.au/ About-Holeproof/Study-Centre/History-of-Socks.asp.

Horai, Joann, Nicholas Naccari, and Elliot Fatoullah. "The Effects of Expertise and Physical Attractiveness Upon Opinion Agreement and Liking." *Sociometry* 37.4 (1974): 601–606.

"How to Choose a Haircut for an Oval Face." *eHow* 3 June 2009 http:// www.ehow.com/how_2216613_choose-haircut-oval-shaped-face.html.

"How to Style Hair for a Heart Shaped Face." *eHow* 12 June 2009 http:// www.ehow.com/how_2217605_style-hair-heart-shaped-face.html.

"How to Whiten Your Teeth." *eHow* 3 June 2009 http://www.ehow.com/ how_3071_whiten-teeth.html.

Howard, Pierce J. *The Owner's Manual for the Brain: Everyday Applica-tions from Mind-Brain Research.* 2nd ed. Austin, TX: Bard Press, 2000.

Hutson, Matthew. "In the Rough: The Science Behind Designer Stubble." *Psychology Today* November/December 2008: 24.

Hutt, Richard. "The Rules." *The Uppers Organization* 22 February 2001. 10 June 2009 http://www.uppers.org/showArticle.asp?article=189.

Jandt, Fred E. *InterCultural Communication: An Introduction.* Thousand Oaks, CA: Sage Publications, 2001.

Johnson, Brett. "Getting to the Bottom of It." *Freshpair* 21 September 2003. 1 June 2009 http://www.freshpair.com/in_the_news/ventura_county _star_20030921.html.

Johnson, David. "2000 Years of the Necktie." *Infoplease* 11 June 2009 http://www.infoplease.com/spot/tie1.html.

Judge, Timothy A., and Daniel M. Cable. "The Effect of Physical Height on Workplace Success and Income: Preliminary Test of a Theoretical Model." *Journal of Applied Psychology* 89.3 (2004): 428–441.

Kaplan, Robert M. "Is Beauty Talent? Sex Interaction in the Attractiveness Halo Effect." *Sex Roles* 4.2 (1978): 195–204.

Katteringham, Kristin. "Wearing the Right Color for Your Skin Tone." *Associated Content: Lifestyle* 30 July 2007. 5 June 2009 http://www.associatedcontent.com/article/328243/wearing_the_right_color_for_your_skin.html?cat=46.

Kaya, Naz, and Helen H. Epps. "Color-Emotion Associations: Past Experience and Personal Preferences." *AIC 2004 Color and Paints, Interim Meeting of the International Color Association* 2004. 12 June 2009 http://www.fadu.uba.ar/sitios/sicyt/color/aic2004/031-034.pdf.

Kim, Ryan. "The World's a Cell-Phone Stage / The Device Is Upending Social Rules and Creating a New Culture." *SFGate* 27 February 2006. 20 October 2008 http://www.sfgate.com/cgi-bin/article.cgi?f=/c/a/2006/02/27/BUG2IHECTO1.DTL.

Lacter, Mark. "How I Did It: Reid Hoffman of LinkedIn." *Inc Magazine* May 2009: 83–84.

Limited Brands. "Limited Brands 2007 Annual Report." 2008. 1 June 2009 http://ww3.ics.adp.com/streetlink_data/dirLPD/annual/HTML1/default.htm.

Lindgaard, Gitte, et al. "Attention Web Designers: You Have 50 Milliseconds to Make a Good First Impression!" *Behaviour and Information Technology* 25.2 (2006): 115–126.

Liptona, Michelle G., et al. "Women Living with Facial Hair: The Psychological and Behavioral Burden." *Journal of Psychosomatic Research* 61.2 (2006): 161–168.

"Liquid Nitrogen Cocktails." *Food Detectives*. Food Network. Scripps Networks Interactive, New York. 24 March 2009.

Lorenz, Kate. "Is a Messier Desk Better?" *CareerBuilder.com*. 24 September 2007. 20 October 2008 http://www.careerbuilder.com/Article/CB-646-The-Workplace-Is-a-Messier-Desk-Better/?ArticleID=646&cbRecursionCnt=1&cbsid=720eac70a7814d348a18f09772251d22-302820270-wb-6&ns_siteid=ns_us_g_PsyMax_Solutions_orga_.

Lorenz, Kate. "Is Your Boss Spying On You?" *CareerBuilder.com* 24 September 2007. 20 October 2008 http://www.careerbuilder.com/JobSeeker/careerbytes/CBArticle.aspx?articleID=718.

Louise, Tegan. "Why Animal Print Fashion Is Popular?" *Ezine Articles* 4 June 2009 http://ezinearticles.com/?Why-Animal-Print-Fashion-is-Popular&id=2279317.

"Magic Eye." Frequently Asked Questions." *Magic Eye* 9 June 2009 http://www.magiceye.com/faq.htm.

Marlowe, Frank T., and Adam Wetsman. "Preferred Waist-to-Hip Ratio and Ecology." *Pergamon* September 1999. 12 June 2009 http://www .fas.harvard.edu/~hbe-lab/acrobatfiles/preferred%20waist.pdf.

Marlowe, Frank T., Coren Apicella, and Dorian Reed. "Men's Preferences for Women's Profile Waist-to-Hip Ratio in Two Societies." *Pergamon* December 2003. 12 June 2009 http://www.fas.harvard.edu/~hbe-lab/ acrobatfiles/profilewhr.pdf.

Martell, Arlene. "How Sexy Lingerie Works—Going Undercover." *HowItWorks* 25 August 2008. 1 June 2009 http://www.howitworks .net/how-sexy-lingerie-works.html.

Massachusetts Institute of Technology. *News: Press Releases* 21 January 2004. 20 October 2008 http://web.mit.edu/invent/n-pressreleases/ n-press-04index.html.

Mazzella, Ronald, and Alan Feingold. "The Effects of Physical Attractiveness, Race, Socioeconomic Status, and Gender of Defendants and Victims on Judgments of Mock Jurors: A Meta Analysis." *Journal of Applied Social Psychology* 24.15 (1994): 1315–1344.

McKelvie, Stuart J. "Perception of Faces With and Without Spectacles." *Perceptual and Motor Skills* 84.2 (1997): 497–498.

"The Meaning of Metals." *EncycloBEADia* 5 June 2009 http://www.fire mountaingems.com/encyclobeadia/beading_resources.asp?docid=8A18.

MobileActive.org. *About MobileActive.org* 20 October 2008 http:// mobileactive.org/about.

Morse, Gardiner. "Why We Misread Motives." *Harvard Business Review* 1 January 2003. 13 June 2009 http://hbr.harvardbusiness.org/2003/01/ why-we-misread-motives/ar/1.

Morton, Jill. "Why Color Matters." *Color Matters* 2005. 4 June 2009 http:// www.colormatters.com/market_whycolor.html.

Murphy, Michael J., Don A. Nelson, and Thomas L. Cheap. "Rated and Actual Performance of High School Students as a Function of Sex and Attractiveness." *Psychological Reports* 48.1 (1981): 103–106.

"NPD Reports U.S. Footwear Industry Takes a Big Step Forward in 2005." *Business Wire* 10 February 2006. 9 June 2009 http://www.allbusiness .com/company-activities-management/sales-selling-sales-figures/ 5370035-1.html.

Nellis, Cynthia. "How to Look Taller and Slimmer." *About.com: Women's Fashion* 10 June 2009 http://fashion.about.com/cs/tipsadvice/ht/ taller.htm.

NIH Obesity Research Taskforce. "The National Strategic Plan for NIH Obesity Research." *US Department of Health and Human Services National Institutes for Health* August 2004. 13 June 2009 http://www.obesityresearch.nih.gov/About/Obesity_EntireDocument .pdf.

Oak Productions, Inc. "Athlete." *The Official Website of Schwarzenegger* 2006. 9 June 2009 http://www.schwarzenegger.com/en/athlete/index .asp?sec=athlete.

Pease, Allan, and Barbara Pease. *The Definitive Book of Body Language.* New York: Bantam Books, 2006.

Persico, Nicola, Andrew Postlewaite, and Dan Silverman. "The Effect of Adolescent Experience on Labor Market Outcomes: The Case of Height." *Journal of Political Economy* 112.5 (2004): 1019–1053.

Pertschuk, Michael, and Alice Trisdorfer. "Men's Bodies—The Survey," *Psychology Today* 1 November 1994. 2 June 2009 http://www.psycho logytoday.com/articles/pto-19941101-000022.html.

Petrini, Jennifer. "Fashion Reincarnated: Styles through the Decades." *Fashion Schools* 27 July 2007. 12 June 2009 http://www.fashion-schools.org/blog/index.php?/archives/8-Fashion-Reincarnated-Styles-Through-the-Decades.html.

Pollick, Michael. "What Is a Clip-On Tie?" wiseGEEK 4 June 2009 http:// www.wisegeek.com/what-is-a-clip-on-tie.htm.

Posthuma, Richard A., Frederick P. Morgeson, and Michael A. Campion. "Beyond Employment Interview Validity: A Comprehensive narrative view of recent research and Trends over Time." *Personnel Psychology* 55.1 (2002): 1–81.

"Pretty Women." *Psychology Today* 1 November 1993. 18 January 2009 http://www.psychologytoday.com/articles/pto-19931101-000002.html.

Sabath, Ann Marie. *Business Etiquette in Brief: The Competitive Edge For Today's Professional.* Holbrook, MA: Adams Media, 1993.

Saether, Linda. "How White Should Your Teeth Really Be?" *CNN Health* 5 September 2008. 3 June 2009 http://www.cnn.com/2008/HEALTH/ 09/05/hfh.teeth.whiter/index.html.

Saltzman, Marc. "Should You Monitor Employee E-Mail?" *Business Tech News* 20 October 2008 http://technology.inc.com/managing/articles/ 200610/emailmonitoring.html.

Sample, Ian. "Why Men and Women Find Longer Legs More Attractive." *The Guardian* 17 January 2008. 5 June 2009 http://www.guardian .co.uk/science/2008/jan/17/humanbehaviour.psychology.

Sandberg, Jared. "Sure, Hold Your Nose, But Colleagues' Odors Pose Serious Problem," *The Wall Street Journal* 21 July 2004. 4 June 2009 http:// online.wsj.com/article/SB109035944035168974.html.

Seitz, Victoria A. *Your Executive Image: How to Look your Best and Project Success—for Men and Women.* 2nd ed. Holbrook, MA: Adams Media, 2000.

Sessions, Karen. "Learn Your Body Frame and Reshape It!" *Critical Bench* 2006. 11 June 2009 http://www.criticalbench.com/reshape_body _frame.htm.

Shenenberger, Donald W. "Removal of Unwanted Facial Hair." *SmartSkinCare.com* 15 November 2002. 8 June 2009 http://www .smartskincare.com/resabstracts/hair-removal_shenenberger_am-fam -physician_20021115.html.

Shoe Tips and Facts." *Designer Shoe Salon* 9 June 2009 http://www .designershoesalon.com/tipsfacts.htm.

"Sign Language: Historical Background." *Sign Genius* 2 June 2009 http:// www.signgenius.com/info-sign-language-01.shtml.

"Silk." *Textiles* 4 June 2009 http://library.thinkquest.org/C004179/ silk.htm.

Silkroad Foundation. "History of Silk." *The Silkroad Foundation* 1997. 4 June 2009 http://www.silk-road.com/artl/silkhistory.shtml.

"16th Century Fashion—The Ruff, a Collar with Meaning." 31 December 2008. 11 June 2009 http://blog.aurorahistoryboutique.com/tag/history- of-the-collar/.

Slack, Alex. "Pop This" *The Harvard Crimson* 12 August 2005. 11 June 2009 http://www.thecrimson.com/article.aspx?ref=508376.

Smith, Jerry. "History of Socks Timeline." 11 February 2006. 8 June 2009 http://www.articlealley.com/article_28545_27.html.

Snead, Elizabeth. "The Beauty of Symmetry." *USA Weekend* 1 June 2003. 3 June 2009 http://www.usaweekend.com/03_issues/030601/030601 symmetry.html.

Snell, Marilyn. "Innovator: Judy Kranzler." *Democratic Leadership Council: Blueprint Magazine* 1 September 1999. 5 June 2009 http://www .dlc.org/ndol_ci.cfm?kaid=110&subid=181&contentid=1234.

Society for the Advancement of Education. "Bosses to Workers: Lose the Flip-Flops." *USA Today* November 2003. 10 June 2009 http://find articles.com/p/articles/mi_m1272/is_2702_132/ai_110531012/.

"Sorry, But You Stink." *hr.blr.com* 14 April 2005. 10 June 2009 http:// hr.blr.com/news.aspx?id=15057.

"The Story of Cotton." 4 June 2009 http://www.cotton.org/pubs/cotton counts/story/index.cfm.

Sutter, Cindy. "Food for Thought: Boulder's Institute for the Psychology of Eating Wants You to Think Differently about What You Eat." *Your Daily Camera Online* 23 February 2009. 13 June 2009 http://www.daily camera.com/news/2009/feb/23/Boulder-Institute-for-the-Psychology-of -Eating/.

Taylor, Rachael. "Famous People and Hairstyles through the Years." *Ezine Articles* 21 October 2006. 3 June 2009 http://ezinearticles.com/ ?Famous-People-and-Hairstyles-through-the-Years&id=334965.

Todorov, Alexander, et al. "Inferences of Competence from Faces Predict Election Outcomes." *Science* 308.5728 (10 June 2005): 1623– 1626.

Tumulty, Karen, and John F. Dickerson. "Inside the Debate Strategies." *Time* 26 September 2004. 14 June 2009 http://www.time.com/time/election2004/article/0,18471,702075-1,00.html.

"Understanding Pronation." *Asics Running* 9 June 2009 http://www.asics.co.uk/running/knowledge/understanding-pronation.

Volin, Kathryn J. *Buff and Polish: A Practical Guide to Enhance Your Professional Image and Communication Style.* Minneapolis: Pentagon Publishing, 1999.

Voros, Sharon. "Weight Discrimination Runs Rampant in Hiring." *Career journal.com, The Wall Street Journal* 2000. 13 June 2009 http://208.144.115.170/myc/climbing/20000905-voros.html.

Vrij, Aldert. "Wearing Black Clothes: The Impact of Offenders' and Suspects' Clothing on Impression Formation," *Applied Cognitive Psychology* 11.1 (1997): 47–53.

Vrij, Aldert, and Lucy Akehurst. "The Existence of a Black Clothing Stereotype: The Impact of a Victim's Black Clothing on Impression Formation," *Psychology, Crime & Law* 3.3 (1997): 227–237.

"Waist." *Noubikko* 12 June 2009 http://www.noubikko.com/noubikko-body/tips/camouflage/waist.htm.

Watson, Kittie W., and Larry R. Smeltzer. "Barriers to Listening: Comparison between Students and Practitioners." *Communication Research Reports* 1.1 (1984): 82–87.

Websense Incorporated. *Key Internet Usage Statistics* 2003. 20 October 2008 http://www.3w.net/lan/internet-use-statistics.html.

Weston Thomas, Pauline "The Wearing of Hats Fashion History General Information." *Fashion Era* 2001. 8 June 2009 http://www.fashion-era.com/hats-hair/hats_hair_1_wearing_hats_fashion_history.htm.

"What Glasses Say About You: Putting Perceptions About People Who Wear Glasses to the Test" ABC News, 2009. http://cosmos.bcst.yahoo.com/up/player/popup/?cl=12304452.

"Why Do Men Have Buttons on Their Jacket Sleeves?" *Big Site of Amazing Facts* 8 June 2009 http://www.bigsiteofamazingfacts.com/why-do-men-have-buttons-on-their-jacket-sleeves.

"Why Do Men Like Big Breasts?" *Breast Options* 10 June 2009 http://www.breastoptions.com/bigbreasts.html.

Wiseman, Richard. "New Year's Resolution Experiment." *Quirkology* 2007. 12 June 2009 http://www.quirkology.com/UK/Experiment_resolution.shtml.

WorldCom Incorporated. "MIA3.pdf." 2001. *Verizon Conferencing* 20 October 2008 https://e-meetings.verizonbusiness.com/meetings inamerica/pdf/MIA3.pdf.

Wyar, Leah. "Your Biggest Beauty Secrets, Spilled." *Fitness Magazine* February 2009: 34.

Zubek, Rachel. "Six Ways to Deal with Digital Bad Manners," *CareerBuilder Jobs* 17 January 2008. 20 October 2008 http://www.careerbuilder.com/JobSeeker/careerbytes/CBArticle.aspx?articleID=702.

Zubek, Rachel. "What Do You Do When the Boss Isn't Looking?" *CareerBuilder Jobs* 6 June 2008. 20 October 2008 http://www.careerbuilder.com/JobSeeker/careerbytes/CBArticle.aspx?articleID=866.

Index

About the Authors

Vu H. Pham, PhD, is a Partner at Spectrum Knowledge, Inc. and works with dozens of organizations from the Fortune 500 to government and nonprofit agencies to boost employee performance and strategic effectiveness. These include Boeing, IBM, Kaiser Permanente, Microsoft, New York Life, Northrop Grumman, PricewaterhouseCoopers, Prudential, Raytheon, and Verizon. He served as a Fellow for the University of California Office of the President and as a visiting scholar at UCLA, and his work has been featured on international media such as CNN, MSNBC, and the Associated Press.

Lisa Miyake is currently a Program Manager at Spectrum Knowledge, Inc. and manages teams for research and training projects for Fortune 500, government, and nonprofit agencies. She is a past Fulbright Fellow and UCLA alumna and currently serves on several boards of nonprofit organizations.

PRINTED IN U.S.A.

DATE DUE

MAY 12 2014

Impressive first impressions : a guide to
the most important 30 seconds (and 30
years) of your career / Vu H. Pham and
Lisa Miyake.

HF5381 .P492 2010
Career